# STRATEGIC BENEFITS REALIZATION

## Optimizing Value through Programs, Portfolios and Organizational Change Management

**Craig J. Letavec,** PgMP, MSP, PMP

J.ROSS PUBLISHING

ISBN-13: 978-1-60427-093-8

Printed and bound in the U.S.A. Printed on acid-free paper.

10 9 8 7 6 5 4 3 2 1

**Library of Congress Cataloging-in-Publication Data**

Letavec, Craig J., 1970-
Strategic benefits realization : optimizing value through programs, portfolios and organizational change management / Craig Letavec, PgMP, MSP, PMP.
pages cm
Includes bibliographical references and index.
ISBN 978-1-60427-093-8 (hardcover : alk. paper)
1. Project management. 2. Organizational change. I. Title.
HD69.P75L474 2014
658.4'012--dc23
2013048433



Direct all inquiries to J. Ross Publishing, Inc., 300 S. Pine Island Rd., Suite 305, Plantation, FL 33324.

Phone: (954) 727-9333
Fax: (561) 892-0700
Web: www.jrosspub.com

# DEDICATION

To my beautiful daughter, who makes me proud and makes me smile every day.

# CONTENTS

# ACKNOWLEDGEMENTS

The process of creating a book is not an easy one. While my passion for project, program, and portfolio management—especially the strategic application of these principles in organizations—is great, passion alone is not sufficient to realize a manuscript that will ultimately become a published work. Support from a number of individuals, who have motivated me over the years, has been critical to helping me continue to write.

I would like to acknowledge the tremendous support and encouragement that I have received over the years from my colleagues and friends in the PMI® Program Management Office Specific Interest Group (now the PMI Program Management Office Community of Practice). From the members of the Board of Directors, who donate countless hours to advance the community and have motivated me to contribute to that community over the years, to the many fine presenters, sponsors, and attendees that I have been lucky enough to interact with as Chair of the *PMO Symposium*, to the many additional members that I have met during six years of service as a member of the Board of Directors, their help has been incredible. They are a tremendous asset to the project management community, and I am thankful to have been lucky enough to contribute to its success.

A timely and relevant case study on the potential application of program management offices in the benefits realization context is presented in Appendix A. Ms. Hayley Douglas, a talented undergraduate student, whom I had the pleasure of advising on an equally timely and relevant research paper she wrote for a prestigious grant competition, contributed the case study there, and I would like to acknowledge her persistence in researching a unique topic in our field and presenting an excellent case study from that work. Ms. Douglas is among the finest undergraduate students I have had the pleasure to advise in my time as an adjunct university faculty member.

Lastly, I am extremely lucky to have the unending support of my wife Jennifer, who has exhibited tremendous patience during many long days, late nights, and Saturdays of writing, revising, and editing. This book would not have been possible without her encouragement and support, and I am extremely lucky to have a partner who is willing to endure the occasionally challenging creative process that comes with envisioning and realizing a book.

# ABOUT THE AUTHOR

Craig Letavec, MSP, IPMA-B, PMP, PgMP, has led major program efforts in a diverse range of large, global companies in a variety of industries, including consumer products, new venture startups, information technology services, and information technology consulting. He has served as an active speaker and author on a range of topics, including program management, implementing effective organizational change management, benefits realization management, and establishing, managing, and building the value of the program management office (PMO) in organizations. He is the author of *The Program Management Office: Establishing, Managing, and Growing the Value of a PMO*, a text noted by the project management community for its specific focus on PMO implementation and development; a co-author of *Program Management Professional: A Certification Study Guide with Best Practices for Maximizing Business Results*; co-editor of the *PMOSIG Program Management Office Handbook;* and a contributor to *99 Things Every Project Manager Should Know.*

Throughout his professional career, he has studied the role of project and program management in organizations, the process of formalizing project and program management practices in organizations, and the many challenges that face organizations and program managers alike. This practical analysis, combined with academic research in the field, has led him to a number of conclusions regarding how organizations can best exploit program management to improve business results.

Craig holds a Bachelor of Science degree from the University of Dayton (Go Flyers!) and a Master of Science in Project Management from George Washington University. As an active teacher, who enjoys educating future project and program managers and business professionals, he has served as an adjunct faculty member in project management in the Master of Business Administration program at Wright State University in Dayton, Ohio and as an adjunct instructor at the University of Dayton. Craig also serves as Vice Chair of the Project Management Institute's Program Management Office Community of Practice and was a founder and general conference chair of the *PMO Symposium*, the largest focused international conference for PMO practitioners.

# INTRODUCTION

The concept of managing benefits is not new. After all, we do many things in business to enhance shareholder value and bring additional return to the business. Whether launching a product, enhancing a process, introducing a new IT system, training employees, or some other project, we act with the goal of making something better. We plan and manage not simply to produce something but to produce something that provides a beneficial return. This, fundamentally, is the essence of a benefit.

What may be new, at least for many organizations, is the notion of a standardized process by which benefits are managed. Historically, many organizations intuitively knew that benefits were important, but, often, the formal management of these benefits was nonexistent, instead relying on traditional project metrics, such as on-time performance and on-budget management, to determine the success of projects. We also intuitively knew that a project that was delivered on time and under budget, but which did not meet the needs of the project's customers, was often a waste of both time and money. The work got done, but—without benefits received—the work was not of much value to the organization.

And therein lies the gap: the gap between the processes associated with *capability creation* and *benefits realization*. The notion of, "if I create it they will come," just doesn't work. We have to clearly articulate the *what*, in terms of the needed capabilities of whatever it is that we're delivering, along with the *why*, which describes the successful integration of the *what* into the business environment. So, fundamentally, managing benefits is really about managing change, ensuring that we have the right capabilities for the right people at the right time and that those delivered capabilities are successfully embedded into the organization in a way that creates value. Equally important, we need to ensure that our processes are proactive enough to understand when desired beneficial outcomes are not likely to be received, ensuring that we can stop efforts when appropriate, in order to limit the risk of needlessly expending organizational resources.

It is the goal of this book to provide a practical introduction to the concepts of benefits realization management, with a focus on a common-sense approach to managing benefits. While more exhaustive works have been written and likely will be written in the future, and while standards and guidelines will certainly continue to evolve, for most people, the extensive tome on the state of practice, or the abstract standard that lacks much practical guidance for how to do the work, is insufficient. This book seeks to bridge the gap, distilling the concepts of benefits realization management down to a palatable level, while additionally providing practical information on how to implement these key concepts in a business organization.

## WHO IS THIS BOOK WRITTEN FOR?

By its nature, this book is designed to be more than a primer and less than an exhaustive review of practice. For the project manager, program manager, or program management office team member or manager, this book will provide a practical overview and advice on how to introduce benefits realization management into your organization. For the portfolio manager, it will provide insight into how benefits metrics can be embedded in the organization's portfolio management practices. For organizational change management practitioners, this reference will provide practical insight into the relationship between organizational change management and benefits realization management, a critical link that cannot be overlooked. The book is written in a way that will appeal to the general business manager as well.

In the interest of transparency, and as noted previously, this book is not designed to be exhaustive, nor is it designed to advocate any particular methodology. The book will reference the implementation of benefits realization management in the context of well-recognized international standards, such as the *Standard for Program Management* from the Project Management Institute, but will extend the concepts of these standards to provide a practical framework, through which an organization can begin to implement benefits realization management principles.

## HOW TO USE THIS BOOK

This reference is divided into relatively compact chapters for ease of reading. While some topics build on each other as the book progresses, the chapters may be used independently if needed. It is suggested to read the introductory chapters in order to gain an understanding of some of the fundamental principles of benefits realization management that will be relevant throughout the book. Beyond these initial chapters, it is possible to focus on areas of greater interest to you, the reader, by skipping among the remaining chapters.

Web Added Value™

This book has free material available for download from the Web Added Value™ resource center at *www.jrosspub.com*

At J. Ross Publishing we are committed to providing today's professional with practical, hands-on tools that enhance the learning experience and give readers an opportunity to apply what they have learned. That is why we offer ancillary materials available for download on this book and all participating Web Added Value™ publications. These online resources may include interactive versions of material that appears in the book or supplemental templates, worksheets, models, plans, case studies, proposals, spreadsheets and assessment tools, among other things. Whenever you see the WAV™ symbol in any of our publications, it means bonus materials accompany the book and are available from the Web Added Value Download Resource Center at www.jrosspub.com.

Downloads for *Strategic Benefits Realization* include templates and tools for organizational change management, key deliverables associated with benefits management, and additional benefits realization management related PgMP® exam preparation questions that build on those contained in Appendix B of this text.

1

# INTRODUCTION TO BENEFITS REALIZATION MANAGEMENT

## INTRODUCTION

This chapter presents an overview of the fundamental terminology of benefits realization management. In addition, it identifies the primary differences between benefits realization management and capability creation, drawing on parallels between projects and programs in the practical business environment.

## WHAT IS A BENEFIT?

Before discussing benefits realization management, it is important to define what is meant by a *benefit*. Definitions of benefits vary, but for the purposes of this discussion, we will focus on the foundational benefits definition found in two well-regarded industry standards in project and program management, as well as a classic dictionary definition.

Beginning first with a dictionary definition, the Merriam-Webster dictionary defines a benefit as "something that promotes well-being" or a "useful aid."[1] We can view something that promotes well-being or a useful aid as representing some sort of desirable outcome or advantage. Perhaps some information system that provides better information to support business decision making, if correctly designed and appropriately implemented, provides a useful aid to business users who have data analysis needs. This notion of a benefit underscores the basic notion of a benefit as providing some advantage. That advantage, however, must be valued by someone in order to truly be a benefit. If one creates a better mousetrap in a world with no mice, it might be proposed that the relative advantage is lost and—although improvement of the mousetrap is created—there is no customer for the better mousetrap and therefore, no advantage. This may seem a simplistic example, and counterpoints could be made, but in essence the point is: benefits need to benefit *someone.*

A second, and more relevant example in a project management context, comes from the definition of a benefit in the Project Management Institute's *Standard for Program Management*, which defines a benefit as, "an outcome of actions, behaviors, products, or services that provide utility to the sponsoring organization as well as to the program's intended beneficiaries."[2] This definition is significantly more focused than the general dictionary definition and is worth digesting a bit. The first notion worthy of mention is the idea of benefits coming from actions, behaviors, products, or services. Benefits have to be delivered by something: It could be a differentiated product that provides a benefit to a user, such as a simpler user experience; it could be a service that offers convenience; or it could be some other form of action that creates value.

These benefits are provided to a sponsoring organization *and* to intended beneficiaries; both are worthy of mention. The idea of a sponsoring organization is not new in our project and program management world. We understand that sponsors are the people who pay the bills and champion the project or program efforts. In our benefits realization management world, the sponsoring organization plays this role, but as indicated by the definition of a benefit, the sponsoring organization expects to get value from the delivered benefits. The sponsoring organization doesn't just want the work to be done; it wants the benefits to be realized. As such, representatives of the sponsoring organization will play a strong role in "benefits realization management."

Secondly, it is expected that utility will be provided to the program's intended recipients. While the use of the word "program" is somewhat specific to a definition that comes from a program management standard, it can be extended beyond programs to the general notion that there are intended customers of the benefits, and those customers need to derive benefits from whatever is created. The diversity of these intended customers may be large. We could imagine a scenario of building a public park. Intended customers of the park may be the general public, and thus the group of intended beneficiaries may be quite large. Will it be possible to build a park that satisfies everyone's needs perfectly? Probably not, but we recognize that benefits may be extended to relatively large stakeholder groups, and while it may not be possible to meet all of their needs perfectly, understanding the intended beneficiaries and their needs will be an important part of the process of aligning the proposed benefits with the sponsoring organization early in the benefits realization management life cycle.

Finally, we can look to the very well regarded APMG-International *Managing Benefits* reference guide, which defines a benefit, as per the UK Cabinet Office, as "the measurable improvement resulting from an outcome perceived as an advantage by one or more stakeholders, which contributes towards one or more organizational objective(s)."[3] I prefer this definition for its simplicity and completeness. It contains some important words. First, and perhaps foremost, is the notion that a benefit is not just an improvement but also a *measurable* improvement. It is unfortunate how many business cases in the world are built largely on intangible benefits. We need to get better. A fundamental notion of benefits realization management that is worth repeating many times is that we need to be able to measure the improvement. Does this mean that we always need to develop complex measurement systems and financial models that are accurate to the second decimal place? Certainly not. But at some minimal level, we need to be able to establish a target and measure against it in order to understand whether the benefits to be achieved will meet the plan. If we don't do this, how will we ever know whether we are heading towards a situation in which what we deliver is not "beneficial enough" to be used? The idea that some benefits are better than no benefits is a dangerous one. We use benefits realization management to fully realize the potential of the benefits we desire, not to create compromises. And while some compromises may be made from time to time, effective measurement helps to limit the risk that we must make compromises down the road—by being the proactive mechanism by which we monitor and manage benefits realization.

The concept of a benefit being valued by a stakeholder has already been discussed, so the second point is the notion of the benefit contributing towards one or more organizational objectives. Some may be flip and say it is obvious that the work we do has to contribute to the organization's objectives. But how often have we found situations where, despite our best efforts, pockets of work occur that appear to be contrary to the general direction of the organization? How often have we encountered cases where managers are doing what is best for them, rather than what is best for the organization at large? It happens. In fact, in the project portfolio management discipline, we often advocate that an initial starting point for implementing portfolio management is to inventory the in-progress projects and programs to determine the extent to which these projects and programs align with the current organizational priorities. Inevitably, this exercise roots out work that probably shouldn't be occurring. As we undertake benefits realization management, we have an imperative to ensure that as we define benefits, we correspondingly ensure the alignment of those benefits with something the organization values, which is often articulated in corporate strategies, objectives, or similar constructs. As these strategies or objectives are cascaded through the organization at large and transformed into actionable initiatives, projects, programs, or other work, benefits realization management may be used as a basis for alignment of work with what the organization values.

And so, the basic notions of a benefit can be summarized in a few key points:

- Benefits are perceived advantages—things that put someone in a better place than they are today
- Benefits must be valued by someone—often a sponsoring organization as well as an end customer of the benefit
- Benefits require alignment with the goals of the organization
- Benefits are delivered through work—project work, program work, operational work, and the like
- Benefits must be measurable—we can't rely exclusively on intangibility

This is a lot. And it's not easy. Throughout the remainder of this book, we will focus on all of these aspects, individually and collectively. But first, it's important to relate benefits to the context of project and program work.

## WHERE DO BENEFITS COME FROM?

One may intuitively understand that benefits do not create themselves out of thin air. In fact, benefits are often the end result of a lot of work that gets done to create them for the stakeholder(s). Consider a large program. Initially, the program may charter certain projects to accomplish work. These projects themselves may not create any benefits at all. Rather, they may create some set of *capabilities* that when integrated together and into the business organization, begin to realize benefits. A practical example may be useful here. Consider an IT system to help a company better process travel expense reports. One component of that system may be a feature that allows employees to submit expense reports electronically versus having to submit paper documents and receipts. Once the programmers have done their work, the system is tested, and the software is delivered by the IT staff to the business users, with the capability to reduce costs and processing times for expense reporting. The capability to enhance user satisfaction through a simpler process exists. These capabilities are created by the IT project itself. Does the IT project realize the benefits? Perhaps not. Only after the appropriate business processes are implemented, the users are successfully trained, the initial bugs are worked out, and the change associated with this new system is successfully embedded in the organization and working properly may the benefits of increased efficiency, reduced costs, or other desirable outcomes be realized.

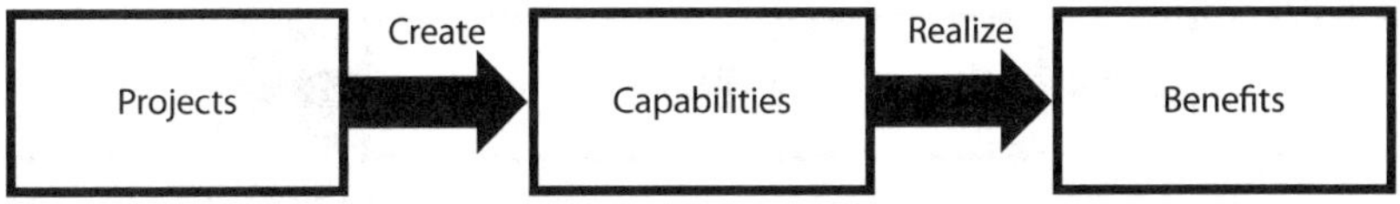


**Figure 1.1** Relationship between capabilities and benefits

So, we have a simple notion that can be summarized in a basic diagram, as shown in Figure 1.1.

As Figure 1.1 demonstrates, the realization of benefits is dependent upon the creation of capabilities, which are often themselves realized via projects. Those capabilities, if successfully embedded in the organization via program and organizational change management, create the relevant benefits of interest to the organization. A further extension of this diagram might describe where the definition of these planned benefits originates, a topic to be discussed separately.

Some benefits realization management literature describes additional terms to distinguish between the tangible outputs of the project, the corresponding capabilities that are created, the results of business change, and the corresponding benefits realization. The commonly used terms are identified in Table 1.1.

These terms can be applied to the general model provided in Figure 1.1, which has been modified in Figure 1.2 to illustrate this relationship.

Figure 1.2 demonstrates the relationship between projects, capabilities, outcomes, and benefits. In this figure, projects produce outputs that are combined to create capabilities. Capabilities are embedded in the business organization through transition, which undertakes the appropriate organizational change management activities to introduce the developed capabilities into the business organization. These capabilities, once transitioned and in use in the receiving business organization, create benefits. The models presented in Figures 1.1 and 1.2 are similar and are presented separately here to enable the reader to understand the common terminology in use in the benefits realization management literature, which does vary from methodology to methodology. However, the essence of projects, business change, and benefits realization are common—despite minor differences in terminology.

**Table 1.1** Benefits realization management terms

| Term | Definition |
|---|---|
| Output | The deliverable created by a project |
| Capability | The set of outputs required to create an outcome |
| Outcome | The result of transition that embeds a capability in the business organization |

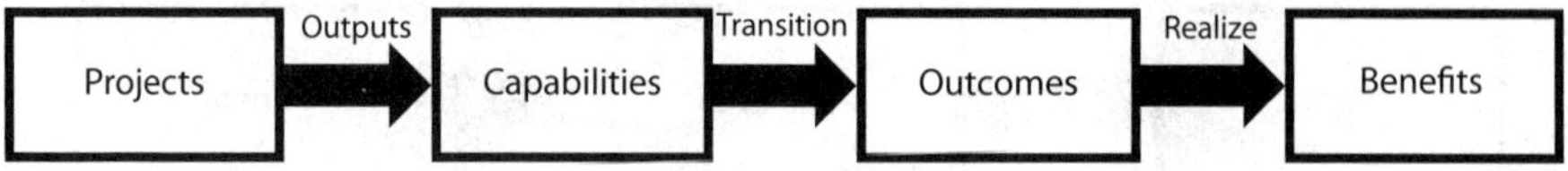


**Figure 1.2** Relationship between capabilities and benefits (modified)

# CHARACTERISTICS OF BENEFITS

A few key characteristics of benefits are relevant to more precisely defining the nature of benefits. These characteristics, while not meant to be an exhaustive list, provide an overview of considerations relevant to the definition of benefits in the project, program, and portfolio management contexts.

## Intermediate and End Benefits

The concept of intermediate and end benefits can be most easily described as a relationship in which the achievement of a final (end) benefit is dependent upon the achievement of one or more intermediate benefits. Figure 1.3 provides an example.

Though a simple example, Figure 1.3 demonstrates the essence of intermediate and end benefits. The end benefit of "increased repeat sales" is not likely to happen on its own. It ultimately occurs as the result of one or more intermediate benefits, such as increasing customer satisfaction. One way that customer satisfaction might be increased is through fewer order processing errors. It is important to note, as the diagram illustrates, that this occurs as a pseudo chain of events, with the achievement of some benefits depending upon the achievement of others. This principle makes effective organizational change management and integration of capabilities into the business environment that much more important. Our ability to realize increased customer satisfaction will be significantly diminished if we do not do a good job of creating the capabilities required to reduce errors and to introduce the corresponding required change into the business environment.

## Disbenefits

It is interesting to note that positive change may come with negative outcomes. The concept of disbenefits refers to an outcome that is viewed negatively by one

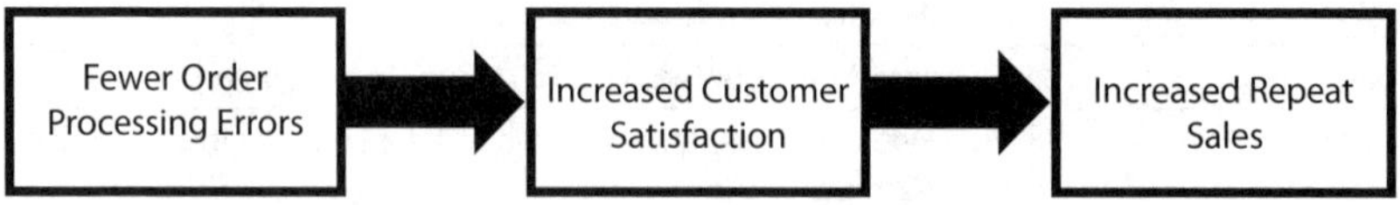


**Figure 1.3** Intermediate and end benefits

or more stakeholders. Disbenefits are a natural occurrence in many business change environments. Sometimes, a positive change for one person or group results in undesirable change for another person or group. Consider an example. It is possible that through implementing a particular tool to make the job of the accounting department easier, you lose some visibility to data that makes the work for the sales operations department a bit more difficult. Weighing benefits and disbenefits against each other is important. If the benefit to the organization of simplifying the work in the accounting department outweighs the additional inconvenience created in the sales operations department, then the organization may consider the disbenefit to be acceptable. Of course, two goals of organizational change management in this context would be to minimize the negative impacts of the disbenefits while also providing the appropriate communication, training, and related processes required to ensure that the sales operations department fully understands the nature of the perceived negative change and is as prepared as possible to accept it.

## Emergent Benefits

There's a saying about "the best laid plans of mice and men," referring to the fact that things don't always go as planned. While the connotation of this adage may be negative in the benefits realization management context, there may be positive outcomes, called emergent benefits, which are not planned from the start but become apparent as time goes on. These emergent benefits, often realized later in the benefits realization management life cycle, while change is being implemented, may represent opportunities for the organization to enhance benefits realization. These opportunities should not be ignored; rather, they should be assessed to understand whether the value of capitalizing on the emergent opportunity outweighs the relevant costs and risks of changing plans that are already in progress. These decisions are not always easy; strong change management processes, combined with sound opportunity analysis processes, must be used to assess the relevant opportunities and risks.

## Tangible and Intangible Benefits

The concept of a tangible benefit represents, at a simple level, a benefit that can be measured. For example, decreased wait time to reach a helpdesk agent could be measured by using wait time data in the helpdesk environment. The concept of an intangible benefit represents a benefit that cannot be measured. As benefits realization management professionals, our goal should be to ensure that we define and manage against tangible benefits whenever possible. If a particular benefit cannot be quantified and measured, then one could argue there is no benefit at all. Though this may be an oversimplification, it is extremely important to point out that there is a large body of evidence suggesting that many problems associated with projects not meeting business needs (especially in industries such as information technology) can be tied to issues with defining and documenting what, exactly, is expected to be realized in terms of benefits—once the systems are implemented, and the measuring and managing to ensure that those desired benefits are realized. It is often the case that quantifying these benefits and defining their associated measures is not impossible, but it is often not easy either.

Consider a proposed benefit, such as "increased ease of use." At first review, it may be difficult to conceive how an increase in ease of use can be measured. There may be no baseline for ease of use in the organization, against which improvement can be measured. There may be no organizational guideline or standard that defines "acceptable" ease of use. These situations can create tempting arguments to the effect that ease of use is simply something we intuitively believe will be a benefit but have no relevant measure for validating. Realistically however, even without a clear baseline, a measurement process can be implemented. Tools, such as surveys, could be used to assess the as-is and to-be states in order to validate that an increased ease of use is attainable, and then to measure whether this ease of use was actually realized at the end of the work. Some organizations fall into a trap of believing that measuring means measuring in dollars. And while monetary analysis is often necessary (especially as part of processes such as business case development), tangible benefits may not always be easily monetized but can very often be quantified, albeit with some effort.

In some cases, certain benefits may be largely intangible and correspondingly difficult to quantify in any relevant way. A benefit, such as increased employee knowledge, may be both difficult to measure in financial terms and difficult to measure on a nonfinancial basis as well. It is recognized that such benefits exist and should not be ignored, but the contribution of these intangible benefits to the organization will be much harder to articulate in a business case or other documentation. In these cases, the intangible contribution should be noted as appropriate with any supporting information to clearly articulate how the benefit contributes to the organization.

## Time Bound Benefits

Many benefits are not tied to specific time validity periods. For example, increasing customer satisfaction may not be something that is only necessary in September. Similarly, increasing productivity may be a desirable benefit that carries well into the future, rather than something with a specific time frame of relevance. Some benefits, by their nature, are relatively time bound. In these cases, the organization may need to assess the specific required delivery periods in order not to miss the "window of opportunity" for seizing a particular benefit.

A related concept that is important to note here is that the value of particular benefits to the organization may change over time. As projects and programs progress, the business world moves along as well. A benefit viewed as critical to the organization six months ago may be relatively inconsequential today. As we will discuss later in this book, this concept is critical. The benefits realization management process must relate closely to the organization's business planning processes in order to ensure that as needs change, the relevant projects and programs responsible for capability creation and benefits realization change as well.

## WHAT IS BENEFITS REALIZATION MANAGEMENT?

Having discussed the topic of benefits in some detail, the concept of benefits realization management can now be introduced. In essence, benefits realization management is the process by which benefits are identified, documented, planned, and managed through to successful delivery. The benefits realization management process typically occurs in a series of phases, over the life of the program that is responsible for benefits realization management. These phases include:

- Identifying potential benefits
- Analyzing potential benefits
- Planning for benefits realization management
- Delivering agreed-upon benefits
- Transitioning benefits to the organization
- Sustaining benefits over time

This list of phases is primarily based upon the Project Management Institute's *Standard for Program Management*, one of the widely distributed standards addressing benefits realization management. While each of these phases will be discussed in more detail in later chapters, it is worth highlighting a few relevant points for each phase here.

### Benefits Identification

The set of benefits relevant to any particular program or initiative may not be obvious at the start. Diverse stakeholder groups, emerging business demands, and other factors may influence which benefits are potentially relevant to the organization. This first phase seeks to identify potential benefits, which will later be validated and elaborated as part of the benefits realization management process.

## Benefits Analysis and Planning

Benefits analysis and planning encompasses the processes required to establish the benefits realization management framework. They also include the processes required to quantify the relevant identified metrics, establish the processes for monitoring benefits, and the work required to integrate benefits realization management activities into the overall program or initiative delivery plans.

## Benefits Delivery

Benefits delivery encompasses the work required to ensure delivery of the planned benefits. This work includes proactive monitoring of the business environment, tracking and management of benefits, risk management, and the required reporting to stakeholders regarding progress.

## Benefits Transition

Benefits transition encompasses the processes required to transition the delivered benefits from the program or initiative team to the operational business organization. Because activities associated with delivery methodologies, such as program management, come to a logical end, the responsibility for benefits must be transitioned to the permanent organization in order to ensure sustainment of the benefits. These transition activities are critically important, as they serve as the foundation for long-term success. Without successful transition, there is a significant risk that benefits, which have been obtained, will erode over time.

## Benefits Sustainment

Benefits sustainment encompasses the activities required to successfully sustain the realized benefits over time. Beyond transition, benefits sustainment seeks to ensure that once the team responsible for benefits realization is assigned to other work, the operational organization is able to successfully maintain what has been created. If not managed well, there is a risk that old ways of working, new inefficiencies, or other factors may begin to affect the realized benefits. This situation could lead to degrading the benefits already realized, resulting in reduced benefits sustainment over time.

# SUMMARY

This chapter provided an overview of the fundamental concepts of benefits and benefits realization management in order to provide a basic understanding of the concepts to be further developed in later chapters. A common definition of benefits and an understanding of the key characteristics of benefits provide an appropriate frame of reference for further discussion. The concepts presented here are generally described in most major benefits realization management methodologies and literature, ensuring that the reader has a background that will allow him or her to speak a language that is common to benefits realization management practitioners.

## REFERENCES

1. From www.merriam-webster.com.
2. Project Management Institute, *The Standard for Program Management*, Third Edition, 2013, 165.
3. Jenner, Steve, *Managing Benefits*, APMG-International, 2012, 15.

2

# BENEFITS REALIZATION MANAGEMENT IN THE PROJECT, PROGRAM, AND PORTFOLIO CONTEXTS

## INTRODUCTION

While it is not the purpose of this book to provide a detailed overview of the fundamentals of project, program, and portfolio management, it is important to briefly discuss the roles of projects, programs, and portfolios in benefits realization management. For a more detailed overview of project, program, and portfolio management, it is suggested that you review a library of standards such as those published by the Project Management Institute (PMI), or other relevant materials, such as the OGC *Managing Successful Programmes* methodology.

## DISTINGUISHING BETWEEN PROJECTS AND PROGRAMS

The distinction between a project and a program is important to discuss, as there seems to be significant confusion in some areas of the business world regarding the use of these terms. For ease of reference, the definitions of a project and a program, as defined by the PMI in *A Guide to the Project Management Body of Knowledge*, are shown here:

- A *project* is a temporary endeavor undertaken to create a unique product, service, or result.[1]
- A *program* is a group of related projects, subprograms, and program activities managed in a coordinated way to obtain benefits not available from managing them individually.[2]

From these definitions, we notice that they are quite different. A program is not simply a large project, and a program is not simply a complex project. This point is made here because, often, things that are called "programs" are really just very large projects.

The distinction lies, for the purposes of this book, in the difference between what we seek to accomplish through project and program work. In a basic sense, a project is really undertaken for the purpose of *capability creation*, in the sense of creating a unique product, service, or result. We create a new widget. We create a better IT system. We install playground equipment for a new park. These activities are projects. They are managed to a budget, a schedule, and a set of requirements in order to create capabilities associated with widgets, systems, or playground equipment.

Programs, more broadly, consider more than capability creation. Programs seek to create capabilities (often via projects) but also to coordinate the integration of created capabilities into the organization in a way that creates benefits. So, where projects focus on capability creation, programs must focus on *benefits realization*, but they can't exist without some link to project work. How do we get the benefit of a happier community without implementing the capabilities that come with new playground equipment? The equipment itself is not enough, is it? Not really. The new park must be marketed to the community. Community concerns about the location of the park, lighting, its operating hours, and so forth must be addressed in order to build community (stakeholder) commitment. The program steering committee, in terms of a City Council or similar body, must be kept apprised of progress, must be engaged in the case of issues, and so forth. While project management could successfully accomplish some of this, the integration of the created capabilities, the required change management activities, and the overriding processes associated with benefits delivery are most often in the realm of program management.

Several additional characteristics that distinguish projects from programs include the degree of change expected. We often expect programs to be evolutionary in nature, changing as the business needs change, whereas in project management, we often expect our project managers to conform to plans (schedules, budgets, etc.). Furthermore, the measures of success may differ between projects and programs. In the project management world, success may be measured in terms of conformance to requirements, adherence to schedule and budget, or other similar measures. In the program management environment, success is more likely to be measured in terms of benefits realization, how successfully the results of the program are integrated into the business environment, and so forth. Finally, because of its larger scope, program planning often relies on high-level integrated planning, whereas project planning often involves a "deep dive" approach to planning that is significantly more detailed than on the program level. There are certainly other distinctions that could be noted, but these highlight some of the key differences that are relevant here.

## UNDERSTANDING PORTFOLIO MANAGEMENT

In general, portfolio management in the context of this book encompasses the activities required to effectively coordinate project, program, and other work in a way that satisfies strategic needs. As a business function, portfolio management often does not "do the work," in the sense of executing projects and programs. Rather, the portfolio management function ensures that appropriate work, aligned to the needs of the organization, is chartered and executed, that the overall body of work is monitored to ensure that needs are being met, and that the portfolio is appropriately adjusted and balanced as business needs change.

The portfolio management function will have key roles at several stages in the benefits realization management life cycle. First, it will be important that the portfolio management function is actively engaged in the business case development process for all of the work within its domain, in order to ensure that the defined benefits associated with the work are aligned with organizational needs and are established in a way that supports tracking and reporting of these benefits over time. While work is being executed, the portfolio management function will need to take inputs from the teams executing the work, regarding planned and actual benefits delivery, as key elements in overall portfolio reporting. As variances from plans to benefits realization occur, the portfolio management function will need to assess the impact of these variances and determine what actions, if any, may be required for adjusting the portfolio. In some cases, a forecast that key benefits realization goals will be missed may require work to be adjusted, postponed, or stopped. Conversely, early delivery of agreed upon benefits may create opportunities to further enhance benefits across the entire portfolio, a desirable situation that the portfolio management team may wish to exploit.

With this basic understanding of portfolio management, we can concisely see the differences between projects, programs, and portfolios in the following table:

**Table 2.1** Comparative overview of project, program, and portfolio management (from the PMI's *Standard for Program Management*—Third Edition)

| | Organizational Project Management | | |
|---|---|---|---|
| | **Projects** | **Programs** | **Portfolios** |
| Scope | Projects have defined objectives. Scope is progressively elaborated throughout the project life cycle. | Programs have a larger scope and provide more significant benefits. | Portfolios have an organizational scope that changes with the strategic objectives of the organization. |
| Change | Project managers expect change and implement processes to keep change managed and controlled. | Program managers expect change from both inside and outside the program and are prepared to manage it. | Portfolio managers continuously monitor changes in the broader internal and external environment. |
| Planning | Project managers progressively elaborate high-level information into detailed plans throughout the project life cycle. | Program managers develop the overall program plan and create high-level plans to guide detailed planning at the component level. | Portfolio managers create and maintain necessary processes and communication relative to the aggregate portfolio. |
| Management | Project managers manage the project team to meet the project objectives. | Program managers manage the program staff and the project managers; they provide vision and overall leadership. | Portfolio managers may manage or coordinate portfolio management staff, or program and project staff that may have reporting responsibilities into the aggregate portfolio. |
| Success | Success is measured by product and project quality, timelines, budget compliance, and degree of customer satisfaction. | Success is measured by the degree to which the program satisfies the needs and benefits for which it was undertaken. | Success is measured in terms of the aggregate investment performance and benefit realization of the portfolio. |
| Monitoring | Project managers monitor and control the work of producing the products, services, or results that the project was undertaken to produce. | Program managers monitor the progress of program components to ensure the overall goals, schedules, budget, and benefits of the program will be met. | Portfolio managers monitor strategic changes and aggregate resource allocation, performance results, and risk of the portfolio. |

## PROJECTS, PROGRAMS, AND PORTFOLIOS TOGETHER

The relationship between projects, programs, and portfolios can be most easily seen in Figure 2.1.

As the diagram illustrates, a portfolio is often the top-level aggregator of constituent project, program, and operational work. In many organizations, there may be sub-portfolios as well that though not shown here, represent additional breakdowns of the work into logical subunits that are useful for more localized analysis and reporting. Constituent programs may be made up of subprograms as well, and will additionally contain representative project work, as well as potentially operational work.

With a basic understanding of the project, program, and portfolio relationship, it is then possible to understand the basic concepts of how benefits should flow within this context. Refer to Figure 2.2 for a first example.

Figure 2.2 represents an important concept—the notion of aggregate desired outcomes being defined on some strategic level and then flowing down to the portfolio level. From the portfolio level, decisions are made as to how to achieve these high-level objectives, and correspondingly, the appropriate projects and

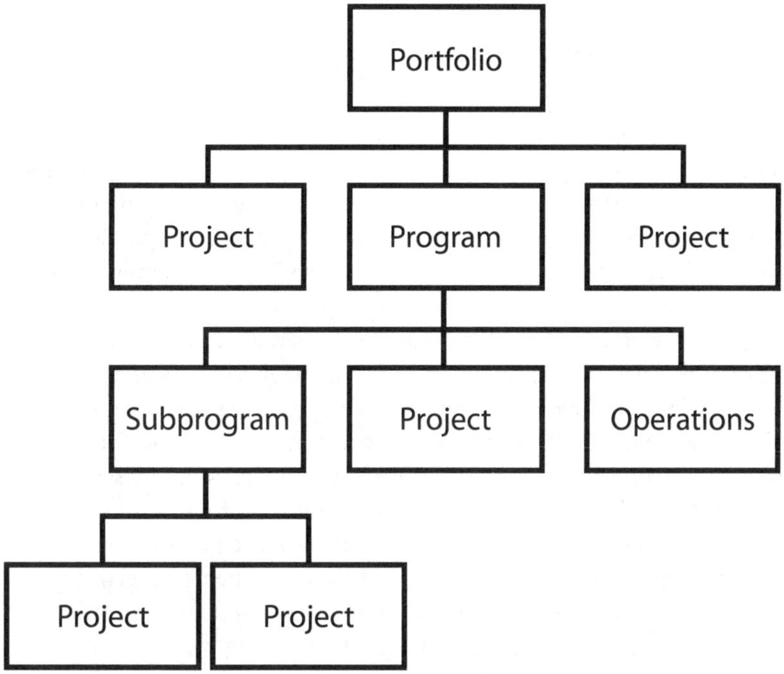


**Figure 2.1** Relationship between projects, programs, and portfolios

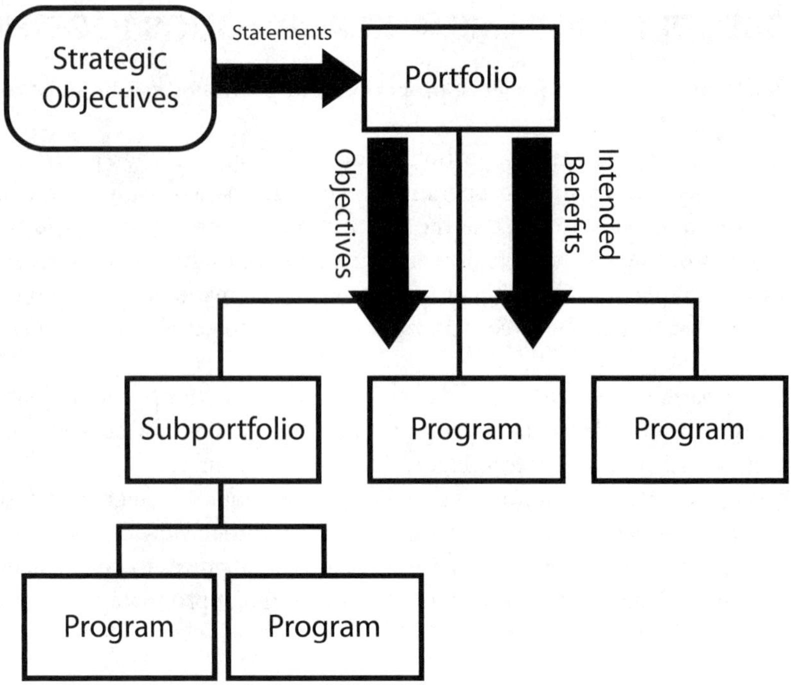


**Figure 2.2** Benefits flow-down

programs are chartered. Within the context of these objectives, high-level notions of required benefits attainment will be included as well. While these objectives will likely not be as detailed as what will be elaborated on the individual initiative level within the benefits realization management context, such guidance provides portfolio and program managers with "guideposts," to help them understand the required attainment from an overall business perspective.

The process works in the opposite direction as well, as depicted in Figure 2.3. In this case, the diagram represents the flow of benefits data from the constituent unit of work level to the management reporting level. As benefits data is created, that data is aggregated within the constituent program level and then aggregated up to the portfolio level, where a composite view—across all in-scope work—is created for stakeholder review. This is an important role for the portfolio management function, as it serves as the high-level governance point for benefits. When benefits attainment is not meeting expectations, or when emergent benefits are identified, the appropriate governance must be implemented, in order to make the best decision for the organization regarding how to handle shortcomings or to exploit potential opportunities. The portfolio management function has visibility across multiple efforts and thus may be able to more holistically analyze

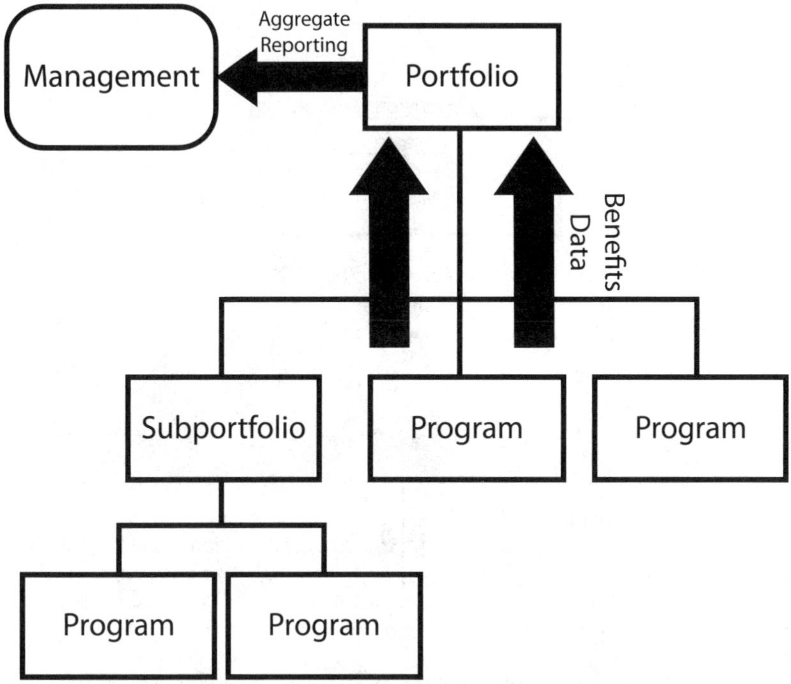


**Figure 2.3** Benefits flow-up

the potential impacts of issues or values of opportunities. Without this portfolio management function, there is a risk that individual program managers or steering committees may make decisions that are in the best interests of the constituent program itself without adequately considering or understanding the broader organizational context.

Finally, beyond these relationships between the projects, programs, and portfolios and the flows between them, it is perhaps useful to understand these concepts in the broader organizational context. Refer to Figure 2.4, which is taken from the PMI's *Standard for Program Management.*

The diagram is best explained from the overall business perspective first. The organizational vision and mission drive organizational strategy and objectives, a fact that is likely not unique in most organizations. From the organizational strategy and objectives, the portfolio management function utilizes concepts from strategic planning as well as processes related to the management of project, program, and portfolio work to establish the right set of initiatives to satisfy the defined organizational objectives. Accomplishing this work often requires changes to the operational processes of the organization (which are represented as the

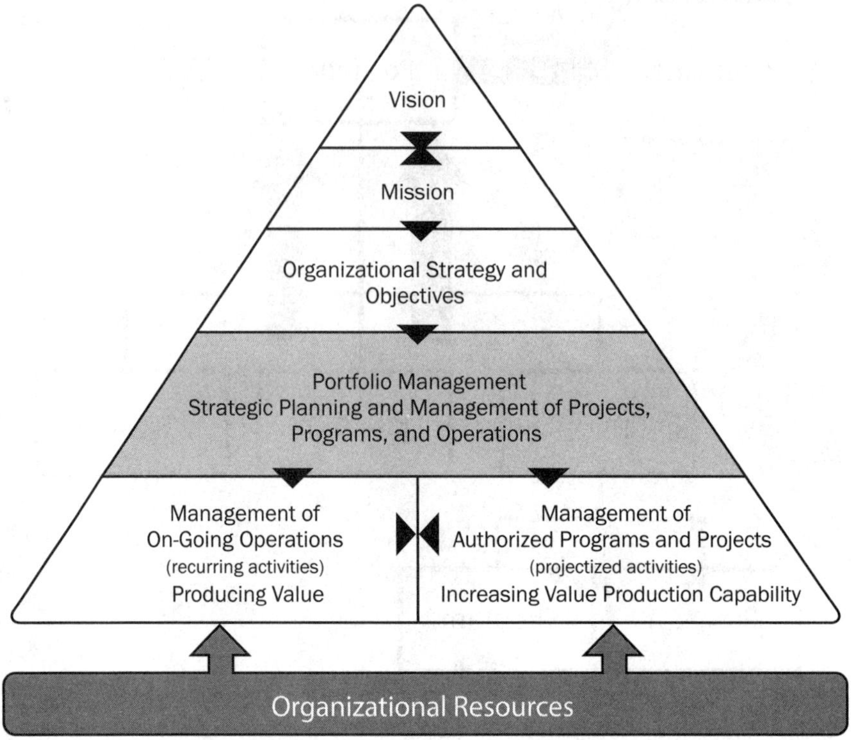


**Figure 2.4** Strategic and operational processes within an organization (from the PMI's *Standard for Program Management*—Third Edition)

ongoing work of the business rather than as temporary in nature like projects and programs) and requires the integration of project and program work in order to accomplish the additional work required to meet the stated business objectives. These operational activities must be integrated with project and program activities so that as change occurs, it occurs in a coordinated way and with the same goal in mind—increased delivery of value. At the bottom of the pyramid are the resources of the organization, which must be allocated across the operational, project, and program work in order to balance the needs of the organization with the organizational capacity to accomplish work.

## SUMMARY

This chapter provided an overview of project, program, and portfolio management in order to provide a foundation for understanding benefits realization management in the context of these important concepts. Organizations will implement benefits realization management on different levels, with some organizations focusing primarily on benefits realization management at the project or program level and others choosing to focus (at least initially) on implementing benefits realization management on the portfolio level. The choice of implementation scope and considerations for implementation of benefits realization management within these various business functions is discussed in further detail in later chapters.

## REFERENCES

1. Project Management Institute, *A Guide to the Project Management Body of Knowledge*, Fifth Edition, 2013, 553.
2. Ibid.

# 3

# BENEFITS REALIZATION MANAGEMENT ROLES AND RESPONSIBILITIES

## INTRODUCTION

This chapter introduces key roles and responsibilities in the benefits realization management life cycle. For simplicity, these roles are divided into two categories. The first category represents those primary roles that are most directly involved in the benefits realization management life cycle. The second category addresses those supporting roles that are important for effective implementation of benefits realization management in the organization. It is certainly not the case that one set of roles is more important than the other. Rather, the distinction is drawn in order to differentiate the roles that are primarily responsible for *doing* the work from those roles that are primarily responsible for either *supporting* the work or *consuming* the outputs of the benefits realization management process.

## PRIMARY ROLES

In the discussion of primary roles within benefits management, we begin with three key roles that most directly form the core "benefits realization team," meaning those key individuals who will drive the implementation of benefits realization management and the realization of benefits on the individual program or initiative level. Each of these roles is important for successful benefits realization management implementation, and as such, certain key characteristics of effective candidates for these roles are identified.

## Program Manager

The program manager role represents the individual who maintains overall responsibility for program leadership. In the benefits realization management context, the program manager will have a variety of responsibilities, including, but not limited to:

- Providing leadership in the development of the benefits realization strategy, liaising with other critical roles and stakeholders in order to ensure stakeholder alignment with and commitment to the strategy
- Providing leadership in the development of the benefits realization plan and associated deliverables, which define how benefits realization management will be implemented within the program
- Managing across the constituent subprograms, projects, and operational initiatives in order to ensure that the capabilities created by these components support the required benefits realization goals
- Monitoring benefits realization management processes in order to ensure that benefits goals are being achieved; proactively conducting reviews, assessments, and other activities to assess progress, respond to issues, and mitigate risks
- Integrating benefits realization management activities into the overall program plans in order to ensure alignment with program governance activities

The program manager maintains an important role as one of the focal points for benefits realization management activities as well as for the program overall. As such, selecting a program manager is not easy. Some characteristics of effective program managers include:

- A change-oriented mindset that enables the program manager to proactively seek value-added change within the program and to appropriately respond to new opportunities as they arise
- A strong business focus that enables the program manager to understand the underlying business drivers and goals for the program and enables the program manager to effectively manage the program to ensure realization of the relevant benefits to support business goals
- An ability to manage throughout the organization, effectively leading the program management team while managing diverse stakeholders, governance bodies, and other entities

- An ability to maintain focus on the broad program while effectively managing more detailed work as appropriate; strong delegation skills to ensure that appropriate work is delegated to competent parties
- Strong negotiation skills and the ability to understand how to effectively manage stakeholder needs and expectations
- A strong background in project and program management and a history of successfully leading large projects and/or programs; appropriate education and certification (e.g., Program Management Professional [PgMP®] certification)

This list is not meant to be exhaustive, but rather indicative of some of the key knowledge and skills that an effective program manager should possess. It will be important to ensure that the program manager is a credible leader who can coordinate the required program management work to successfully implement benefits realization management into the business organization.

## Senior Responsible Owner

The senior responsible owner is a representative of the program's sponsoring organization and maintains overall responsibility for ensuring that the program delivers the identified benefits. The senior responsible owner is often a relatively senior member of the organization's management, with the ability to allocate resources, make decisions to resolve issues, and represent the business community that is primarily involved in receiving the benefits created by the program. In this context, the senior responsible owner most often undertakes responsibilities, including, but not limited to:

- Representing the sponsoring group and providing leadership within the sponsoring group to support advancement of the program and realization of planned benefits
- Supporting the development of the benefits realization strategy and benefits realization plan by providing key business input, ensuring effective implementation of the plans and compliance with the plans during the overall benefits realization management life cycle
- Leading benefits reviews and supporting validation of benefit realization with appropriate business stakeholders
- Managing expectations within his or her sphere of influence and ensuring that the business organization maintains support for the program and the benefits goals
- Providing key input to important program decisions that affect benefits delivery

The senior responsible owner plays an important role in providing business leadership support for the program, which is crucial for ensuring success. Characteristics of an effective senior responsible owner include:

- Appropriate seniority within the organizational structure to influence business stakeholders and members of the sponsoring organization
- Strong ability to influence throughout the organization, ensuring that program and benefits realization management goals are appropriately understood and agreed upon by appropriate parties
- Thorough awareness of the business environment and changing business needs
- Commitment to the program and its benefits objectives
- Ability to make decisions and, as appropriate, to allocate resources to support decisions and changing program needs

This is by no means an exhaustive list. It is of the utmost importance that the senior responsible owner role is appropriately positioned within the organization to exert influence, as needed, to support the program's goals, is empowered to make decisions that affect the program, and is able to allocate resources, as needed, to provide support for the program. It is also important to note that the senior responsible owner must be a single empowered individual. There is a tendency in some organizations to "manage by committee," empowering steering committees, sponsor boards, or other such entities to make collective decisions, but not empowering a single person to act as the ultimate decision maker. In a dynamic environment, such as the program environment, management by committee rarely works. The senior responsible owner role exists to maintain accountability for the program as well as to support the program management team in advancing the program's goals. The program manager should be able to rely on the senior responsible owner to provide leadership and decision making in a timely manner without excess reliance on the "monthly steering committee meeting." This is not meant to discount the role of a sponsoring board or steering committee in the program management context. It is important that such stakeholder groups are engaged throughout the program life cycle. However, the program manager must be able to count on the senior responsible owner to make decisions outside the context of these boards and meetings, as required, in order to keep the program moving forward in a fast-paced business environment.

## Business Change Manager

The business change manager is a fundamental role that is, unfortunately, either not staffed or staffed inappropriately in many organizations. The role of the business change manager is to ensure that the capabilities created as part of the program efforts are effectively embedded into the organization and that the corresponding benefits, associated with the business change created by capability creation and integration into the business environment, are realized. Often, these critical responsibilities are relegated to the program manager or program management team, who may not be well enough equipped to undertake them. This is not because the program manager and program management team are not competent to do the work. Rather, it is because they are often not an integral part of the business functions being impacted by the change. Instead, they are part of the project and program management function of the organization, moving from program to program. The business change manager role is best filled by a *business* team member who has credibility in the business environment and can influence the business recipients of the change. The program manager and program management team cannot effectively do this in many environments.

The business change manager has a variety of responsibilities within the program environment which are related to benefits realization management. These include, but are not limited to:

- Facilitating identification and quantification of program benefits; engaging the business stakeholder community in order to establish consensus and alignment
- Effecting business change to support benefits realization, utilizing sound organizational change management practices
- Proactively monitoring the business environment for changing business conditions, resistance, or other factors that may influence attainment of benefits realization goals
- Supporting the creation of the benefits realization plan, ensuring that the required business change activities and processes are represented within the plan
- Developing and maintaining key benefits realization management artifacts, including benefits profiles
- Supporting ongoing sustainment of benefits as appropriate

Finding an effective business change manager is not always easy. Desirable characteristics include:

- A strong change orientation and desire to effect change within the business organization
- An understanding of (or ability to learn) basic organizational change management principles and techniques
- Appropriate seniority within the organization to enable the business change manager to effect change
- Excellent written and oral communications skills, including strong presentation skills

- Strong negotiation skills and an ability to effectively build consensus
- A fundamental understanding of project management techniques

## Program Management Team

The program management team is another important set of individuals who provide overall support for effective delivery of the program work. The size and composition of the program management team may vary widely, depending upon the specific nature of the program being undertaken, and it is not possible to provide an exhaustive list here. However, from a benefits realization management perspective, the program management team (perhaps through a program support office) will provide support to the program manager and business change manager to:

- Support data aggregation and management to provide benefits realization management reporting
- Interface with relevant enterprise program management office staff and portfolio management staff to support benefits realization management reporting
- Track and manage benefits realization management-related issues and risks
- Support benefits realization management-related communication via established program communications processes, defined in the program's communications management plan

## Effort Allocation to Primary Roles

Determining the appropriate allocation of effort to the primary roles within the program and benefits realization management context is not always easy. Many factors, such as the size and complexity of the program, could affect the number of roles required and the allocation of these roles. However, two requirements are almost always clear. First, the program manager should be assigned on a full-time basis to support the program. Second, the business change manager should be assigned on a full-time basis to support the program.

The reasoning behind these allocations is straightforward. In both cases, the scope of effort necessitates the allocation. The program manager is responsible for the overall delivery of the program, of which benefits realization management activities are but one important part. It is shortsighted to believe that someone working part-time can handle the overall program management effort for a program of any meaningful size. Even with effective deputies, it is unlikely to be a sustainable model. Focus and attention must be paid to the many aspects of program management, which are within the purview of the program manager, on a daily basis.

In the case of the business change manager, it is common for the business change manager to be given this role in addition to his or her regular duties. This is a tremendous mistake. The business change manager must be focused on managing change and ensuring the realization of benefits. This often requires taking someone who is a reasonably tenured employee out of his or her regular job function and assigning him or her, perhaps for an extended period of time, to the business change manager role. This can be as worrying for the employee as it is for the organization. Specifically, the employee may feel that he or she:

- Is not qualified to perform the role because he or she has no formal training or experience as a business change manager
- Will not have a "home" to come back to in the organization once his or her duties as business change manager are fulfilled
- Will not have appropriate empowerment or influence to truly drive change within the organization (this is especially prevalent in relatively change-adverse business cultures)

The appropriate management, often including the senior responsible owner, must work to ensure that the business change manager is appropriately empowered, that the role of business change manager is viewed as a valuable opportunity for a highly qualified staff member, and that adequate training is provided to support the business change manager in his or her role. It is certainly possible to hire qualified consultants to support business change management work, but ultimately, the organization will be best served by empowering one of its own staff, who is credible and respected by his or her peers, to lead the relevant benefits realization and business change management efforts.

## SUPPORTING ROLES

Beyond the primary roles responsible for the majority of the work within the program and benefits realization management domains, certain supporting roles often exist to support the program management team, as well as to ensure governance and coordination across the numerous initiatives of the organization. Several of these key roles follow:

### Benefit Owner

The benefit owner is the individual responsible for the realization of a particular benefit. Because the business change manager has overall responsibility for realization of all benefits, he or she must rely on a team of individuals who can tactically work at the individual constituent benefit level to provide focus on the achievement of individual benefits. This individual will be responsible for supporting the implementation of the appropriate business change, as well as for reporting data to demonstrate the realization of benefits. This role may not be a full-time role for each benefit owner; however, the benefit owner must have sufficient capacity and empowerment to effect change. Desirable characteristics of benefits owners include, but are not limited to:

- A solid understanding of the business environment and culture of the business area(s) where change will be implemented
- A strong change orientation and desire to effect change within the business organization
- Understanding of (or ability to learn) basic principles and techniques of organizational change management
- Appropriate seniority within the organization to enable the benefit owner to effect change

The role of benefit owner is crucial and is listed here as a supporting role, primarily to distinguish the three "key" program management roles defined in the relevant program management literature. Certainly, clear benefit ownership and accountability for realization of individual benefits will be required in order for benefits realization management to be successful. This ownership and accountability must rest with a specific, named individual who serves in the benefit owner role. Assigning benefit ownership to groups is not appropriate, as a group of individuals maintains no individual accountability for ensuring that required work is completed.

## Program Office

A program office provides program support functions to a specific program. Often established in large programs, the program office assumes a significant administrative and business support role within the program, enabling the core program management team to focus its attention on day-to-day management of the core work. In some cases, program offices exist to support multiple programs, sharing costs and resources across these programs in order to capitalize on economies of scale, create consistency of process, or for other beneficial purposes. In the benefits realization management context, the program office may provide support, including, but not limited to:

- Providing data management activities to support gathering and reporting data concerning benefits realization
- Supporting periodic benefits reviews and program governance reviews
- Performing document management and maintenance activities to ensure that key benefits realization management artifacts (e.g., the benefits

realization plan) are available to all stakeholders and are appropriately document controlled
- Supporting the program manager and program management team in maintaining updates to benefits registers and other benefits realization management artifacts
- Supporting the business change manager by providing support for program change communication, training, and associated activities

While this list is not all-inclusive, the key point is that the program office may provide important support to ease business management and administrative support burdens within the program, a necessary function in many large programs.

## Program Management Office

A program management office (PMO) is an organizational entity that maintains responsibility for governance of the processes, tools, and techniques used by the program management staff, ensuring that consistent ways of working are implemented across initiatives for the benefit of the organization. There are numerous other tasks that a PMO may perform, but for the purposes of the discussion here, it is important to note the role of the PMO in defining standard organizational processes for benefits realization management activities. It is inefficient and a disservice to the organization to have individual programs and other initiatives defining their own ways of working. The problems with this approach are many, but the primary problems that are created and that limit effective benefits realization management include:

- Lack of a standard process may lead to individual program management teams defining their own process artifacts, creating unnecessary work and limiting the opportunity for reuse
- Inability to effectively manage stakeholder expectations across multiple programs if stakeholder groups are provided with different templates, reports, or other artifacts that represent the same business use (e.g., three different benefits realization plan templates in use)
- Lack of consistency in documenting benefits, measures, and related items can make it difficult to reuse artifacts from benefits realization management activities later
- Varying degrees of detail on benefits attainment may make it difficult to aggregate benefits data across multiple programs or initiatives

The job of the PMO is not easy. Especially in large organizations, managing and maintaining consistent ways of working can be a challenge. Different business groups may perceive that they have different business needs and that these needs require the use of specialized tools or processes. Employees may empower themselves to create their own "better" processes. These situations, among others, can make it challenging for the PMO to maintain control. As a general note of advice, the PMO should maintain a specific minimum set of process standards but permit some reasonable amount of tailoring of these processes to the specific needs of different business or program teams. While this tailoring must be controlled, ensuring some flexibility will go a long way toward maintaining process compliance and deriving value from the PMO.

In some organizations, the PMO may assume certain functions that are directly related to benefits realization management. These functions could include aggregating and reporting data on benefits attainment across programs (especially in organizations where a separate portfolio management function does not exist), supporting tools used for benefits reporting, and providing support for benefits reviews or other checkpoints. While the majority of the benefits realization management work will occur at the program level, effective PMO support can make the program management team's job easier and should be leveraged as appropriate.

## Portfolio Management Office

The portfolio management office maintains responsibility for one or more portfolios of work within its sphere of influence. This includes the processes associated with managing the portfolio itself, as well as providing reporting and analysis regarding portfolio health; leading portfolio governance activities, such as periodic reviews; and maintaining an effective resource allocation across initiatives that best meets business goals. The portfolio management office may also create and enforce standardized processes for executing portfolio management as a business function, if there is no program management office that provides the standards and processes to be used as part of its scope.

In the benefits realization management context, the portfolio management office serves several distinct functions. These include:

- Managing business case review and approval, including ensuring that appropriate benefits targets, measures, and associated data are included and validated within the business case
- Maintaining the portfolio-level benefits realization plan, which encompasses the required realization across numerous programs and initiatives, and communicating required benefits realization goals to the programs
- Providing portfolio-level reporting on benefits realization, gathering data from the constituent portfolio elements (programs), and aggregating this data for portfolio-level reporting
- Leading portfolio-level resource allocation and resolving allocation conflicts to minimize disbenefits to affected portfolio elements

At the individual program level, interfaces with the portfolio management office will likely include providing support to portfolio-level data aggregation and reporting, liaising with the portfolio management office to keep the portfolio management office staff apprised of situations that may affect benefits realization, working with the portfolio management office to overcome resource constraints that may affect benefits realization, and ensuring the continued alignment of the program to the organization's priorities as described in the portfolio.

The last point is especially important. As business needs change, the composition of the organization's portfolio should change as well. In this context, the effect of portfolio composition changes on the organization's benefits realization needs may change also. While the portfolio management office may maintain primary responsibility for understanding these impacts across the overall portfolio, individual managers of constituent portfolio elements should also maintain awareness of these changes. As these individuals are the closest to their constituent work, they may be better equipped than the portfolio management office to identify and assess potential new opportunities that their constituent portfolio elements could capitalize on to positively affect benefits realization. These opportunities may not be immediately apparent to the portfolio management office team.

Additionally, in some organizations, the portfolio management office may maintain a specific role for a *portfolio benefits manager*, who maintains responsibility for ensuring that a consistent approach to benefits realization management is implemented across the portfolio. This role may also serve the important function of identifying opportunities to optimize benefits realization across the portfolio. Specific duties of the portfolio benefits manager include, but are not limited to:

- Maintaining a set of practices for implementing benefits realization management across the portfolio, including standardized templates, processes, and tools to support consistent benefits realization management implementation
- Participating in business case development to ensure that appropriate benefits are identified, quantified, and validated to ensure achievability and alignment with organizational benefits realization management policies
- Supporting program managers and business change managers by providing coaching and mentoring on effective benefits realization management practices
- Conducting benefits audits and reviews to ensure consistent application of benefits realization management practices across constituent portfolio elements
- Providing consolidated benefits reporting for the portfolio, leading analysis of benefits data to identify risks

While this role is not strictly necessary, it is often beneficial, especially in large portfolios, to have an individual who is specifically focused on supporting benefits realization management on the portfolio level. This ensures an appropriate focus on benefits realization management, provides support to the program teams, and ensures process consistency across all portfolio elements.

## SUMMARY

This chapter provided an overview of important roles that support effective benefits realization management. Making decisions to fill these roles with the most qualified staff is an important component for successful benefits realization management implementation. While benefits realization management may be relatively new to the organization, it is certainly possible to train qualified resources to support implementation, and providing these resources with new skills and opportunities may be welcomed by staff seeking new challenges. Where appropriate, involvement from external consultants to support some of the roles mentioned in this chapter may be appropriate and should support building competency within the organization itself, enabling the organization to be self-sustaining in the future.

# 4

# A BENEFITS REALIZATION MANAGEMENT LIFE CYCLE

## INTRODUCTION

This chapter provides an overview of a benefits realization management life cycle. For the purposes of this chapter and the later chapters that provide more in-depth discussion and practical guidance for implementation of the various stages of the life cycle, the life cycle presented in the Project Management Institute's *Standard for Program Management* will be used as the basic reference model. This is not the only available model. Proprietary models exist within organizations that augment, extend, or perhaps vary significantly from the standard presented by the Project Management Institute (PMI). The esteemed *Managing Successful Programmes* methodology from the UK Cabinet Office is an additional excellent reference on program management, with a significant focus on benefits realization management. Other resources exist online and in other places. The selection of the PMI's standard is based primarily on the global reach of the standard and the relative completeness of the standard as presented. It's a great starting point. This chapter and subsequent chapters, while primarily relying on the *Standard for Program Management*, will be augmented with resources drawn from other sources and the author's own experiences, providing a picture of the standard model as well as additional detail to assist readers with practical implementation of the model in their own organizations.

## BENEFITS REALIZATION MANAGEMENT IN THE PROGRAM LIFE CYCLE

Figure 4.1, depicting benefits realization management in the context of program management, provides a starting point for elaborating the major phases required for effective benefits realization management.

The top of the figure illustrates major domains within the broader context of program management, including domains related to program definition, program benefits delivery, and program closure. These domains are embedded within the overall program management approach, and specific benefits realization management activities, which will be described in detail later, are performed within these phases to support benefits realization management.

The arrow below the program domains demonstrates that benefits realization management is a process that extends beyond the program itself. We know this is true, as certain activities related to benefits sustainment must be carried out after the program is finished in order to ensure ongoing benefits realization. Similarly, initial thinking regarding potential benefits associated with a particular undertaking may take place well in advance of formal program initiation, as "back of the napkin" sketches of potential investments are considered by organizational leaders and as business cases are developed and reviewed.

Below the arrow, we find the five major domains within the benefits realization management life cycle. The arrows between Benefits Analysis and Planning and Benefits Delivery depict the circular interaction between these domains, representing the fact that it will be necessary during benefits delivery to perform some amount of incremental benefits analysis and planning, either to respond to identified risks or issues or to capitalize on potential opportunities. Below the domains are representative activities that must be performed. In the following sections, each of the five domains will be briefly described, along with the key activities typically performed within these domains in order to provide an overview of the full benefits realization management life cycle.

### Benefits Identification

Benefits identification includes the activities required to identify appropriate benefits and to quantify these benefits with business stakeholders. Benefits identification requires significant knowledge of the organization's business environment, competitive environment, industry, external influences, and related drivers that may impact the organization, as well as a strong understanding of the organization's strategies and business objectives. Specific activities to be undertaken

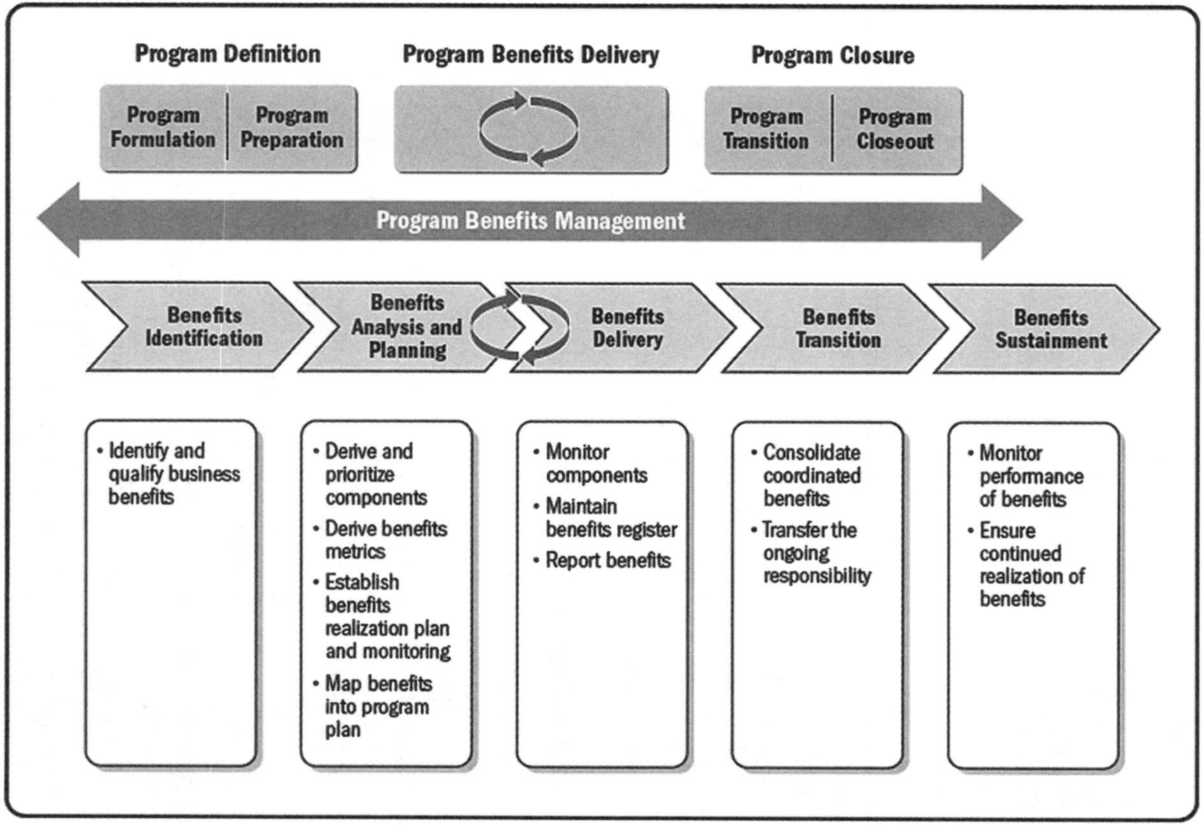


**Figure 4.1** Program life cycle and program benefits management (from the PMI's *Standard for Program Management*—Third Edition)

during benefits identification, according to the PMI's *Standard for Program Management*, include:

- Defining the objectives and critical success factors for the program
- Identifying and quantifying business benefits
- Developing meaningful metrics and key performance indicators (KPIs) to measure the actual delivery of benefits and planned benefits
- Establishing processes for measuring progress against the benefits plan
- Creating the tracking and communications processes necessary to record program progress and report to stakeholders[1]

There is quite a bit of work to do in this phase. Beyond identifying and quantifying benefits themselves, the appropriate metrics, measurement processes, and reporting mechanisms must be established. This is critically important, as doing it successfully builds the foundation for managing benefits delivery throughout the remainder of the life cycle. If the results of this work are largely intangible statements of benefits without firm metrics or measurement systems to support them, it is likely that realization of benefits will be hindered. As already stated, intangible benefits are less desirable from a benefits realization management perspective, as they offer no guidepost against which attainment of benefits can be concretely determined.

## Benefits Analysis and Planning

Benefits analysis and planning includes the activities required to formalize benefits realization management within the program (via the benefits realization plan) as well as the additional activities required to formalize appropriate processes and tools to measure benefits realization. This fundamental phase solidifies the foundation for success that was first built during benefits identification by formally establishing the plans for benefits realization and the monitoring and controlling framework that will be used to ensure that the established framework is effective. Specific activities to be undertaken during benefits analysis and planning, according to the PMI's *Standard for Program Management*, include:

- Establishing the benefits realization plan that will guide the work through the remainder of the program
- Defining and prioritizing program components, including component projects, subprograms, and their interdependencies
- Defining the KPIs and associated quantitative measures required to effectively monitor the delivery of program benefits
- Establishing the performance baseline for the program and communicating program performance metrics to the key stakeholders[2]

There is much important work to be done in this domain. First, the benefits realization plan must be established, which will provide the guidance necessary for the program management team and other stakeholders to execute benefits realization management activities. While this plan will be based on existing organizational process assets—if they exist (perhaps via a template provided by a project management office, or PMO, or other entity)—it will likely need to be tailored, to some extent, to the unique needs of the particular program in which it will be used. This tailoring is perfectly acceptable, as long as the tailoring itself is done in a standard way and is reviewed and approved by appropriate governing bodies or other stakeholders. Tailoring is not necessarily a risk, but uncontrolled tailoring does present a risk to effective governance and delivery.

Beyond the benefits realization plan, the relevant program components must be defined and prioritized. In the benefits realization management context, it is important to understand how these program components contribute to benefits realization, as well as how the interdependencies between them potentially impact benefits realization. This will be discussed in more detail in Chapter 6. Additional work to be completed within this domain includes definition of KPIs and relevant measurements and measurement techniques to ensure that it is possible (and, if possible, easy) to measure and assess performance. Lastly, a performance baseline is established, so that measurement comparisons can be made against an approved baseline for tracking and reporting purposes.

## Benefits Delivery

Benefits delivery includes the activities required to proactively ensure that the established program benefits are delivered. This likely sounds obvious to you. And to some extent, it is but—much as many project managers tend to "forget" some of the basics of project management when project work gets difficult, or a project gets behind schedule or over budget—so does it occasionally occur in the benefits realization management world that the program management team takes its eyes off the execution of the benefits realization plan when issues or realized risks divert their attention to other matters. It's not a healthy situation. A consistent focus on benefits delivery is absolutely critical. Specific activities to be undertaken during benefits analysis and planning, according to the PMI's *Standard for Program Management*, include:

- Monitoring the organizational environment (including internal and external factors), program objectives, and benefits realization to ensure that the program remains aligned with the organization's objectives
- Initiating, performing, transitioning, and closing component projects and subprograms and managing the interdependencies between them

- Evaluating program risks and KPIs related to program financials, compliance, quality, safety, and stakeholder satisfaction in order to monitor the delivery of benefits
- Recording program progress in the benefits register and reporting to key stakeholders as directed in the program communication plan[3]

Reading these bullet points may cause you to think that the primary work in this domain encompasses the basics of program delivery, in which we monitor the environment, do the work, evaluate ourselves, and communicate. At a simple level, this is exactly what it is. The key point to understand here is that the integrated nature of benefits realization management necessitates that its work will be performed within each of these activities. For example, transitioning and closing components will require performing benefits transition activities. Evaluating risks will include a focus on the risks to benefits delivery. The transversal nature of benefits realization management requires that many of the standard processes of executing program work be viewed with a "benefits lens" in order to ensure successful benefits delivery.

## Benefits Transition

We recognize that simply creating capabilities that have the potential to deliver benefits is not enough. Through benefits delivery, we ensure that the capabilities created deliver the benefits anticipated. Benefits transition encompasses the activities required to transition these benefits from the program to the operational areas of the business. According to the PMI's *Standard for Program Management*, activities in this domain include:

- Verifying that the integration, transition, and closure of the program and its components meet or exceed the benefit realization criteria established to achieve the program's strategic objectives
- Developing a transition plan to facilitate the ongoing realization of benefits, when turned over to the impacted operational areas[4]

The verification activity contained within benefits transition is the final check to ensure that the program component being transitioned has fulfilled the established benefit realization criteria. If this is the case, then the program must document the attainment, as well as the plan for ensuring ongoing benefits realization. This documentation is provided so that the operational area receiving the delivered benefits has a guide to ongoing benefits realization that operates after the program is formally closed.

## Benefits Sustainment

In the typical project management context, we tend to not think about the notion of "life after the project." When the project closes, the project team moves on, and whatever the project delivers remains in the organization that received it. In the program management context, we take a more holistic view, by including benefits sustainment activities as part of the program management work, with an eye on ensuring that the appropriate activities are undertaken to position the achieved benefits for long-term sustainment. This work differs slightly from the benefits transition work discussed in the previous section. In the benefits sustainment context, we assume the successful transition of the benefits from the program to the operational organization, ensuring that these benefits are appropriately embedded in the operational organization. In benefits sustainment, there is a stronger focus on ensuring the long-term viability of benefits realization, which positions the benefits for long-term effectiveness. According to the PMI's *Standard for Program Management*, activities in this domain include:

- Planning for the operational, financial, and behavioral changes needed from program recipients (individuals, groups, organizations, industries, and sectors) to continue monitoring performance
- Implementing the required change efforts to ensure that the capabilities required during the course of the program continue when the program is closed and the program's resources are returned to the organization
- Monitoring the performance of the product, service, capability, or results from a reliability and availability-for-use perspective and comparing actual performance to planned performance, including KPIs
- Monitoring the continued suitability of the developed product, service, capability, or results to provide the benefits expected by the customers owning and operating it. This may include the continued viability of interfaces with other products, services, capabilities, or results and the continued completeness of the functionality
- Monitoring the continued availability of logistics support for the product, service, capability, or result in light of technical advancements and the willingness of vendors to continue to support older configurations
- Responding to customer inputs on their needs for product, service, capability, or results of support assistance or for improvements in performance or functionality
- Providing on-demand support for the product, service, capability, or results either in parts, improved technical information, or real-time help desk support
- Planning for and establishing operational support of the product, service, capability, or results separate from the program management function without relinquishing the other product support functions
- Updating technical information concerning the product, service, capability, or improvement in response to frequent product support queries

- Planning the transition of product or capability support from program management to an operations function within an organization
- Planning the retirement and phase out of the product or capability, or the cessation of support with appropriate guidance to the current customers
- Developing business cases and the potential initiation of new projects or programs to respond to operational issues with the deployed product, service, or capability being supported or public acceptance/reaction to the improvement
- Developing business cases and the potential initiation of new projects to respond to legislative changes, political and economic, socioeconomic changes, cultural shifts, or logistics issues with a deployed product, service, capability, or results being supported.[5]

There are quite a number of activities here. In short, benefits sustainment is primarily focused on making sure that whatever is created (product, service, capability, or result) continues to create value and, where actual performance versus planned performance varies unfavorably, understanding the impact of the variances on continued benefits realization and the required actions, if any, to correct variances. Because the program management team may not exist forever, the work associated with benefits attainment may, from an ongoing business perspective, reside in the operational organization. In this case, the program management team is obligated to ensure a solid foundation for benefits sustainment as part of the program benefits sustainment activities. In some cases, members of the program management team responsible for the development of the product, service, capability, or result may transition into a program office role responsible for the ongoing development, maintenance, and support of the developed product, service, capability, or result, even after the formal program is concluded.

## RELATIONSHIP BETWEEN THE BENEFITS REALIZATION MANAGEMENT LIFE CYCLE AND ASSOCIATED LIFE CYCLES

The benefits realization management life cycle described in this chapter represents one view of the overall life cycle of a program, and more broadly, one life cycle within the larger context of organizational project management (OPM). The relationship between the benefits realization management life cycle and several associated life cycles is described in the following sections.

### Relationship to the Program Management Life Cycle

This relationship is, perhaps, the easiest to describe. The discipline of benefits realization management is most closely associated with program management and is, therefore, tightly integrated into most major program management methodologies. It is important to recognize that while benefits realization management is an essential component for effective program management, from the program manager's perspective, it can become one (among many) of the various items that the program manager must manage in the course of program delivery. This can create a risk that when "push comes to shove," the benefits realization management work gets overtaken by work that is deemed more urgent. This situation seems to be especially prevalent when programs are troubled and the program management team is focused on addressing budget, schedule, customer, resource, or other challenges.

## Relationship to the Portfolio Management Life Cycle

Benefits realization management, while not directly addressed as a core domain of portfolio management in standards such as the PMI's *Standard for Portfolio Management*, is clearly a data provider and data consumer within portfolio management and, furthermore, reliant on the portfolio management process as part of initial benefits identification and throughout the portfolio management life cycle. These relationships manifest themselves in several ways.

One can think of this first in the context of initiation of any organizational investment that is a responsibility of the portfolio management function within an organization. As part of the process of choosing between potential investments, portfolio managers need to work with business managers to assess trade-offs—based on potential risks, rewards, resource mixes, strategic goals, and other factors. This typically occurs as part of a business case analysis and review process. An integral part of the business case, from a benefits realization management perspective, will be the initial assessment of anticipated benefits, rationales for investment, investment analysis, and related facts and data that provide the justification for investment. While program management literature may suggest that business case development and approval falls within the responsibility of the program, the reality is that the portfolio management function plays a significant role in business case development and review in many organizations, with formal approval of business cases and chartering of initiatives occurring on the portfolio management level and then flowing down to the program management function for direct execution and management. From a strategic alignment and resource allocation perspective, this makes perfect sense. And, rightfully, the necessary "balancing act" to manage the all-too-common environment in which the organization has more initiatives it would like to do than it has resources to commit to doing necessitates that these trade-offs be assessed on the organizational (portfolio) level.

We can also think of the benefits realization management relationship to portfolio management in the context of portfolio management data aggregation requirements. As benefits realization management activities progress, data is generated. This data is generated to support reporting that is required on the program level in order to keep program stakeholders informed regarding benefits attainment, risks to benefits attainment, additional opportunities to realize benefits, and so forth. The types of data, frequency of reporting, and related logistics should appear in the benefits realization plan. This generated data will also be of interest to the portfolio management team for aggregation with benefits data from other programs. This aggregated data will be used to support consolidated benefits reporting on the portfolio level, portfolio level decision making required to respond to issues and exploit opportunities, and for other purposes. The portfolio management office must coordinate with the program office and/or program management team to ensure that:

- Portfolio level reporting requirements are understood, documented, and accounted for within the relevant program plans
- Early warning or related procedures for raising awareness of key risks and issues are understood
- Frequency, format, and means of communicating data from the program level to the portfolio management office are understood and agreed upon
- Review cadences are established
- The role of the program manager or other program management team members in portfolio-level reviews is understood

The maturity of portfolio management processes varies widely from organization to organization. As such, different programs in different companies may encounter varying levels of data and collaboration requirements with the portfolio management office. Where portfolio management is well established, standard governance for reporting and related processes may exist, and support may be provided to the program team (either via people or systems) to enable easy management of required data. In other organizations, less formal processes may be in use. The important consideration for program managers, business change managers, benefit owners, and others regularly involved in benefits realization management activities is ensuring that whatever data is provided and reported is an accurate representation of the true picture of benefits realization. Incomplete data, skewed data, incorrect interpretation, and other associated factors may come into play and must be handled appropriately.

## Relationship to the Project Management Life Cycle

In the project management context, it is important to understand that while the project manager and project team are primarily responsible for capability creation rather than benefits realization, these key stakeholders in program delivery must understand the relationship between their work and the overall program goals, including benefits realization goals, as well as the relationship between their work and other constituent work in the program. In other words, it is important for the project manager and the project management team (and the program management team as well) to understand the interdependencies that exist within their environment as well as the impact of these interdependencies, if not managed well, on overall results.

Additionally, it is imperative that the project manager (and potentially, key members of the project team as well) obtains a basic understanding of benefits realization management principles as well as the specific benefits realization management implementation standards in use in the organization where he or she is managing projects. Because the project manager is closest to the direct delivery work of the program, he or she is well positioned to survey the project environment and to proactively identify situations in which project issues or risks may be placing benefits realization at risk. These situations may be remedied within the project environment or as appropriate, escalated to the program level via escalation procedures established in the program management plan. It is important to stress, again, that basic principles of benefits realization management must be provided (in the form of training) to project managers operating in a benefits realization management environment. Failing to make this important link between the project and the program is a critical mistake that can result in a number of undesirable consequences, including:

- Lack of sufficient "early warning" from projects regarding risks to benefits realization
- Reduced visibility into opportunities to leverage change for additional benefits realization (recognizing that project managers may be better equipped to identify some emergent opportunities than the program management team)
- Reduced ability for the team to proactively manage the project to support benefits realization, if understanding of how benefits realization management is being used on a broader level is not established
- Reduced awareness of the importance of dependencies between projects and the operational organization

## Relationship to Organizational Project Management Processes

While perhaps not a life cycle per se, the relationship between benefits realization management and the OPM framework within the organization is worth noting. As we have seen, benefits realization management operates in a broader organizational context and interfaces with other processes and life cycles of the organization in order to operate effectively. At a broader organizational level, OPM exists to ensure the appropriate governance and maturity management, guiding all processes associated with project, program, and portfolio management, as well as associated processes, in a way that provides consistent delivery and organizational value from their execution.

In the benefits realization management context, we are concerned primarily with ensuring the alignment of our benefits realization management activities with these organizational processes, as well as with ensuring that the processes are flexible enough to be tailored to the unique needs of specific organizational initiatives. While more on this topic will be discussed in Chapter 7, this notion of flexibility to ensure the appropriate ability to tailor processes is important. Excessively rigid methodologies have proven, time and time again, to be inadequate in creating long-term value for the organization. While advocating "agile" approaches is not necessarily appropriate, clearly some degree of flexibility in ensuring that processes are *appropriate* for a particular initiative is important. Striking this balance is not easy, but organizations must be prepared to understand how much process, standardization, and compliance activity is necessary to balance risk with reward. This is particularly relevant in benefits realization management, where the size, scope, impact, and importance of any particular program or initiative that implements benefits realization management must be considered when deciding whether, and to what extent, interfaces between benefits realization management activities and other organizational life cycles and processes must be undertaken.

## SUMMARY

This chapter provided an overview of the benefits realization management life cycle, with a focus on the fundamental work that is undertaken at each phase within the life cycle. This information will be elaborated, for each phase of the life cycle, in the following chapters. Having a fundamental understanding of the life cycle in general is useful as background information for a more detailed discussion, as well as enabling the reader to relate the fundamental benefits realization management life cycle phases to other related concepts presented in this book. Additional detail, regarding the relationship between the benefits realization management life cycle and associated life cycles, provides a context for understanding how benefits realization management fits within project, program, and portfolio management.

## REFERENCES

1. Project Management Institute, *The Standard for Program Management*, Third Edition, 2013, 36.
2. Ibid, 37.
3. Ibid, 39–40.
4. Ibid, 41.
5. Ibid, 43–44.

# 5

# BENEFITS IDENTIFICATION

## INTRODUCTION

Fundamental benefits identification and quantification processes are included in this chapter. The benefits realization management benefits identification process exists to ensure that appropriate benefits are identified and quantified by stakeholders in order to ensure appropriateness, based on business need, and to make the appropriate quantifications required to understand the value that will be delivered to the organization. To some extent, this is an alignment process. Especially in larger initiatives, different business stakeholders may have significantly different ideas of the benefits that the initiative should realize, which may be based on individual perspectives or on differing understandings of the overriding purposes and goals of the program. Through benefits identification, we seek to understand the range of potential benefits that *could* be achieved, the nature of these benefits, and their relative importance. With this information, informed decisions can be made regarding the particular qualified benefits that should be carried forward for further planning and realization.

## BEGINNING WITH THE END IN MIND

Before discussing benefits identification practices in detail, it is worth noting one important point regarding the benefits identification process. Benefits come from many places. When commencing benefits identification on the program level, there will likely be a tendency to look at already formalized statements regarding benefits first. These may come from the portfolio management process or other business planning processes in the form of data from business cases, governance committees, program chartering documents, such as program mandates, or from other sources. These sources often provide an excellent *starting point* for benefits identification but are seldom sufficient for benefits analysis. The reasons for this are several.

First, there may be a time lag between the production of these deliverables and the initial program benefits identification work. It is possible that these initial deliverables could have been created as part of an annual planning process that concluded a number of months ago. Or, they could have come from deferred initiatives that are now deemed to be of a higher priority to the organization. The revalidation of these business cases and the corresponding benefits may be far from assured. As such, it is possible that these deliverables contain outdated information or perhaps more likely, information that minimally needs a thorough review and revalidation by the relevant stakeholders.

Additionally, given that any business case is subject to the conditions of the business environment, it is important to recognize that the current business environment may differ from the business environment at the time the initial artifacts containing benefits statements were developed. One might reasonably assume that such changes were vetted prior to receiving an authorization to begin detailed program planning, but it would not be out of the realm of possibility that such vetting did not take place, took place considering the perspective of only a few stakeholders, or took place but only on a cursory level. These situations have the potential to create situations wherein the relevant environmental business factors either are not considered or are not considered in a way that supports effectively analyzing their impacts on the ability of the program to successfully realize the relevant benefits. While it is not the intent to provide specific examples here, there are a number of cases in the business literature in which products have been brought to market, only to "miss the mark" because either the market moved while the product was in development or product development was initiated without the proper background understanding required to validate that the product was appropriate.

Finally, it is worthy of note that stakeholders change. During business case development and approval, there will certainly be input from a variety of business stakeholders, but as time goes on and people and roles in organizations change, it is entirely possible that the stakeholders who originally approved the business case are not the same stakeholders who are now organizationally relevant. For this reason, it is necessary to ensure that appropriate stakeholder identification takes place at the benefits identification stage to validate existing assumptions regarding the stakeholder mix as well as to ensure the appropriate involvement of currently relevant stakeholders as part of benefit identification, qualification, and review.

These points underlie a basic notion that the world changes. As we begin the process of identifying benefits, we must look holistically at the business environment, the business drivers, the stakeholder community, and the existing planned benefits and determine where differences might exist that would cause us to think differently about what we are able to realize, or potentially whether this particular program is positioned for success. Starting with the end business goals and solution in mind and then considering the various factors impacting the ability to achieve these goals in the context of the business environment, may cause us to consider different solution options, different approaches to planned benefit realization, different problems to be addressed through the program, or other factors. All of these viewpoints could impact benefits identification and qualification. As such, benefits identification and qualification must be *supported* by artifacts that provide details on desired benefits attainment but must not be exclusively supported by these artifacts. Benefits realization management activities at this stage must not only be positioned to leverage what has already been done but also to take a fresh look at the program and the business environment in order to ensure, to the extent possible, that the benefits identification process holistically considers a variety of information sources and inputs.

## BENEFITS IDENTIFICATION

Benefits identification includes the steps required to identify and quantify benefits that are aligned with stakeholder needs and to the objectives of the organization. The process encompasses more than creating a list of benefits; it includes, but is not limited to:

- Using group facilitation, brainstorming, and other techniques to identify appropriate benefits
- Qualifying identified benefits to ensure appropriateness
- Developing metrics and measures that ensure the identified benefits can be measured—during and following realization
- Determining how the program measurement system will be structured and used
- Defining appropriate data management and communications processes to ensure that benefits realization management data is provided to stakeholders as needed
- Ensuring that the appropriate governance and change management procedures are in place to manage changes to identified and qualified benefits, tracking mechanisms, performance indicators, and other factors

## TOOLS AND TECHNIQUES FOR BENEFITS IDENTIFICATION

A variety of tools and techniques are available to support benefits identification. Some are general management tools that are widely used in businesses, consulting, and in other areas and are described here at a high level. Additionally, some techniques specific to benefits realization management must be addressed here.

### Benefits Register

A common tool for documenting identified benefits and associated data is the benefits register. The benefits register format may vary from organization to organization, but it is generally designed to capture key data about benefits for tracking and reporting purposes, similarly to the risk register used in project management. The benefits register is designed to be used as a living document rather than as a static representation of the benefits landscape. As such, a resource must be tasked with the responsibility to manage and maintain the benefits register. This resource may be part of the program management team, a dedicated benefits manager, if one exists, a member of the program office, or some other role, but it is critically important that he or she be responsible for the *proactive ongoing maintenance* of the benefits register, ensuring that it is consistently available and regularly updated. An example of a benefits register format can be found in Table 5.1.

Each of the components in the example benefits register is briefly described below:

- Benefit ID—A unique identifier for each benefit, which is used for referencing and tracking purposes
- Description—A concise statement of the specific benefit to be achieved, written in the clearest possible business language
- Measures—Specific measures that will be used to quantify the benefit
- Measurement method—The methodology (e.g., survey, data collection, etc.) and frequency of measurement to be employed
- Key performance indicators—The target values, thresholds for achievement, or similar indicators of progress and completion
- Status—A descriptive status (e.g., "Planned," "On Track," etc.) or indicator (e.g., Red, Amber, Green) that provides a high-level summary of status versus plan; status indicators, such as "Not Started," "Deferred," and the like, may be used as appropriate
- Timeline—The period of planned realization, target realization date, or other time frame relevant to stakeholders

**Table 5.1** Sample benefits register

| Benefits Register | | | | |
|---|---|---|---|---|
| | **Benefit A** | **Benefit B** | **Benefit C** | **Benefit D** |
| Benefit ID | | | | |
| Description | | | | |
| Measures | | | | |
| Measurement Methods | | | | |
| Key Performance Indicators | | | | |
| Status | | | | |
| Timeline | | | | |
| Risk Rating | | | | |
| Benefit Owner | | | | |
| Notes | | | | |

- Risk rating—A high-level indicator of risk associated with achievement of the benefit; this may be a qualitative rating (e.g., "High," "Medium," "Low") or a quantitative ranking based on a scale (e.g., 1 to 5)
- Benefit owner—The specific individual responsible for the benefit
- Notes—Additional detail regarding benefits status, risks, or other data relevant to stakeholders

While the data in the benefits register may seem straightforward, it is important to note several points that assist in creating a more useful benefits register. First and foremost, a focus on the measures, measurement methods, and key performance indicators (KPIs) is important. The old consulting phrase, "you cannot manage what you cannot measure," comes into play here. As part of benefit identification and qualification, you must be able to validate that you can create a reasonably valid measurement system, as well as one or more relevant KPIs that can be used to assess benefit attainment. While these items may be refined during this and subsequent phases of the benefits realization management life cycle, if there is a struggle to identify these items initially, it is worth considering whether the identified benefit is appropriate and appropriately defined.

Additionally, status indicators and risk ratings are important in this context. A qualitative status indicator and qualitative risk indicator provide the program management team and stakeholders with important information regarding the overall state of each benefit. These indicators do not need to be overly complex. While some may desire a high degree of quantification, the reality is that in the project, program, and portfolio management world, there are many examples of complex and ineffective status reporting mechanisms. As the primary purpose of the benefits register is to assist the delivery team in benefits tracking, indicators that qualitatively support the team in understanding where to focus and that provide a basis for initial data sorting and aggregation for reporting are largely appropriate. Additionally, and especially in the case of the risk rating, processes may exist elsewhere in the organization's methodologies to support more in-depth analysis. It is not necessary to repeat or augment those procedures here. If program risk management procedures provide risk analysis, with respect to benefits realization management goals, then a high-level summary from those processes will be sufficient. It is appropriate to err on the side of simplicity within the benefits register.

## Benefit Profile

It is often difficult to capture all of the desired data about a particular benefit within the benefits register. For this reason, many organizations utilize a subsidiary document, known as a benefit profile, for the purpose of elaborating more data about a benefit than can be effectively captured within the benefits register. An example of a benefit profile can be seen in Table 5.2.

The benefit profile repeats a significant amount of the data found in the benefits register but provides the opportunity for benefit owners and other team members to provide additional detail that could not be effectively captured within the benefits register. Furthermore, the benefit profile provides supporting data not found in the benefits register.

There are many formats for benefit profiles, and it is impossible to specify a single format that would be useful under all circumstances. As a general guideline,

**Table 5.2** Sample benefit profile

| Benefit Profile | |
|---|---|
| Benefit ID | |
| Document Date | |
| Benefit Owner | |
| Description | |
| Measures | |
| Measurement Methods | |
| Key Performance Indicators | |
| Costs | |
| Dependencies | |
| Risks | |
| Issues | |
| Notes | |

organizations should start with a simple benefits register and profile format that captures minimal data, as proposed in these examples. Over time, as the organization becomes more adept at benefits realization management, the benefits register and profile templates can be enhanced to support additional data gathering and reporting needs. A simple, easy to navigate template will provide significant value early in the implementation of benefits realization management.

## Benefits Workshop

The purpose of a benefits workshop is to bring together key stakeholders for a focused, facilitated session that is structured to support initial benefits identification and qualification. I have used versions of this workshop and believe in its effectiveness for several important reasons:

- Focused workshops with participants "in the room" are often more efficient for gathering and qualifying initial benefits than remote methods or meetings because the facilitated session provides a format and structure to focus discussion and drive results
- Engaging stakeholders together provides an opportunity for multiple viewpoints to be heard and for consensus to be reached, supported by a trained facilitator to ensure that progress is made and opinions are voiced and valued
- Workshop participants are able to learn from each other, build on each other's ideas, and identify additional opportunities for benefits realization that may not be possible without having diverse stakeholder groups in the room together; such collaboration is unlikely when multiple stakeholder groups are addressed at differing times, through the normal flow of meetings, conference calls, and the like
- Engaging people in the process helps to build support and a sense of ownership among them, supporting the often used phrase, "people tend to support what they themselves create"

The agenda for a benefits workshop must be developed collaboratively between the program management team and the facilitator. Where possible, there should be clear roles for the program management team, the stakeholders, and the facilitator; ideally, the facilitator is a neutral third party who represents neither the program team nor any specific stakeholder group. Effective facilitators must be adept at benefits realization management and have excellent facilitation skills. Resources from an organization's program management office or portfolio management office may be qualified to fill this role.

For reference, a sample agenda for a benefits workshop may be found in Table 5.3. Bear in mind that the length of the workshop and the specific time allocated

**Table 5.3** Sample benefits workshop agenda

| **Benefits Workshop Agenda** | |
|---|---|
| **Topic** | **Time** |
| Introductions | 10 Minutes |
| Objectives | 10 Minutes |
| Program Overview | 30 Minutes |
| Benefits Realization Management Approach | 15 Minutes |
| What About? | 60 Minutes |
| Benefits Brainstorming | 120 Minutes |
| Benefits Ranking and Prioritization | 120 Minutes |
| Conclusion and Next Steps | 15 Minutes |

to any particular activity may vary, depending upon the program's size and scope. As such, specific times are not included in the sample agenda. My experience with these types of workshops suggests that half a workday would be the minimal time investment for effectively conducting a benefits workshop, and in many cases, one business day or more is preferable.

The workshop is logically divided into several key sections:

- Introductions—Introductions of all participants need not be lengthy, but it is important to understand the roles of workshop participants
- Objectives—The facilitator should briefly describe the key objectives of the workshop, which should minimally involve initial identification and qualification of benefits
- Program overview—An overview of the program or initiative to be analyzed should be provided by the program manager or other key member of the program management team in order to level-set expectations regarding the scope of the program and to address high-level scope questions as required
- Benefits realization management approach—A team member familiar with the organization's standard benefits realization management processes should provide a brief overview of the organization's methodology, as well as any specific guidance that workshop participants should consider as they identify and qualify specific benefits
- What about?—This is a brainstorming exercise that asks participants to write down their questions. Participants then share these questions, and the facilitator engages the experts in the room to answer questions that can be answered, to note questions that cannot be answered for follow-up, and identify areas of confusion or concern regarding the program, its goals, scope, etc.

- Benefits brainstorming—Working in small teams, participants brainstorm potential benefits and document these benefits on note cards or sticky notes (see Figure 5.1 for an example of a format to be used for this exercise)
- Benefits brainstorming debrief—The facilitator leads a review of the identified benefits, moving from team to team and asking a representative to briefly discuss the identified benefits. The facilitator attempts to identify common themes and to create initial "groupings" of benefits, using the note cards or sticky notes as a basis
- Ranking and prioritization—Participants are assigned to one or more groups of benefits to perform an initial qualitative ranking and prioritization, again using the note cards or sticky notes. New benefits may emerge during this exercise, and these additional benefits can be documented using additional note cards or sticky notes
- Debrief and conclusion—The initial ranking and prioritization is summarized by the facilitator. An opportunity for feedback from participants is provided, and the facilitator works with participants and the program manager to identify next steps and follow-up items for after the workshop.

There could be many variations on this agenda. However, this example provides a basic construct to achieve the following basic goals:

- To provide the opportunity for stakeholders to engage in a workshop setting and build relationships
- To ensure clarity regarding the program or initiative among stakeholders
- To enable stakeholders to ask questions and surface issues and misunderstandings
- To obtain an initial identification and qualification of benefits to support creation of an initial benefits register

To support the workshop, a standardized format for capturing identified benefits and qualification data may be useful. The example in Figure 5.1 provides a format that can be produced easily (and relatively inexpensively) on customized sticky notes, or copied on heavy paper to produce note cards.

The card provides basic information, such as the benefit name and a brief description of the benefit, as well as a place to document initial thoughts on relevant measures and KPIs. Additionally, a benefit owner may be identified, and an initial high-level risk rating provided, to support qualification. The card could be enhanced by an organization to include initial qualification criteria as well. As an example, a basic grid such as in Figure 5.2, could be included on the reverse side of the card or as a replacement for the KPIs and risk rating in the example shown in Figure 5.1.

| | |
|---|---|
| Benefit Name: | |
| Description: | |
| Measures: | KPIs: |
| Owner:<br>Stakeholders: | Risk Rating: H M L<br>Risk Notes: |

**Figure 5.1** Sample benefit card

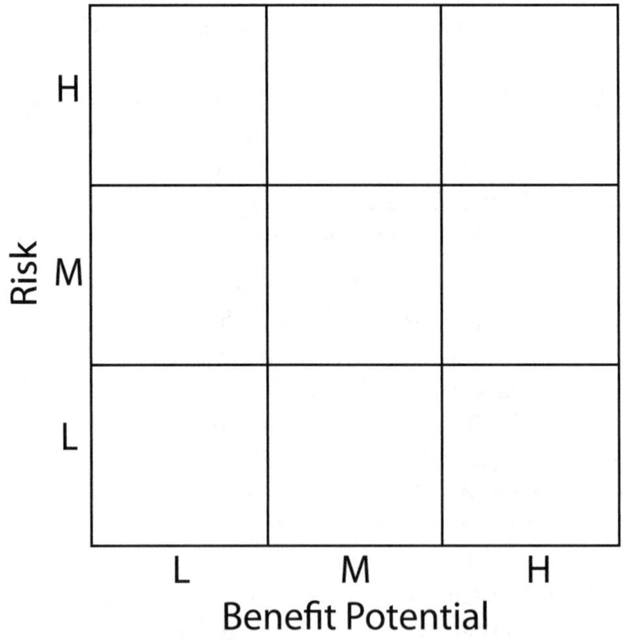


**Figure 5.2** Simplified qualification grid

In this case, the qualification grid asks the participant to rate the benefit in terms of its potential and risk to benefit attainment on a "High," "Medium," or "Low" scale. In order to ensure consistency, the facilitator should define the relative meaning of "High," "Medium," and "Low" for participants, such as "Low benefit means less than $1 million in cost avoidance," and "High benefit means greater than $5 million in cost avoidance," or some similar scale, which will depend upon the specific nature of the program.

## Benefits Brainstorming

If a formal benefits workshop cannot be conducted, a simple brainstorming technique can be used to identify potential benefits. This technique relies on first identifying current challenges and then using those challenges as the basis for developing a set of statements of associated benefits that can be achieved through change. The brainstorming exercise can be performed individually or with teams and involves asking four basic questions and identifying their answers. A document with the graphic depicted in Figure 5.3 can be produced to facilitate this exercise, or a depiction of the graphic can be placed on a whiteboard in a meeting room to set up the exercise, which asks participants to answer four basic questions related to the business scenario under analysis.

As Figure 5.3 depicts, participants are asked to identify current challenges, change opportunities, and practices that should be discontinued and then to make statements regarding how these changes produce value. The results of the "What Do We Get?" question form the basis for identifying benefits that may be achieved through change. Though this exercise may be simple, it is a powerful tool that permits participants to consider challenges and opportunities in their own frames of reference. If this exercise is conducted individually, the individual results should be consolidated into a single document. If brainstorming is performed in a group setting, a single set of answers to these questions will result. In either case, while the outputs of this exercise do not typically create a complete picture of change needs and associated benefits, the technique can be used as a relatively quick and simple way to identify potential business change needs and benefits for further elaboration. Figure 5.4 provides an example of the benefits brainstorming format with associated outputs.

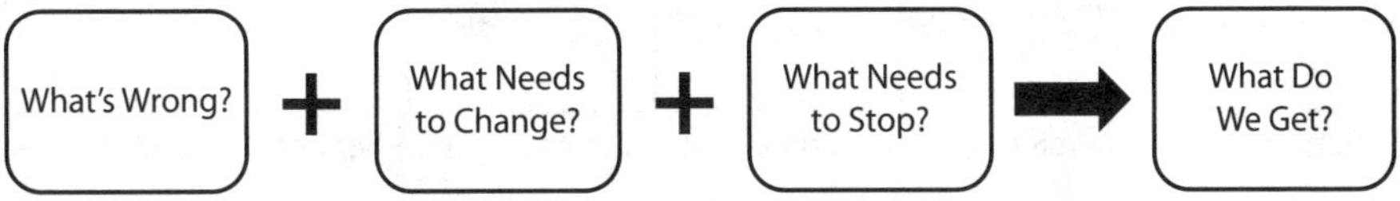


**Figure 5.3** Benefits brainstorming example

## Benefits Map

A benefits map seeks to depict the relationship between outputs of constituent work, capability creation, outcomes, benefits, and organizational objectives graphically. The benefits map approach is used in many organizations that have adopted benefits realization management and is referenced specifically in literature in the field, such as the *Managing Successful Programmes* guide. The example in Figure 5.5 best illustrates the benefits mapping approach.

It is often easiest to create a benefits map by working from right to left, starting with the objective and moving backward. However, for some people, it is easier to begin with the project view and work forward toward the objective. In this example, reading from right to left, we would state that the objective of increased sales revenue is achieved through the benefit of improved customer experience. Improved customer experience is enabled by decreasing the time to first customer contact, which is the result of the outcome of sales leads being assigned

**Figure 5.4** Completed benefits brainstorming example

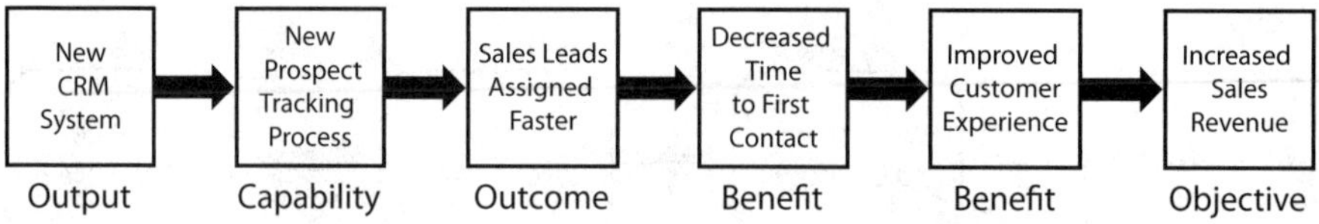


**Figure 5.5** Benefits map example

faster. Sales leads are assigned faster because a capability exists to better track and understand prospects—the result of implementing a new customer relationship management system.

This is a simplistic example, and there would likely be far more capabilities, outcomes, and benefits associated with the implementation of a customer relationship management system. While a more complete diagram might contain a number of additional capabilities, outcomes, benefits, and objectives, the simplified example here provides a single view into one pathway through the map. Once this mapping technique is understood, it is possible to create benefits maps that are much more complex. However, it is important to note that it is seldom the goal to use a benefits map for every potential benefit. Rather, the map is useful as an exercise for either high-level analysis of key benefits or for specific elaboration of already qualified benefits. Additionally, it would not be uncommon to have multiple maps for a single program, with different maps representing unique business objectives or created capabilities. Determining the level of detail to be elaborated is largely a team decision, based on the needs of the particular program being analyzed, but it is generally good practice to start simple and then determine the benefit of additional elaboration. One often finds that a simple, high-level map is sufficient for "telling the story" to key stakeholders. Details regarding benefits and attainment, will be documented in other artifacts, such as the benefits register; therefore, the benefits map may serve as a supporting artifact for discussion and communication purposes, rather than as a tracking and reporting mechanism.

## BENEFITS QUANTIFICATION

As discussed in Chapter 1, it is desirable to ensure that identified benefits are quantified. The goal of benefits identification is to establish the appropriate quantitative benefits targets, KPIs, and measurement systems to support benefits realization during the program life cycle for the identified and qualified benefits. Through benefits identification, the program management team will reach consensus with relevant stakeholders regarding which of the identified benefits will be included within the scope of benefits realization management—based in part on qualitative analysis and in part on benefits quantification. Some of these benefits may have already been elaborated as part of business case development, but others may emerge as benefits identification activities are undertaken.

An important point to understand in this context is that quantification is an exercise that often, but not always, leads to quantification in monetary terms. In some cases, while one might wish to quantify a particular benefit based on a monetary value, it may not be possible to do so. Some benefits clearly lend themselves to monetary quantification. A benefit of "increased sales revenue" is an example. It is certainly possible to perform analysis to determine the amount of additional revenue to be created from activities that support this benefit.

In other cases, however, it may not be so easy. Consider a benefit such as "increased productivity." Analysis could clearly quantify an amount of productivity increase (for example, planning a five percent increase in productivity), which may be translated into additional units of product per hour, or some other basis. However, uniquely linking these additional units of production and subsequent sales—that can be expressed in monetary terms—exclusively back to increased productivity could be problematic, as there are many factors that could impact the connection, such as events outside of the program, which could also be responsible for increased sales (e.g., marketing factors). This is not an insurmountable obstacle from a benefits realization management perspective, but it is worth noting in order to highlight the point that not all benefits will be able to be translated directly to a "bottom line" monetary value.

Within the context of benefits quantification, it is possible to create complex models and mechanisms, geared toward extremely precise quantification. For organizations that have undertaken benefits realization management activities for some time, the precision approach may be entirely appropriate. However, for organizations that are taking their first steps towards establishing benefits realization management as a business practice, a more simplified approach is usually better. A three-step approach is described here to assist the reader in applying a practical quantification framework to their benefits realization management initiatives.

## Baseline Performance

The first step in the quantification process is to ensure that an appropriate baseline exists, or can be created, to establish current performance against which improvement will be measured. Without this data, it is difficult to truly quantify the benefit achieved. Thus, even if a quantified benefit is established, the organization may struggle with providing conclusive proof that the defined benefit was achieved. Where possible, this performance baseline should rely on existing data that is readily available for capture and use. It is not desirable to build a baseline measurement system unless absolutely necessary. Historical data, if available and reliable, is appropriate for establishing the baseline performance. If such data is not available, some data gathering activities may be required, but this can be time-consuming (perhaps requiring several performance periods before an effective baseline can be established). In these cases, proceeding without an established baseline may be appropriate, but data will need to be collected as work progresses to ensure that appropriate comparisons can be made to support data analysis.

Consider, as an example, a benefit of reducing cost to process an expense report in a corporate travel and expense department. The manager of this department may already have data to understand the cost per submitted expense report (cost per transaction). Or, if needed, historical data on departmental personnel and associated costs could be used, along with historical data on expense report transaction volumes, in order to establish a baseline cost. The team responsible for benefits realization management will need to weigh the value of precision in this analysis, perhaps making some trade-offs between the amount of data cleansing undertaken and the value of an additional one or two cents of accuracy in the established baseline cost. Let us assume, for the purposes of this example, that the cost per transaction for processing expense reports is $52.50. This will be important data for determining improvement potential.

## Determine Improvement Potential

This step is an estimating and forecasting activity. It is unlikely that an extremely precise model for the specific quantified benefit to be achieved will be able to be developed in a timely and cost-effective manner, and for most organizations beginning benefits realization management activities, such precision is unnecessary. While we would like the improvement potential estimate to be more accurate than a "back of the napkin" or "order of magnitude" estimate, we recognize that very accurate estimates consume time and money and therefore permit a reasonably accurate but not necessarily perfect estimate.

There are a number of techniques that can be used to establish improvement potential. These include:

- Expert judgment—Relying on experts (e.g., consultants, internal business experts, etc.) to provide a basis for quantification from industry data, company experience, or other factors
- Benefits workshops—Expanding the benefits workshop to include focused discussion by small teams to develop quantification estimates
- Pilots—Utilizing small-scale examples and extrapolating the improvement potential on a larger scale from data obtained in the pilot
- Modeling techniques—Some improvements lend themselves to process modeling or other types of modeling that can be used to quantify expected benefits
- Consensus estimating—Relying on estimates from team members or other relevant stakeholders to establish an "average" view of expected benefits to be obtained

These and other techniques may be used in combination to establish an appropriate estimate. Some additional factors to consider, when quantifying benefits, include:

- Ensuring that benefits realization is appropriately understood from a time bound perspective. Realization is seldom a "big bang." One should reasonably expect that some ramp-up would be required before full realization is achieved. Such ramp-up must be planned for in benefits quantification, to clarify both when full realization will be achieved and the duration of the ramp-up period. Similarly, any potential ramp-down effects should be understood, if they affect the overall benefit quantification.

- Ensuring that the effects of disbenefits are considered. It is often easy to see the upside of a particular benefit, but its potential downsides must also be considered, along with their relevant offsetting effects on benefits realization potential.
- Ensuring that the quantification considers only the direct benefit created by the program. It is possible that some benefit contribution will come from other initiatives or changes within the organization, which are outside the scope of the program or would occur whether the program took place or not. These effects are often discounted, since they skew the view of the benefit in relation to the program itself.

## Validate Benefits

The third step involves ensuring that appropriate stakeholders review and approve the quantified benefits. The importance of, and required time commitment to, effectively executing this phase should not be underestimated. It is absolutely critical that the quantifications are reviewed and deemed appropriate by key stakeholders and that buy-in is obtained. The quantified benefits become the basis for management and measurement in the benefits realization management life cycle, and—if these quantified bases are not agreed upon by key stakeholders before further work commences—there exists a significant risk that the data may be "conveniently" questioned later.

Benefits validation may not be a simple task. Factors such as differing stakeholder viewpoints, a large number of impacted stakeholders, and others may require a significant amount of review and negotiation. In some cases, it is possible that the senior responsible owner may need to be directly involved to overcome potential blocking from stakeholders. Although discussed briefly later but beyond the scope of this book, it is critically important that the stakeholder identification and analysis take place because these activities enable the program management team to understand the roles, attitudes, and influences of stakeholders. This analysis assists the team in understanding how best to build consensus between differing stakeholder groups and helps to clarify which stakeholders are required to provide input to and concurrence with the benefits.

With validation activities complete, the relevant data should be merged, and the benefits register and benefits profiles should be considered "final," for the purposes of this phase. The next phase, benefits analysis and planning, uses the outputs of this phase as key inputs to more detailed benefits realization planning.

## SUMMARY

This chapter addressed the critical processes of benefits identification and quantification, including the relevant activities required to perform baselining, validation, and other activities to support the description of quantified benefits, which will serve as the basis for further benefits realization management activities. The processes described in this chapter are critically important, as effective benefits identification forms the foundation for successful benefits planning by ensuring that further planning work is focused on those benefits that have been identified, qualified, quantified, and validated by the program management team and relevant stakeholders. These are processes that should not be rushed: taking the time to identify the right and relevant benefits to the business at this stage minimizes risk of rework later and provides an initial validation point with stakeholders to ensure that the correct benefits will be focused on as detailed planning progresses.

# 6

# BENEFITS ANALYSIS AND PLANNING

## INTRODUCTION

Benefits analysis and planning encompasses the activities required to formalize the benefits realization management processes in a benefits realization plan, as well as the work required to put into place appropriate processes and governance in order to control benefits realization activities during program execution. While this phase is primarily a planning phase, it creates the foundation upon which successful benefits realization management during subsequent program execution is built. While practitioners intuitively know the importance of proper planning for project and program success, this phase often receives less attention as additional project and program planning activities, such as scheduling and budgeting, begin to create demands on the program team's time. Unfortunately, insufficient benefits planning leads to numerous potential issues, as benefits realization, measurement, and other activities take place later in the program life cycle.

This chapter provides a specific focus on establishing the benefits realization plan as a key document for managing benefits realization management; describes the additional work required to prioritize program components and understand the dependencies between program components; discusses further definition and analysis of key performance indicators (KPIs), and their relationships to the measurement system that will be in place to measure and track benefits attainment; and describes activities required to formalize a performance baseline. Some of this work has been started already. During benefits identification and quantification, efforts were made to build a foundation to support measurement and tracking as well as to include activities that support baseline analysis for establishing a clear baseline in this phase. Thus, this phase builds on the prior work and focuses on the successful integration of benefits realization management activities into the overall program plans.

## THE BENEFITS REALIZATION PLAN

The benefits realization plan is a subsidiary plan included as part of the overall program management plan. Its purpose is to ensure that defined ways of working are established with respect to benefits realization management activities as well as to formalize the planned benefit delivery, the required organizational change activities to support benefit delivery, and for additional purposes. Ideally, the organization maintains a master template for a benefits realization plan, as part of its organizational process assets and ensures that individual programs rely on this master template as a starting point for developing the benefits realization plan. Appropriate tailoring should be permitted so the template can be customized to the needs of specific programs, but the general framework for how benefits realization management activities are expected to be executed in the program, based on organizational governance principles (perhaps established by an organizational program management office), should be standardized within the template.

A benefits realization plan typically includes the following key sections:

- Formalization of roles and responsibilities related to benefits realization management, and assignment of those roles and responsibilities to team members
- Benefits and associated benefits detail, such as plans for realization, assumptions, risks, and other key data (likely sourced from the associated benefit profiles)
- Benefits metrics and detail regarding how metrics data will be captured and managed
- Schedule that details when benefits will be realized
- Plans for benefits reviews, as well as proposed review times (often on a cadence or milestone basis)
- Benefits reporting requirements, formats, and information distribution mechanisms to ensure that program stakeholders are kept informed of benefits realization management activities
- Transition plans that describe how capabilities will be transitioned to the operational organization

- Validation activities and criteria for determining the processes by which benefits will be formally recognized as achieved
- Dependencies within the program related to benefits realization, as well as external dependencies that may impact benefits realization
- Descriptions of sustainment activities required to ensure that the realized benefits will be maintained after the program concludes

The list of required activities may seem elaborate at first glance, and to be sure, creating the benefits realization plan is a significant amount of work. However, this work is largely related to other program planning activities that must be undertaken and in some cases, simply extends existing documentation. As a general point of guidance, organizations that are beginning benefits realization management implementations in program environments should focus on creating a benefits realization plan that meets the needs of the program and the organization in a minimal way and evolve the benefits realization plan template over time. A pilot approach may be appropriate, leveraging a template from popular methodologies or online resources as a starting point, to provide a means for the organization to become familiar with the types and formats of information that best meets the program's and the organization's needs.

It is important to understand the criticality of several sections of the benefits realization plan. First, the elaboration of the time required for planned benefits realization should not be ignored. While it is nice to have benefit profiles that indicate planned attainment, the mapping of benefits delivery to the overall program schedule, the integration of tracking that delivery's timetable, and the production of a time-phased plan for benefits realization is crucial for effective tracking as well as for effective expectation management. It is a clear reality that the attainment of benefits does not happen overnight. Because capabilities will be delivered at different times, because delivery of end benefits may require the delivery of several capabilities and their intermediate benefits, and because stakeholders will expect to see progress in benefits realization as part of their continued commitment to the program, the program management team must have good information to support when benefits are expected to be realized. Figure 6.1 from the Project Management Institute's (PMI's) *Standard for Program Management* demonstrates the relationship between costs and benefits across the program life cycle.

As depicted in the diagram, the cost profile of the program begins to trail off as benefits transition and sustainment activities begin to pick up. During this period, benefits delivery continues, building on the initial program benefits deliveries that now must be transitioned and sustained. In order to create this diagram for a program, the cost profile must be established (and is established as part of program cost management); similarly, the benefits delivery profile must be established as well. It is only possible to create this diagram if delivery of benefits is

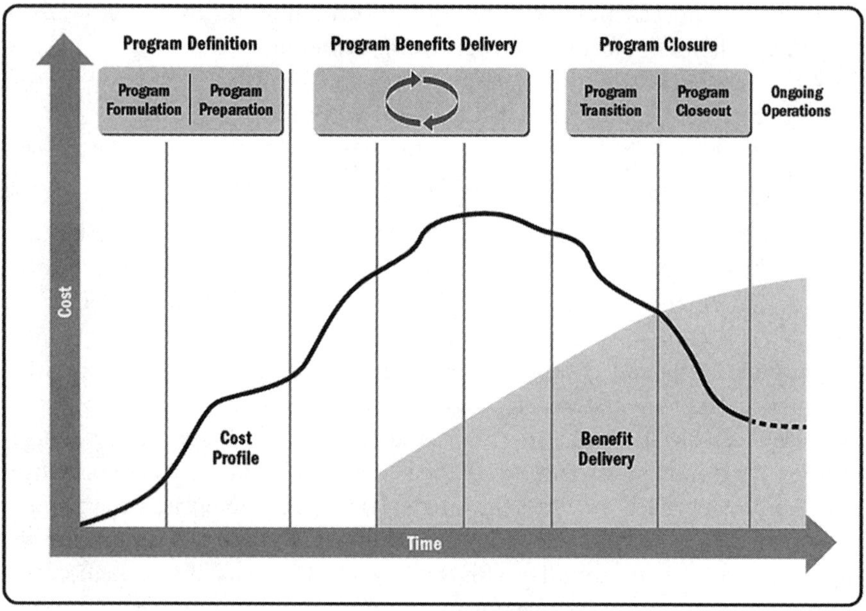


**Figure 6.1** Example cost and benefit profiles across the generic program life cycle (from the PMI's *Standard for Program Management*—Third Edition)

understood on a time-scale basis. It is also important to note that benefits delivery activities commence well into program delivery, when a significant amount of investment has already been made (as depicted in the diagram). As such, the program management team must understand the relationship between actual delivery and the time-phased baseline that is established, so that appropriate business decisions can be made if benefits delivery is not forecasted to meet expectations.

Additionally, sufficient detail regarding metrics, KPIs, measurement techniques, and related topics must be included. Measurement is not easy in the benefits realization management environment. It is important to keep the measurement system relatively simple in initial benefits realization management implementations. But simple does not necessarily imply easy. Data collection challenges and other issues often face organizations implementing benefits realization management. Overcoming these challenges or, minimally, developing plans to address potential challenges as they occur is extremely important. The benefits realization plan should clearly articulate specific targets, milestones, measurements, measurement frequencies, data sources, and all relevant information that supports ensuring that timely, accurate, and useful data is available to support benefits realization management and reporting. If the program is incapable of providing believable data to stakeholders regarding benefits realization management progress and benefits attainment, it will face a significant uphill battle; furthermore, the individuals attempting to implement benefits realization management on a broader organizational scale will similarly face an uphill battle in convincing stakeholders of the value of benefits realization management as an organizational process.

Finally, transition and sustainment activities should be elaborated in the benefits realization plan in enough detail that expectations regarding the types of activities that will take place, the roles of program team members and the receiving organization, and specific criteria for establishing that the transition is complete are clear. Specific processes for these important benefits realization management activities are not described here, as both benefits transition and benefits sustainment are addressed in Chapters 8 and 9. However, it is important to underscore the fact that these activities are specifically related to benefits realization management but must be in the overall program plan in order to ensure that schedule, budget, risk, and other considerations related to benefit transition and sustainment are included.

## COMPONENT IDENTIFICATION AND PRIORITIZATION

Component identification and prioritization include the processes required to define the program components that will be responsible for capability creation and benefit delivery (often in the form of projects) as well as the additional work required to prioritize these components according to the business objectives. Often, the benefits identification process produces a long list of benefits. Although the organization may wish to realize all of these benefits, further detailed planning and mapping of the work required to achieve them may reveal that resource constraints limit the ability of the organization to take advantage of all benefits opportunities. As such, prioritization is used to ensure that the best mix of benefits is considered for inclusion in the program plans, given organizational constraints.

As a starting point for component identification and prioritization, a program roadmap may be developed. The program roadmap seeks to identify key program components that will create the required capabilities for benefits realization, depict these key components and their associated milestones on a timeline, identify relevant dependencies between them, and provide high-level documentation of risks and issues that may impact plans. A sample graphical depiction of a program roadmap is provided in Figure 6.2.

The roadmap in Figure 6.2 depicts a series of swim lanes (sometimes referred to as tranches) with bars depicting constituent work to support relevant

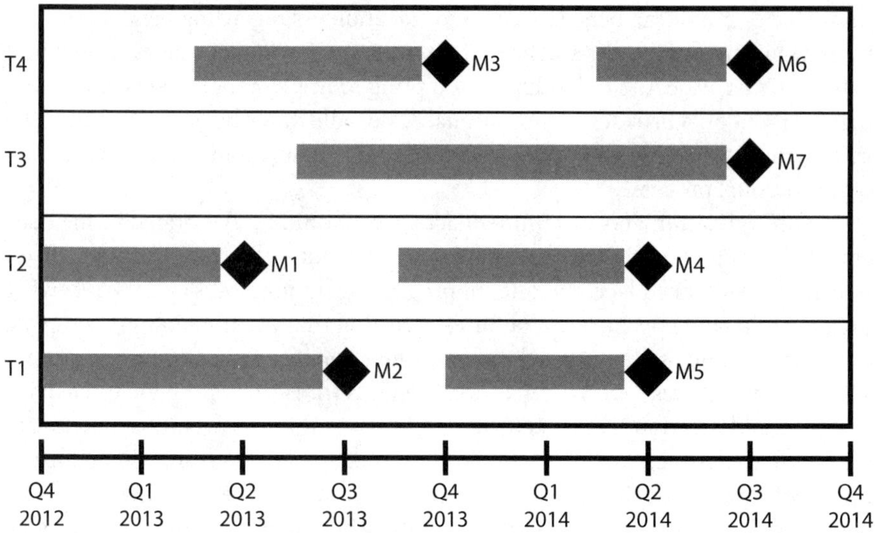


**Figure 6.2** Sample program roadmap

milestones. The overlap between the bars, or the linkages between milestones, may represent dependencies that must be managed in order to ensure successful delivery. This provides a high-level view of work, milestones, and timelines. From a presentation standpoint, it is useful for providing stakeholders with a representative view of key work as well as a high-level timeline and identification of key dependencies. From a practical work management standpoint, however, the usefulness of the visual program roadmap is limited, and more detailed schedules are subsequently developed.

Because of the limitations of the graphical format, the program roadmap is often supported by a document or similar artifact with additional detail. This document typically contains such information as:

- High-level definition of the constituent program components (e.g., projects). These descriptions are intended to provide details of the work to be undertaken but not to replicate more detailed scope statements.
- Definition and description of dependencies between program components and relevant descriptions of how these dependencies will be managed. It is important to document potential effects on benefits realization that these dependencies create.
- Milestone descriptions and measures that indicate milestone achievement.
- Relevant high-level assumptions and risks. These statements should highlight key risks and assumptions and are not meant to replace the more

detailed descriptions of assumptions and risks found in other program artifacts.

- Statements regarding anticipated benefits achievement (especially as related to milestones) and important KPIs that will be used to indicate success.

Because the program roadmap is both a management and a communication vehicle, striking a balance between enough information to support communication and too much information is critical. Some of the detail contained within the program roadmap is duplicated and elaborated in other documentation (e.g., benefits data in the benefits realization plan). Therefore, it is advisable to summarize key elements of the graphical program roadmap as part of the supporting documentation but not to repeat the detail contained in other program artifacts.

## A Note on Interdependencies

An important theme in program management is work integration. Often, programs require managing multiple concurrent efforts in a coordinated way, ensuring that the appropriate "synchronization" takes place to deliver the required capabilities and benefits at the required time. In this context of interdependent work, management of interdependencies is critical. Numerous types of interdependencies can exist both in the context of capability creation (e.g., requiring that certain projects are managed in a coordinated way in order to ensure that the work associated with them is delivered at the right time) and in benefits realization (e.g., certain benefits being delivered together or in a coordinated way in order to realize a greater end benefit).

It is tempting to treat management of these interdependencies as primarily a scheduling exercise; clearly, ensuring that the required work is understood from a scheduling and delivery standpoint is important. However, in the benefits realization management context, these interdependencies must be understood in terms of how they affect benefits realization. For example, as part of planning for benefits realization, we seek to understand when benefits will be delivered so that we can create the time-phased plan for when program costs will be incurred and when benefits will be realized. If some risk exists with respect to this plan, or if some issue exists that causes plans to change, understanding the schedule impact of these changes is important, but understanding the extent to which these potential changes impact the ability of the organization to realize planned benefits according to the benefits realization plan is critical as well. In some cases, there may be no effect on benefits realization. In some cases, the effect may be significant. In isolation, a particular schedule slippage, scope change, or other factor may not appear to be significant. However, work interdependencies may make the impact more significant.

The point to be made here is: work integration and understanding how changes in one area of the program potentially affect other areas of the program is important from a benefits realization standpoint, as decisions regarding how to address risks and issues must consider the effects on benefits realization. If a slippage of a particular project results in a 2% reduction to one benefit in the overall program, then the program management team may decide to accept the slippage and its corresponding reduced benefits realization. If a slippage in one project in a particular program will result in another project in the program failing to deliver on time, resulting in an 80% reduction in benefit realization, then the program management team may take a different approach to managing it. An understanding of the interdependencies between work and the corresponding benefits realization is critical to being able to effectively analyze and react to changes. Organizations beginning benefits realization management should ensure that time is spent clarifying and documenting relevant interdependencies in order to provide visibility to these interdependencies and their corresponding impacts.

## ESTABLISHING MEASUREMENT AND MONITORING

In the benefits realization management context, the activities related to establishing measurement and monitoring include the activities required to formalize the KPIs for the agreed prioritized benefits, formalizing measurement processes to provide data for assessing achievement against the plan, and establishing a monitoring framework to consistently execute required measurement and monitoring activities and to report progress to relevant stakeholders.

### Types of Measures

Many different types of measures exist to support measurement activity. While most benefits realization management literature focuses on distinguishing quantitative from qualitative measures, often advising establishing quantitative measures whenever possible, other characteristics of measures exist and are worth noting. These different types of measure are summarized in Table 6.1.

Selecting the most appropriate measure requires thought and experience, and the data contained in Table 6.1 can be helpful for thinking about the types of measures that may be most useful for benefits realization management.

The examples of quantitative versus qualitative and financial versus nonfinancial measurement types are fairly straightforward. Direct versus indirect measurement are relatively simple but often confused. A direct measure is a measure that can be used to directly support a benefit. For example, measuring units produced per hour could be a direct measure of productivity. Indirect measurement

**Table 6.1** Measure types

| Measure | Example |
|---|---|
| Quantitative | Time Saved |
| Qualitative | Customer Perception |
| Financial | Cost Reduction |
| Nonfinancial | Increased Productivity |
| Direct | Dollars saved as an indicator of cost reduction |
| Indirect | Student job placement rates as an indirect measure of academic success |
| Leading | System implementation leading to better customer service |
| Lagging | Increased revenue resulting from improved customer service |

applies when a particular measurement is an indicator of something else. For example, the percentage of repeat customers could be an indirect measure of customer satisfaction. Leading versus lagging measures refer to whether the measure leads to the attainment of something or it is a measure of the impact of something that has already occurred.

In most organizations implementing benefits realization management, quantitative versus qualitative and financial versus nonfinancial measures will be the starting point, and finding the right balance will be key. It is unlikely that purely quantitative financial measurement will be possible; thus, it is important to find the right mix of measures for performance management. Quantitative and financial measures are ideal in many cases, but well thought out qualitative and nonfinancial measures can be used effectively. Regardless of the mix, alignment with stakeholders is crucial to ensure that the measures are agreed upon.

## Measure Development Example

A basic example, which extends Chapter 5's example of reduction in cost per business transaction for expense report processing, can be used to illustrate the process and its importance. That example established a current baseline cost per transaction for expense report processing of $52.50. Let us assume that through the process of defining the improvement potential, it is found that through systems implementation and organizational change, the cost per business transaction can be effectively reduced to $38.50—a significant decrease. This data could be considered on an individual transaction level or aggregated together into a total improvement potential by considering the number of business transactions per year. For the sake of simplification, it will be assumed that the number of business transactions is fixed at 10,000 per year. This will yield a current baseline cost of $525,000 per year. Assuming successful realization of the desired benefits, this cost should be reduced to $385,000 per year, yielding a savings of $140,000.

Now consider the data that is relevant from a measurement and monitoring perspective. Table 6.2 provides a summarization.

In this example, key data related to the benefit's baseline, KPI, target, and measurement methodology are included to clarify the specific performance target as well as the measurement system. Organizations may choose to capture this data differently—or potentially, to capture data different from that shown in the table—but as a recommendation for organizations beginning to implement benefits realization management, this table represents the key data that should be available as part of establishing measurement and monitoring. For simplicity, this data is often in the benefit profile and extracted for measurement and monitoring planning.

The limitation of this example is that it addresses only one benefit. Repeating this example for many benefits will result in a variety of KPIs, measurement requirements, and associated data, which must be managed together in a coordinated way. A measurement plan is useful for this purpose.

## The Measurement Plan

Although not often described as a key benefits realization management deliverable in benefits realization management literature, the development of a measurement plan is extremely valuable, especially for organizations that are starting benefits realization management activities. The measurement plan is a program-level deliverable that is included as part of the benefits realization plan and provides key data to support ensuring that measurement is carried out appropriately. A sample format for a measurement plan can be seen in Table 6.3.

**Table 6.2** Representative measurement and monitoring example for benefit

| Attribute | Data |
| --- | --- |
| Benefit | Reduced expense report processing cost |
| Baseline Volume | 10,000 transactions per year |
| Baseline Cost | $525,000 per year |
| Key Performance Indicator | Cost per transaction |
| Benefit Target | $385,000 (26% reduction) |
| Measurement Method | Transaction cost analysis |
| Measurement Frequency | +30, +60, +90 days from go-live |
| Measurement Owner | Director, Travel and Expense |
| Assumptions | Assumes 10,000 transactions per year volume |

**Table 6.3** Sample measurement plan

| Data | Example |
|---|---|
| Benefit ID | A21 |
| Measure | Cost per transaction |
| Baseline | $8.00 |
| Baseline Date | March 1, 2013 |
| KPI / Target | $5.00 |
| Measurement Type | Direct / Financial |
| Measurement Method | Observation / Calculation |
| Measurement Frequency | Weekly |
| Measurement Owner | B. Jones |
| Start Date | December 1, 2013 |
| End Date | July 1, 2014 |

The measurement plan summarizes data about performance and measurement across all required measures and provides a single document (often a spreadsheet) that can be used for measurement management and for integrating measurement activities into program plans. It is also possible to extend the measurement plan format to capture key measurement data to be used during benefits delivery.

## Characteristics of Good Measures

It is worth noting a few characteristics of good measures, as many organizations struggle with establishing appropriate measures when initiating benefits realization management activities. Over time, organizations typically become better at elaborating measures that are relevant to their needs and relatively simple to produce.

First and foremost, any established measure must be able to be supported by data—ideally, by existing organizational data. To the extent possible, one should rely on existing information systems, data sources, and/or processes already in place to gather measurement data. It is time consuming and does not add much value to create measurement activities solely for use during benefits realization management activities within the program. It may be appropriate to create such activities, if they will be transitioned and used as part of benefits sustainment, but the appropriateness of performing this work and the relative risk and reward of doing so must be considered. Thankfully, most organizations capture more data today than ever in history, providing rich potential for measurement supporting data that already exists.

Additionally, the data used for measurement in benefits realization management must be reliable. Characteristics of trustworthy information include:

- Accuracy—the data is free from error
- Timeliness—the data represents current business conditions
- Correct granularity—the data has the level of detail required for the analysis
- Worth its cost—the data is not overly expensive to capture and use for benefits realization management purposes

These characteristics are important for determining whether a particular measure should be utilized for benefits realization management purposes. Bear in mind that data collected and analyzed as part of measurement and monitoring will be used as the basis for significant reporting, including reporting to steering committees and other key stakeholders regarding benefits attainment. If the data cannot be trusted, then it is extremely difficult to validate actual benefits realization. If an organization has data management challenges, the organization must be aware of these challenges and their potential impacts on its ability to reliably report. If necessary, compromises may have to be made to reduce some measurement activity. One is better off with less measurement that is trustworthy than with suspect data—attempting to cleanse it and transform it into credible reporting.

Finally, data to support measurement must be sufficiently available. Statistical sampling principles can be used to determine sample sizes for some measures, but a general "common sense" test is often sufficient to determine whether enough data will be available to support measurement. If there is a question whether sufficient data will be generated, the program management team must assess the importance of the measure as well as the value and potential cost of gathering additional data in order to provide credible data to support measurement and analysis. This analysis will most likely manifest itself in a cost/benefit analysis and in a discussion regarding the impact of having more versus less data. There is not a single right answer. Some organizations will take a "something is better than nothing" approach, while others will insist on more rigid adherence to organizational standards, statistical sampling rules, or other criteria when determining data sufficiency. For organizations beginning to implement benefits realization management, a general guideline is to start with a small set of reliable measures that pass the test of trustworthiness, rather than to produce an elaborate set of measures that may be difficult or costly to reliably capture. Keeping this process simple will still yield important information to support your benefits realization activities.

## SETTING THE PERFORMANCE BASELINE

The final important step in benefits analysis and planning is establishing a relevant performance baseline for benefits realization. This exercise is not entirely different from setting schedule baselines in scheduling or from cost baselines in earned value management, since the goal is to establish a standard against which actual performance can be measured. This baseline considers the time-phased quantified benefits that have been agreed upon by stakeholders and documented as part of the benefits realization plan, program roadmap, and established measurement system. This baseline provides the basis for reporting and should be shared with stakeholders as part of regular benefits realization management reporting. A graphical illustration of the baseline will probably look like Figure 6.1, showing the relationship between investment and benefit realization with respect to time. Figure 6.1 depicts the (not unique) situation in which benefit delivery does not outpace cost incurred during the program itself. The baseline may be bound to the time constraints of the program; as such, additional value delivered in subsequent years from ongoing sustainment will not be part of the baseline in these cases, as additional benefits will not be realized during the program lifetime.

## COMMUNICATING PERFORMANCE

While program communication management practices will be included as part of the overall program management plan, it is worth briefly noting a few points regarding planning for benefits realization management communication. Benefits information is among the most critical information to report to stakeholders. Effective communication of benefits information requires planning that is specific to benefits realization management communication. In developing communication requirements for benefits realization management communication, the following points are important:

- Stakeholder analysis must be performed—It is critical that stakeholder needs, with respect to benefits realization management communication, are understood and documented. Different stakeholders will have different needs at different times, depending upon the impact to them at different points during the benefits realization management life cycle. For example: stakeholders potentially impacted by disbenefits may require different communication than stakeholders actually impacted by benefits. The clear imperative is to tailor the messaging to the audience.
- Informational communications must be formalized—Communications primarily meant to inform stakeholders regarding benefits realization

management activities (e.g., regular status reports) must be formalized with respect to format, delivery medium, delivery cadence, and other factors.

- Action-oriented communication must be focused—Communications regarding issues affecting benefits realization, requests for decisions or support for decisions, and other communications requiring action from stakeholders must be focused, both in audience and message. This requires the program management team to ensure that such communications clearly articulate the specific situation requiring attention and the specific action or recommendation requiring attention and to target these communications towards specific decision makers. Time being of the essence, this is not an area where general communications will be effective.
- Communications must be an integral component of program reporting—It is essential that benefits realization management-related status and communications are built into regular program reporting and review. A disconnected process, of providing benefits realization management communications apart from regular program communications and review, can lead to confusion or lack of messaging clarity. This does not imply that some communication will not occur separately, but is noted here to state that integration is important.

It is appropriate, during benefits analysis and planning, to include benefits realization management-related communications requirements in the benefits realization plan as well as to integrate key components of benefits realization management-related communications into the overall program communications plan. If not already provided by the organization, standard templates should be developed to support consistent communication of routine information. For organizations establishing benefits realization management as a business practice, these templates can be piloted in initial benefits realization management work, refined through lessons learned, and leveraged as reusable organizational process assets in subsequent work—once their appropriateness and completeness is established.

## SUMMARY

This chapter addressed important considerations in benefits planning. Effective planning supports ensuring that the further work to be performed in program execution is appropriately integrated into program plans so that desired benefits realization goals are met. A key component of this planning is the creation of the benefits realization plan. Formalizing a specific plan for benefits realization management activities ensures an appropriate focus on these activities. While the benefits realization plan is no substitute for more detailed planning on the overall program level, its focus on benefits realization management is important, and as appropriate, components of the benefits realization plan will be integrated into broader program planning to ensure a strong alignment between this plan and the overall program management plan.

7

# BENEFITS DELIVERY

## INTRODUCTION

Benefits delivery ensures that the program optimizes delivery of benefits through the work required to actively manage benefits delivery in the context of the overall program. To this point, much of the benefits realization management work that has been completed is related to planning. Now, the focus shifts to leveraging the plans created in order to ensure that benefit realization is optimized, disbenefits are minimized, emergent benefits are analyzed, and the relevant monitoring, review, and reporting activities are undertaken to support benefit realization.

It is important to note that although the focus of benefits delivery is primarily on executing the work to support benefits realization, benefits realization management is a cyclical process. As such, it is possible that as changes in the program or environment occur as new opportunities are uncovered, or as issues and risks present themselves during execution, it may be necessary to perform additional benefits identification and planning activities to support a changing benefits landscape. This activity is natural and should be considered a normal course of business in most programs. While excessive change is not desirable, some change is expected, and appropriate changes to the benefits realization plan should be considered through sound change management practices in order to take advantage of opportunities, respond to issues, and minimize risks.

## MAINTAINING BENEFITS ALIGNMENT

An important component of benefits delivery is maintaining alignment with organizational objectives. The alignment of the program and the corresponding benefits with organizational objectives will have been established as part of program approval via appropriate portfolio management and governance processes. However, it is well known that the business environment (both internal and external) can change at a rapid pace. As such, it is critical that regular assessments occur to ensure continued program alignment with the business environment and organizational strategies. There are a number of roles that will have responsibility for participating in this process:

- Benefit owners—Survey the business landscape to understand the impact of changes on benefit realization as well as new opportunities to potentially exploit emergent benefits
- Senior responsible owners—Maintain a holistic understanding of the program and its benefits objectives as well as the organizational environment and external business environment, which may best position them to understand the impact of changing business strategies and industry trends on the program and its associated planned benefits
- Portfolio managers—Together with portfolio management offices, when implemented, they should proactively scan the entire portfolio to understand the impact of changes in portfolio components on benefits realization, identify opportunities to exploit benefits across programs, and understand changing business priorities and their impacts on portfolio components and benefits realization across the portfolio
- Program managers—Must ensure they understand the relationship of the program to other relevant organizational initiatives as well as to the organization's strategies, objectives, and business environment, and should proactively scan this environment to identify and understand potential changes that impact benefit delivery

There are other roles that may participate in this process as well; however, these four roles are key to actively ensuring continued benefits alignment with organizational strategies and objectives. As situations arise that potentially affect strategic alignment and benefits realization, the program management team must work together with the senior responsible owner and as appropriate, program and organizational governance bodies to:

- Understand the impact of potential changes on the program and benefits realization
- Forecast, to the extent possible, the impacts of the changes on current and future benefits realization plans
- Understand contingency actions that can preserve benefits realization, minimize disbenefits, and exploit opportunities
- Develop plans to respond to the changing business environment

- Execute appropriate change management activities (e.g., change authorization, change communication, etc.) in order to approve changes and integrate changes into relevant plans and artifacts

Critical to the success of this process is proactive scanning of the environment and analyzing opportunities in a timely manner. Too often these activities lag behind changes in the environment, which unfortunately results in either missed opportunities or continued investment in activity that does not support the current business strategies and landscape. While some people contend that the strategic and portfolio management functions of the organization maintain primary responsibility for proactive scanning and action, the reality is that while these bodies certainly play a key role, there cannot be a disconnect between their work and the people doing the work, who are primarily parts of the program management teams. Communication and collaboration must be two-way, supported by status reporting and formal communication but also including regular meetings, reviews, and informal collaboration opportunities that present the results of organizational and environmental scanning, updates to business strategies and goals, and opportunities to exploit emergent benefits. The important role of portfolio management in the benefits realization management context, together with elaboration on this link, is described in Chapter 12.

## BENEFITS TRACKING AND REPORTING IN BENEFITS DELIVERY

Tracking and reporting during benefits delivery requires the integration of processes—found in the benefits realization plan, measurement plan, and other program plans—to collect and consolidate data for use by the team in managing benefits delivery as well as for production of status and other reporting for program stakeholders. The scope of potential reporting is large. Put simply, there are a multitude of metrics, measures, statuses, and other informational elements that could be reported, and the potential stakeholders to report this information to is also a large group. We recognized, as part of the previous phase, the importance of developing a benefits realization management communications plan to be integrated into the overall program communication plan. Now is the time to put that plan to use. Additionally, now is the time to leverage the measurement plan to capture and manage the required data for reporting.

A summary of all relevant benefits information may be included as part of a benefits realization report. This report, often a constituent component of the overall program communications plan, provides the high-level "dashboard" view of benefits realization management activities on a program level. Information commonly included in this dashboard includes:

- Brief executive summary (potentially including "Red," "Amber," and "Green" indicators) highlighting the overall benefits realization position for the program
- Status of benefits realization versus plan (either per benefit or aggregated by program tranche or benefit type)
- Revised benefit realization forecast, based on current business and program conditions, and including explanations for relevant variances
- High-level risk analysis, with a focus on highlighting key risks to benefit realization
- Summary of important issues and potential disbenefit situations, with corresponding high-level plans to address them
- Summary of benefits opportunities (e.g., emergent benefits)

This dashboard is not meant to be a detailed report. Rather, it is designed to support broad distribution and easy consumption of the most relevant information regarding benefits realization management activities. It should to some extent, be used as an exception report, highlighting positive and negative variances, key issues and risks, as well as plans to address these situations. The dashboard should be updated on a regular basis (weekly, at most, and monthly, at minimum) and should be distributed to the relevant stakeholders who were identified in the stakeholder analysis.

## Benefit Realization Management Reviews

The benefits realization report can serve as a key input to regular reviews as well. From a benefits realization management perspective, several types of reviews are of interest. Overall benefits realization management activities and statuses should be encompassed in a program benefits review, which may be part of regular program review meetings (e.g., steering committee meetings) or a separate meeting that is specifically focused on benefits realization management activities. For organizations that are newly implementing benefits realization management, a separate meeting is strongly advised to enable a focus on benefits realization management activities. Regardless of whether this review occurs in a separate meeting or in a regular program review, the benefits realization management review should focus on the key topics contained in the sample agenda provided in Table 7.1.

Note that the times indicated in the agenda are only a general guideline. Organizations that combine benefits realization management reviews with regular steering committee or other reviews may have far less time to devote to benefits realization management review. Additionally, program size and complexity, as

**Table 7.1** Sample program benefits realization management review meeting agenda

| Benefits Realization Management Review Agenda | | |
|---|---|---|
| **Topic** | **Owner** | **Time** |
| Overall Benefits Realization Management Status | Program Manager | 5 Minutes |
| Executive Feedback | Senior Responsible Owner | 5 Minutes |
| Benefits Realization vs. Plan | Benefit Owners | 15 Minutes |
| Forecast and Analysis | Program Manager | 15 Minutes |
| Emergent Benefits Reviews | Benefit Owners | 10 Minutes |
| Business Change Highlights | Business Change Manager | 5 Minutes |
| Issues and Risks | Program Manager | 10 Minutes |
| Look Ahead | Program Manager | 5 Minutes |
| Summary and Next Steps | Program Manager | 5 Minutes |

well as the frequency of the reviews, may impact the time allotted as well. As a general rule, formal review on a biweekly or a monthly basis is appropriate, assuming that other informal reviews and day-to-day management of the benefits realization management process occurs.

Also, note that the scope of the agenda provides an opportunity for all key members of the benefits realization management team to provide input regarding relevant activities within their areas of responsibility. Specifically, this meeting is designed to focus on realization versus plan as well as benefits forecasting and analysis. Review of emergent benefits and business change activities are included at a high level to summarize key points regarding these activities.

## Benefits Reviews

Another important component of benefits tracking and reporting is the benefits review. The purpose of benefits reviews is to undertake regular review of identified and prioritized benefits during benefit delivery in order to provide assurance, identify issues and risks, and as appropriate, make updates to benefit profiles (and other documentation) to support a current picture of benefits. The benefit owners will play a strong role in these reviews, representing their assigned benefits. Reviews should include relevant program leadership and benefits stakeholders and should be conducted either at an established cadence (e.g., monthly) or minimally, at milestones identified in the program road map. Benefits reviews should minimally include the following activities:

- Assessing benefit realization versus plan on a per benefit basis, and identifying factors that are affecting (or could affect) realization

- Reviewing benefit profiles and updating based on changing business conditions or other factors
- Assessing risks to benefit realization and defining mitigation activities to ensure that risks remain within acceptable tolerances
- Reviewing planned benefit transition and sustainment activities to ensure that plans remain aligned with organizational needs
- Validating continued alignment of benefits with the benefits realization plan and with organizational strategies and objectives
- Reviewing the established measurement system and assessing suitability of the measurement system for benefits realization management needs, adjusting when necessary
- Assessing overall benefits realization management effectiveness and prioritizing opportunities for improvement

The main focus of the benefits review should be on specific benefits, with emphasis on those benefits to be realized in the near term, and those benefits whose realization is either occurring or recently completed. A cursory review of benefits planned for realization in later periods may be included, but the benefits review meeting should be primarily focused on near-term objectives.

A secondary, but important focus in the benefits review meeting should be on the effectiveness of benefits realization management as a business process. This task includes reviewing the measurement system and overall benefits realization management business processes as a whole and identifying opportunities for improvement, which should be reviewed by the program management team and implemented as appropriate. While this activity could occur in overall benefits realization management reviews generally, the reason for inclusion in benefits reviews is that the audience of the benefits review is closer to the actual day-to-day benefits realization management work and thus in a better position to assess process effectiveness and identify improvement opportunities.

Attendees at benefits review meetings will likely include benefit owners, benefit stakeholders, and key members of the program management team, including the program manager and business change manager. As appropriate, additional parties may be invited to support discussion or decision making.

## MANAGING WORK AND INTERDEPENDENCIES

Benefits delivery requires completion of the program activities required to successfully create the required capabilities, embed those capabilities in the organization, and realize the corresponding benefits. As these activities primarily involve execution of project work, a component of benefits delivery is ensuring that the relevant component projects are initiated, managed, and transitioned in a way that supports benefits delivery, as well as ensuring that relevant interdependencies between these activities are actively managed. These practices are not specific to benefits realization management; therefore, extensive discussion of them is beyond the scope of this book. It is worth noting, however, the critical importance of ensuring an understanding of the relationship between capability creation and benefits realization and that, as work is performed, any relevant risks or issues related to capability creation are understood in a benefits realization management context. Additionally, it is important to note the value of effective transition activities, as constituent program components are completed. This topic is addressed in detail in the following chapter.

## BENEFITS MONITORING

Active monitoring of benefits realization is an additional important component in benefits delivery. In this context, monitoring refers to the actions required to survey the program environment, gather data, identify issues and risks, and support reporting. Activities related to monitoring and controlling are covered relatively well in most program management literature. In the benefits realization management context, the importance is the specific focus on monitoring to ensure that realization meets the identified benefits realization targets. A significant amount of monitoring activity will take place as part of measurement, utilizing the measurement plan to ensure that appropriate data is captured and made available for analysis and reporting. Additional monitoring activities may occur, using techniques such as environmental surveying, "management by walking around," and similar methods.

When implementing benefits monitoring in new benefits realization management environments, the following suggestions may be helpful:

- Leverage what you already have—if program management is an established business practice, utilize the existing tools, techniques, and templates for program monitoring and controlling as the basis for benefits monitoring. Integrating specific benefits monitoring activities into existing monitoring frameworks is much easier than creating these techniques from scratch.
- Choose wisely—when starting implementation of benefits realization management, you may wish to constrain detailed monitoring activities to the "critical few" benefits that deliver the most benefit from the program and spend less time on the many additional benefits that are smaller contributors. Taking the time to effectively monitor these critical few benefits will produce better results than attempting to apply equal amounts of monitoring to all benefits, especially in resource-constrained environments.

- Focus on what matters—variances are going to occur. This is the nature of the world, and the benefits realization management environment exists in that world. Attention should be paid to indicators that significant variances may occur. Some normal variation from established benefits realization targets may not require the same amount of attention as other variances. Clear definition of acceptable variances in the benefits realization plan allows appropriate understanding and management of variances.
- Keep your eyes on the prize—benefits monitoring should occur with the end in mind. It is tempting to "dive into the details," when performing monitoring activities, in the hope of getting "the answer" to a particular issue, risk, or variance. It is important to consider the big picture and the amount of work necessary to get "the answer." Especially when starting to implement benefits realization management, "good enough but not perfect," may very well be appropriate. Maintain focus on the big picture.

## RISK MANAGEMENT ACTIVITIES

Most of the prevalent literature on project, program, and portfolio risk management takes a holistic view of risk—as an uncertain event that can impact one or more objectives. In this context, risk can be viewed either negatively (as an obstacle—the traditional view) or positively (as an opportunity). Risk management is a part of program management in general, and each program will implement relevant activities (via the program management plan) to address program risks. As such, the purpose here is not to attempt to describe risk management activities as a part of the overall program management life cycle. Rather, the focus of this section is on specific risk management activities related to benefits realization management, which must be considered during benefits delivery.

Recall from previous chapters that risk has been mentioned in several places. Risks will be identified as part of benefit identification. Relevant risks to benefits delivery will be included in benefit profiles. Risk reviews will be part of benefits realization and benefits reviews. So, there is no question that if effective benefits realization management processes are being followed, the relevant risks should be documented (via the benefits register as well as in the program-level risk register and reporting), and proactive risk management activities should be planned, to keep risk within acceptable tolerances. Within benefits delivery, the focus is on several specific risk factors that affect benefits realization management activities:

- Risks associated with realizing benefits—these risks could be associated with capability delivery (e.g., delivering capability late, thus impacting benefit delivery), associated with organizational change management (e.g., inability to successfully embed capabilities in the organization in a way that realizes benefits), or associated with other factors

- Risks associated with disbenefits—these risks could be associated with amplified disbenefits from poor organizational change management or other factors, associated with stakeholder acceptance of disbenefits from poor communication and understanding of change, or associated with other factors
- Risks associated with emergent benefits—these risks could be associated with failure to identify and analyze potential emergent benefits or associated with forecasting failures that overestimate the benefit potential of emergent benefits, leading to poor decisions regarding which emergent benefits to exploit
- Risks associated with interdependencies—these risks could be associated with failure to identify and adequately manage interdependencies, or associated with technical or other factors within the interdependencies
- Risks associated with program dynamics—these risks could be associated with budget and cost considerations in benefits realization (e.g., budget overages that cause benefits to be realized at an excess cost)

A recommended approach for management of these specific risk factors involves several activities. First and foremost, the program management team must ensure that benefit-related risks are integrated into the overall program risk management processes so that appropriate visibility, tracking, management, and reporting of key benefit-related risks are proactively managed via the program risk management processes that are established in the program management plan. This includes documenting risks both in the benefits register as well as in the program risk register (unless software tool implementation supports consolidation of this data in an automated way) and including relevant benefits risks in the regular risk reporting and review processes for the program.

Beyond the risk management processes established for the program, it is recommended that organizations perform regular reviews that are specific to benefits realization management risks, using benefit profiles, the benefits register, and the benefits realization plan as key inputs. Some organizations establish specific benefits realization management risk registers as subsidiary registers to the overall program risk register to support this process. These specific risk registers often extend the program-level risk register by adding additional data fields and more detailed comments and analyses specifically for benefits realization management purposes. Extending the existing program-level risk register enables easier aggregation of the benefits realization management risk register into the overall program risk register for reporting purposes, yet still enables the more detailed tracking and management of risks that some organizations prefer. For

**Table 7.2** Benefits realization management risk review meeting agenda

| Risk Review Agenda | | |
|---|---|---|
| **Topic** | **Owner** | **Time** |
| Meeting Overview | Risk Manager | 5 Minutes |
| Top Risks | Risk Manager | 10 Minutes |
| Emerging Risks | Business Change Manager | 10 Minutes |
| Mitigation Planning | Risk Manager | 20 Minutes |
| Opportunity Identification and Evaluation | Business Change Manager | 10 Minutes |
| Conclusion and Next Steps | Risk Manager | 5 Minutes |

organizations beginning to implement benefits realization management, this approach may be preferable, as it forces a specific focus on benefits risk management and provides a mechanism for detail to be codified, so it does not get "lost" among many data points.

Risk reviews should focus on the primary risk areas mentioned here and should include opportunities for planning actions to ensure that proactive measures are being taken to ensure that benefits realization management risks are being managed appropriately. A sample agenda for a benefits realization management risk review meeting can be found in Table 7.2.

The agenda for the benefits realization management risk review contains standard elements from most risk review meetings, including a focus on top risks (via a review of the risk register), identification of new (emergent) risks, and mitigation planning. Additionally, considering the holistic view of risk management, some time is spent on opportunity identification and evaluation to permit a specific focus on discussion of opportunities for additional benefit realization.

Participants in this benefits realization management risk review should include key members of the program management team as well as the business change manager, benefits owners, and other stakeholders who require visibility into benefits realization management risks. These participants could include project managers from constituent program components as well as business stakeholders.

## SUMMARY

This chapter described the work required to support delivering planned benefits. While a significant amount of this work will occur in tight integration with program delivery—as opposed to discrete, stand-alone activities—it is important to recognize the need for a specific focus on maintaining benefits alignment with organizational goals, tracking, monitoring and reporting, managing risks, and other activities required to effectively support benefits realization. The program management team must ensure appropriate focus on these activities, relying on benefit owners, the business change manager, and other key benefits realization stakeholders to support timely monitoring and managing of benefits realization. Risk and issue management will be important at this stage, as will effective communication with stakeholders to ensure that appropriate communication of benefits attainment, risks, issues, and other important topics are addressed.

8

# BENEFITS TRANSITION

## INTRODUCTION

This chapter addresses benefits transition. Benefits transition includes the activities required to appropriately transition benefits from the delivery program to the receiving business organization in a way that ensures that they are embedded in the business organization and sustained over time. The importance of this work cannot be overstated. Effective transition positions delivered capabilities and realized benefits for long-term success. Ineffective transition may create inefficiencies in the business organization or transition challenges that require extra effort from the program management team. These situations can create challenges for long-term benefits sustainment as well as potential additional program costs, as transition issues are addressed during the program. Transition activities include a strong organizational change management component; therefore, the additional guidance on organizational change management provided in Chapter 11 should be referenced to assist in ensuring that appropriate organizational change management activities are integrated into transition planning and execution. These activities will include managing stakeholder expectations, performing readiness assessment, managing resistance, and others.

## DETERMINING TRANSITION SCOPE

In most programs, transition is not a one-time activity. Over the course of the program, there may be multiple points at which transition activities occur, as capabilities are created, delivered, and integrated into the business organization toward benefits realization. Some incremental benefits may be realized during the program, while other benefits may not be realized until long after the program concludes. Understanding the nature of these various deliveries and their corresponding transition activities is an element of determining the scope of transition planning. The primary sources of information for determining the transition scope and associated timeline of required transition activities are the program plan and its associated deliverables, such as the program schedule. Analyzing these deliverables in the benefits realization management context, additionally considering benefits realization plans and associated deliverables, will enable the program management team to determine when transition activities will be required.

## DETERMINING TRANSITION SUCCESS

Successful transition involves two important components. The first is the successful integration of delivered capabilities into the business organization. This is the traditional view of a transition, in which the outputs of the project or program are given to the business for use. In many organizations, transition activities required to embed delivered capabilities into a business organization are well established, as such "implementation" activities are common in most project and program management environments. Similarly, the required practices to determine the associated activities to manage successful integration and to perform such integration are usually established in the organization's project and program management methodologies.

The second component of determining transition success relates to whether, and to what extent, the transition achieved the planned benefits. This is the component of transition success that is new to most organizations that are implementing benefits realization management. The program management team's focus, in transition management, must include the activities required to ensure that the benefits planned, through integration of delivered capabilities into the business organization, are realized. As such, transition is not complete until the required benefits validation and realization reporting activities are conducted, which provide stakeholders with data demonstrating successful benefits realization. In some cases, this work may not be possible within the program itself, as some benefits may not be planned for realization until after program completion. In these cases, the program management team will need to devise acceptance criteria and applicable benefits measures to be used as indicators that the transition positioned the organization to realize the anticipated benefits in the future.

# REQUIRED TRANSITION ACTIVITIES

Transition is a multi-step process that requires several important activities, including:

- Transition planning
- Transition initiation
- Transition management
- Transition review
- Benefits validation
- Benefits realization reporting

In the following sections, each activity will be described, identifying its key components, followed by a discussion of integrating these activities into a consolidated transition plan.

## Transition Planning

Transition planning involves the activities required to develop a transition plan that considers the needs of the organization, as well as the program responsibilities for managing transition. Transition planning activities will guide the additional work to be performed and should include the planning activities required to ensure that:

- Stakeholders who should participate in transition activities are engaged
- Appropriate transition documentation, training materials, and associated artifacts are planned for release to the business organization
- Appropriate readiness planning and associated processes are in place to validate readiness for transition
- Acceptance processes and criteria are identified to ensure that acceptance can be performed in a formalized way

Transition plan development is covered in more detail in a later section of this chapter, so discussion of this topic is limited here. However, this section is provided in the interest of ensuring that the entire set of activities required as part of transition management is described.

## Transition Initiation

Transition initiation is performed as capabilities are prepared for delivery to the receiving business organization. As noted previously, transition activities will likely be performed multiple times over the life of the program; therefore, transition initiation activities will be performed as required in order to ensure that as capabilities are prepared for delivery, the business organization is ready to receive them. A balance must be struck in this activity, ensuring that capabilities are delivered as required, but that capability delivery does not create undue stress on the receiving business organization. As such, transition management must consider how to best integrate new capabilities, while still ensuring that normal business operations are maintained. This is an important organizational change management consideration, which requires engagement from the business change manager, program management team, and stakeholders of the receiving business organization to ensure that transition planning considers the effects of transition on ongoing business operations. Contingencies should be established for temporary additional staffing, job role changes, or other activities to ensure that focus is on transition as well as on management of the day-to-day work in the receiving business organization.

An additional consideration in transition initiation is mobilizing the resources required to support transition. This activity could involve members of the organization's human resource department, training and development organization, or other functions that can provide support to ensure that stakeholder concerns are managed, transition issues are addressed in a timely manner, and other required support is available to the receiving business organization to ease the impacts of transition. These activities are part of organizational change management and will be considered in the transition plan as well as in the program's overall organizational change management plan.

## Transition Management

Transition management includes performing the actual transition work. This activity primarily involves executing the activities required to transition developed capabilities into the receiving business organization. The focus in transition management should be on the appropriate monitoring activities that are required to ensure that:

- Delivered capabilities are transitioned to the receiving business organization as planned, and appropriate acceptance criteria are met
- Transition issues are identified and proactively resolved
- Benefits realization considerations are understood, and required monitoring activities—to ensure that transitioned capabilities are positioned to realize planned benefits—are implemented
- Transition activities do not negatively impact normal business activities

The role of the program management team is to ensure that the appropriate monitoring of transition activities is in place and is executed to ensure successful transition. The team will rely on the developed transition plans as well as on measurement and monitoring techniques to ensure that transitioned capabilities are positioned to support benefits realization.

Transition management also requires a focus on change management. It is possible that during transition, there will be issues or risks that require the program management team to adjust transition plans. While change is reasonably common in program environments, focus must be placed on ensuring that changes requested during transition do not unduly impact the receiving business organization or benefits attainment targets. It is easy to make compromises in response to perceived issues in the receiving business environment during transition; however, the program management team must balance the need to minimize disruption to the receiving business organization with the overarching need to prevent such changes from delaying or otherwise impacting benefits realization.

## Transition Review

A transition review occurs after the transition activities to identify improvement opportunities and document lessons learned. These lessons learned may be applicable to later transition activities within the program as well as to other programs. Identified lessons learned should be shared both with the program management team and with the organization's program management office, or other entity, which is responsible for the central management of lessons learned for the benefit of the organization. Identified improvement opportunities to be implemented within the program itself should be integrated into program management plans, utilizing appropriate change control mechanisms.

## Benefits Validation

Benefits validation is the process of measuring benefits to compare actual benefits attainment against the plan. This activity may not occur immediately following transition, as there may be required measurement activities that must occur in order to develop data for understanding benefits realization. As such, it is possible that transition activities will conclude upon confirmation of successful transition to the receiving business organization, even though validation of benefits is not yet possible. This situation is perfectly acceptable; however, the program management team must ensure ongoing focus, during further program activities, on measurement and data analysis that supports understanding whether planned benefits attainment goals are met.

Benefits validation requires a strong partnership with business stakeholders as well as a focus on ensuring that the identified key performance indicators (KPIs) and measures, which were defined as part of benefit identification and planning, are utilized to validate benefits realization. Credible measurement and reporting of achieved benefits is crucial.

### Benefits Realization Reporting

This activity provides reporting to stakeholders regarding the results of transition activities and corresponding benefits realization. Reports include results of transition activities, results of measurement and benefits validation activities, and other information given to stakeholders and provide data on benefits attainment. As appropriate, additional reporting to stakeholders may include residual risks that are to be transitioned to the receiving business organization, as yet unrealized benefits that will be transitioned to the receiving business organization or to a portfolio management function, which will continue benefits realization tracking after the completion of the program, or other information. Reporting may also include reviews to provide information to stakeholders, to respond to issues or risks, as well as to finalize the transition, secure sign-off, and conclusion of transition activities. These reviews are used as an additional opportunity to gather stakeholder feedback and lessons learned, which can be integrated into later transition activities within the program. The type, format, and timing of these reviews should be captured in the transition plan.

## DEVELOPING A TRANSITION PLAN

A key component of transition management is the development of a comprehensive transition plan that guides the program management team and the receiving business organization in transition management activities. A sample table of contents for a transition plan can be found in Table 8.1.

As shown in Table 8.1, there are five essential components to a general transition plan. As appropriate, organizations may choose to augment this template with additional sections or details to meet their individual transition needs, based on the types of work they typically undertake. Additionally, organizations may have existing transition plan templates in use in the project or program management environment that may be able to be used directly or modified to meet the needs of transition management in a program and benefits realization management context. In the following sections, each component of the transition plan will be discussed.

It is important to note that multiple transition plans may be developed, depending upon the nature of the program and its associated work. It is perfectly acceptable to develop detailed transition plans that match the delivered capabilities rather than to use a generic transition plan that is not tailored to the unique transition needs or particular capability integration needs.

**Table 8.1** Sample transition plan

| Section | Contents |
|---|---|
| Overview | • Transition Scope<br>• Transition Plan Objectives<br>• Reference Documents<br>• Outstanding Issues |
| Transition Planning | • Transition Schedule<br>• Roles and Responsibilities<br>• Resource Requirements<br>• Transition Risks<br>• Sustainment Plans |
| Transition Delivery | • Rollout Plans<br>• Testing Requirements<br>• Acceptance Requirements<br>• Risks and Mitigations<br>• Communication Plans |
| Benefits Delivery | • Key Performance Indicators<br>• Measurement Requirements<br>• Acceptance Requirements<br>• Communication Plans |
| Transition Approval | • Transition Approvals |

## Overview

The overview section of a transition plan provides a concise summary of planned activities, including the transition scope, transition objectives, relevant reference documents that underpin the transition plan, and statements of known issues that may impact successful transition. Confirmation of the transition scope and objectives is a critical component of this section and is useful for ensuring stakeholder alignment with transition objectives. Identification of known transition issues is included in this section to enable stakeholders to understand issues that may impact transition and corresponding actions to resolve them.

## Transition Planning

The transition planning section includes the transition schedule, as well as identification of transition resource requirements and roles and responsibilities. Additionally, documentation of relevant transition risks and associated mitigation plans are included here. This section may be quite detailed, as it presents the key planning activities that have taken place to ensure a successful transition. These activities should be detailed from the perspectives of both the program management team and the receiving business organization in order to capture the required work of both parties during transition. Utilization of effective project and program management practices related to schedule management, defining and aligning roles and responsibilities, and other similar topics should be undertaken here to ensure that the relevant planning deliverables are included within the transition scope.

Transition planning will also include elements of benefits sustainment planning, which is discussed in the next chapter. Within the transition plan, the activities required to ensure that realized benefits are sustained over time should be included, as sustainment is an important component of successful transition. Turning over capabilities and realized benefits without appropriate processes to enable the receiving business organization to sustain benefits over time may lead to reduced benefits in the long run, which is not desirable. The program management team will work with the receiving business organization to define the required sustainment activities as well as the role of the program in providing support for long-term benefits sustainment. As the program will not have responsibility for long-term benefits sustainment in most cases, helping to build a firm foundation for benefits sustainment within the receiving business organization is important.

## Transition Delivery

Transition delivery includes the activities required to execute transition. These activities include rollout planning activities, which underpin the transition schedule; testing and acceptance requirements, which are used to measure transition success, as well as the additional required measurement activities necessary to support testing and acceptance; discussion of relevant transition delivery risks and associated mitigation activities to manage risks; and required communications plans, which ensure appropriate communications as the transition progresses.

Transition delivery represents the most critical phase of transition management, as this is the phase in which the transition work occurs. As such, the program management team may wish to elaborate additional detail here, in order to manage stakeholder expectations, as well as to ensure a clear understanding of how transition work will progress and how transition success will be validated. Validation is especially important. Clear alignment between the program management team and the receiving business organization on the transition success criteria must be reached in order to ensure that stakeholder expectations are managed and that the transition is completed according to the plans agreed upon. Absent clear success criteria, transition activities may be prolonged by stakeholders with unreasonable expectations regarding what the program management team will provide during transition. Readiness assessment and associated processes are important for ensuring that, as the organization prepares for transition, there is sufficient focus on the receiving business organization's ability to accept the transitioned capabilities.

## Benefits Delivery

This section elaborates on portions of the benefits realization plan, identifying specific actions, both during and following transition, to be undertaken toward effective benefits delivery. Data, including required measurements and KPIs, benefits acceptance requirements, and relevant plans to communicate benefits realization status to stakeholders, must be given here. Of specific interest are the acceptance criteria used to formally gain stakeholder sign-off on all benefits planned for realization within the scope of transition. For benefits planned for realization after transition (and potentially after the program's end), acceptance of the responsibility for ongoing activities to support later benefits realization by the receiving business organization is required. The program management team documents the acceptance criteria from the benefits realization plan but may further tailor these criteria or provide specific detail regarding acceptance activities in the benefits delivery section of the transition plan.

## Transition Approval

Transition approval is the final section of the transition plan and defines the process by which the overall transition will be formally closed. Transition approval signifies acceptance by the receiving business organization that the program has fulfilled its transition obligations and that the receiving business organization is prepared to take over any remaining transition items as well as to perform the required sustainment activities to continue to realize benefits. Formal approval is often achieved through both a review and a document that serves as a program artifact. The purpose of the review is to address outstanding issues as well as to document relevant process improvements or lessons learned that may be used in future transition activities. The purpose of the transition approval document is to provide an artifact documenting the outcomes of the transition review and includes official acceptance that the transition is complete from a representative of the receiving business organization.

In cases where transition approval cannot be obtained in a timely manner—due to stakeholder expectations, issues that cannot be resolved in a timely manner, or other similar situations—involvement from the senior responsible owner may be required, as it is not advisable to permit transition to continue for extended periods of time—especially if the majority of the transition completed successfully, and the remaining issues are relatively minor. In such a case, specific actions to be taken by the program management team and/or the receiving business organization may be documented as part of the transition approval, indicating actions and timelines to complete residual items, but permitting the program management team to conclude formal transition management activities.

## MANAGING TRANSITION ISSUES

Transition can be one of the most difficult aspects of any program, as it is often the time when the most stakeholders are actively engaged, when the most organizational change management work is done, and when the receiving business organization is required to take ownership of change. Numerous issues may arise during transition, and the program management team must be prepared to quickly assess potential transition issues and address identified issues in a timely manner. While it is not possible to enumerate all possible transition issues, common categories include:

- Issues from capabilities not delivering their required functionality. These issues are often proactively addressed through appropriate acceptance testing prior to transition.
- Issues related to managing organizational change. These issues may relate to managing stakeholder expectations, managing resistance, or managing successful change integration. These issues are best addressed through proactive organizational change management planning and execution of the organizational change management plan as well as through appropriate environmental scanning and stakeholder feedback activities to understand sources of concern, resistance, or other factors.
- Issues related to benefits realization. Planned benefits are occasionally not realized in the receiving business organization. In these cases, the program management team must assess the impacts of reduced benefits realization and put into place, together with stakeholders, appropriate mitigations or other actions to respond to benefits realization challenges.
- Issues related to the transition itself. Poor or nonexistent transition planning, transition planning that does not involve affected stakeholders, or other issues related to the transition activities themselves are best resolved proactively with appropriate transition planning and by securing agreement to transition plans from stakeholders prior to initiating transition activities.

Effective management of transition issues requires attention from the program management team—specifically from the business change management team—for those transition issues that are primarily business change issues. Establishing a specific transition issue log is often appropriate, utilizing existing issue log formats when available, in order to provide specific focus on proactively managing transition issues. This issue log should be reviewed with the program management team and representatives of the receiving business organization as part of regular transition planning and execution meetings, with a focus on ensuring timely resolution of issues or if necessary, timely escalation of issues to the senior responsible owner for resolution.

## SUMMARY

This chapter addressed the primary activities of benefits transition. Because transition considers both capabilities and benefits, the chapter included discussion of both facets of transition as well as of the importance of appropriate transition planning and execution. The transition management plan is an effective deliverable for managing stakeholder expectations, as well as for ensuring that the program management team has plans in place to ensure a successful transition. Unfortunately, many otherwise successful programs are challenged in transition, and the program management team must place sufficient focus on transition planning and execution to ensure that transition activities are completed in an organized way. Ensuring that all impacted stakeholders understand their roles and responsibilities during transition and are committed to performing the required transition activities is important for success.

# 9

# BENEFITS SUSTAINMENT

## INTRODUCTION

Benefits sustainment represents the final phase in the benefits life cycle. The purpose of benefits sustainment is to ensure that the receiving business organization is equipped to sustain benefits after transition has been completed and that the appropriate support for benefits sustainment is in place. It is important to note that sustaining the transitioned benefits typically falls outside of program responsibilities. As the program will eventually terminate, benefits sustainment ensures that the post-transition foundation is established for the receiving business organization to sustain benefits for itself. Activities to be positioned for ongoing responsibility by the receiving business organization include: monitoring activities to assess ongoing product, service, or results performance against the plan (including benefits realization goals), establishing processes and infrastructure to provide service and support, and ensuring that processes are in place to manage ongoing product, service, or result transformation over time.

In general, benefits sustainment involves four key sets of activities. Planning activities build the foundation for benefits sustainment by ensuring that processes and infrastructure are established, post-transition, to ensure the success of benefits sustainment in the receiving business organization. Monitoring activities include the activities within the organization required to monitor the product, service, or result to ensure continued suitability, viability, and performance of the delivered product, service, or result. Supporting activities include ongoing support for the product, service, or result. Finally, evolving activities include the activities necessary to eventually sunset, upgrade, or otherwise evolve capabilities in order to meet stakeholder expectations. The following sections will briefly describe key activities that are typically included within the planning, monitoring, supporting, and evolving activity sets, recognizing that the key focus should be on building a foundation for long-term benefits sustainment rather than on detailed management of this work within the receiving business organization.

## BENEFITS SUSTAINMENT PLANNING

One of the key components required for successful benefits sustainment is assisting the receiving business organization in understanding and preparing for benefits sustainment. An implicit assumption is often made that the receiving business organization will somehow "know how" to sustain the benefits over time. While transition activities ensure, to some extent, that this knowledge exists, and while regular involvement of business stakeholders throughout the benefits realization management life cycle should ensure a good understanding of the anticipated benefits and activities required to sustain them, formalization of the plans and structures required for benefits sustainment is important.

### Performance Monitoring Planning

An essential component of successful benefits sustainment is an established monitoring system that enables continued benefits realization to be monitored in the receiving business organization. As previously discussed, some benefits may not be realized until after the formal benefits realization management activities associated with the program come to an end, and some benefits may be currently being realized with plans for additional realization well into the future. Since the program will no longer be there to perform ongoing monitoring activities, it is incumbent upon the receiving business organization, either directly or via some business support function established to support it, to monitor and control benefits realization. While more detailed steps associated with this ongoing monitoring will be discussed in the next section, within performance monitoring planning, it is important to ensure that:

- Clear accountability for performance monitoring and achievement of benefits realization management objectives is established within the receiving business organization
- Processes are established and formalized to define the types of monitoring required as well as the specific responsibilities for performing monitoring activities and reviewing results
- Key performance indicators (KPIs) related to performance monitoring are understood and accepted by the receiving business organization

- Processes are established for review of actual results and as appropriate, for responding to deviations from planned results are agreed upon

These activities will require coordination between the program management team and a representative of the receiving business organization to ensure that the planned activities are appropriately agreed upon and embedded within the business processes of the receiving organization. This point is especially critical and underscores the importance of effective business change management during benefits sustainment planning. Simply "throwing the work over the wall" from the program to the receiving business organization is rarely successful. Active involvement from business stakeholders, benefit owners, the business change manager, and other key members of the program management team is required in order to ensure that the established plans are understood, agreed upon, and successfully integrated into the organization.

## BENEFITS SUSTAINMENT MONITORING

Monitoring activities focus on monitoring the product, service, or result in the context of the business environment to ensure that the product, service, or result meets the needs of stakeholders and that the planned benefits to the organization are realized. This monitoring may be focused within the receiving organization or may extend beyond the business organization—depending upon the nature of the product, service, or result. For example, benefits associated with internal changes to realize efficiency may only require monitoring within the receiving business organization, whereas monitoring a product that has been deployed into the marketplace may involve gathering data from customers, suppliers, or other stakeholders outside the organization in order to effectively gauge the suitability of the capabilities delivered and the benefits realized. It is not possible to propose a universal monitoring scheme. However, monitoring activities will generally include some combination of the following:

- Monitoring performance of the deployed capabilities and ensuring that the performance of the delivered product, service, or result meets established KPIs
- Analyzing variances from planned performance and establishing corrective action plans to address variances
- Monitoring the business environment to ensure that as needs change, the impacts of these changes on the product, service, or result are understood and if appropriate, corresponding product, service, or result changes or enhancement opportunities are evaluated

- Ensuring that supporting functions continue to be available to meet business needs

Within this context, a strong awareness of changing business needs and a changing business environment is critical. Over time, planned benefits realization may be hindered by advancements in the marketplace, technological advancement, or other factors external to the organization. For example, if a key supplier declares bankruptcy, then the materials needed to provide product support to customers may not be available. Similarly, customers' needs may change due to external factors, and these changes may impact the organization's ability to realize benefits with planned sales, service contracts, or other factors. Monitoring must include being aware of these changes, understanding their impacts on planned benefits realization, and implementing plans to respond to them. While not all such conditions will be external to the business organization, it is necessary to be aware of both the internal and external business environment and to monitor for changes of interest, regardless of their origins.

The program management team must ensure that the processes associated with these activities are understood and that, to the extent possible, the monitoring activities do not place an undue burden on the receiving business organization. Balancing risk and reward is crucial, as it is possible to establish either formal and detailed monitoring systems or less rigorous systems. A clear linkage must exist between the monitoring activities and the value of the data received, so that appropriate data is available for analysis but that data is not simply collected for the sake of collecting data. Linkages to relevant KPIs are the clearest to establish. If monitoring is established that is not linked to a relevant KPI, its value must be validated, and if possible, a relevant KPI must be developed.

## SUPPORTING BENEFITS SUSTAINMENT

Supporting benefits sustainment refers to the set of processes required to ensure that the required support for the delivered product, service, or result is readily available and effective. This may include technical support, operational support, or other support required to ensure that stakeholder needs are being addressed. In this context, support often includes:

- Establishing support functions within the operational business organization and/or transitioning to existing support functions
- Responding to stakeholder questions, concerns, and complaints in order to provide support for delivered products, services, or results
- Assessing stakeholder perceptions and inputs to plan for product enhancements

- Communicating relevant information to stakeholders in order to keep them informed of product changes, enhancements, or tips for more effective use

In this context, a stakeholder may be thought of as a customer who uses a delivered product, service, or result. Customers will likely be primary stakeholders, but other stakeholders, such as suppliers and partners, should not be ignored. These stakeholders, who may be responsible for providing support on behalf of the business organization, may be critical components of an end-to-end support process and required in order to meet end customer needs. One can imagine examples, such as product resellers who provide first-line operational support for an organization's delivered products. These resellers must be kept abreast of recommended support practices, changes in support recommendations, updates to technical documentation, or other changes that impact their ability to service their customers and by extension, the organization's customers.

Additionally, it is important to note that for many organizations, these supporting activities will be integrated into existing support organizations. These organizations likely have standards, processes, and tools they use to support customers as well as mechanisms to gather and act on customer feedback. The program management team must understand the standards, processes, and tools used within these support organizations and ensure that any developed documentation, support processes, or other support mechanisms align with the standards of that support organization. Doing so will minimize potential rework and ensure that the delivered product, service, or result integrates more easily into the existing support environment.

Finally, it is important to ensure that the necessary processes for analyzing and responding to customer feedback are integrated within the supporting processes. The reality of the current business environment necessitates that organizations regularly and proactively manage customer feedback from a variety of sources—both within and beyond the organization's control. Formal mechanisms of the organization—such as customer satisfaction surveys, reviews of support requests, and analyses of commonly reported product or service failures—are mechanisms of the organization used to assess customer feedback. However, mechanisms outside the organization—such as product or service reviews posted on external websites, social media interactions, and other forms of feedback originating and propagating outside of the business organization—must also be managed. While these sources of feedback may be difficult to directly control, responding to feedback from these sources must be considered. The program management team should ensure that as part of establishing sustainment plans, these external feedback mechanisms are not ignored.

## EVOLVING PRODUCTS, SERVICES, AND RESULTS

Evolving refers to the processes undertaken during benefits sustainment to plan for eventual changes, enhancements, or other modifications to delivered products, services, or results. These changes may be driven by customer needs, expectations, recommendations, or complaints as well as by changing business conditions, regulations, or other such factors. While some evolution is natural, it is important to consider the potential impacts of evolution on benefits realization, as some evolution may result in enhanced benefits realization, while other evolution may result in disbenefits. For this reason, development and analysis of appropriate business cases is critical.

These evolutionary activities are often the responsibility of the receiving business organization, and this is, perhaps, the area within benefits sustainment where the program management team responsible for transition and initial sustainment activities will have the least influence. These activities however, may result in new projects or programs that implement change, sunset products, correct technical or other deficiencies, or create new product or service enhancements, based on market or stakeholder needs.

## SUMMARY

This chapter addressed the important role of benefits sustainment in ensuring that transitioned benefits are maintained over time. While benefits sustainment activities are often outside the scope of the program management team, given its temporary nature, providing support for effective sustainment in the receiving business organization is an important component of the benefits realization management life cycle. Appropriate planning and monitoring activities should be included within the benefits realization plan to ensure that the receiving business organization is equipped for success—long after the program concludes.

10

# DESCRIPTIONS FOR PRIMARY BENEFITS REALIZATION MANAGEMENT ROLES

## INTRODUCTION

This chapter provides practical guidance for benefit owners, senior responsible owners, and business change managers. As these critical roles are often undertaken by individuals who are not experts in benefits realization management, the nature of the roles and how to be successful in them is worthy of discussion in the hope that this guidance will reach individuals serving in them. The information provided here is a starting point for becoming familiar with each particular role and for successfully supporting benefits realization when serving in one of them.

## BENEFIT OWNERS

This section addresses the important role of benefit owners. A particular program may involve multiple benefit owners throughout its life cycle so the role of the benefit owner may have to be explained multiple times to different people. Additionally, benefit owners are often representatives of the business organization and may not be familiar with benefits realization management. Therefore, education and training is often necessary to acclimate benefit owners to their roles.

## What Does a Benefit Owner Do?

Benefit owners support the realization of a particular benefit within a program. In this capacity, the benefit owner serves as the representative of the benefit and its realization, providing support for organizational change management related to realization of the benefit, ensuring appropriate management and measurement during benefits realization, supporting benefits planning, and other duties. In many organizations, a benefit owner will support the program in a part-time capacity but will be an integral part of the organizational change management and benefits realization management teams within the program. Key activities undertaken by a benefit owner include:

- Supporting the creation of the benefit profile for the particular benefit the owner represents, including working with the business change manager and other key stakeholders to ensure concurrence with the profile
- Leading business change management related to the benefit, as part of the business change management team within the program and in coordination with the business change manager and other key change stakeholders
- Representing the benefit in benefits reviews and other formal checkpoints
- Supporting the development of appropriate key performance indicators (KPIs) and measurement mechanisms to provide data and reporting regarding benefits realization
- Managing the collection of data to support benefits realization reporting
- Supporting validation that the planned benefit has been achieved
- Supporting transition and sustainment activities as part of program transition

While the senior responsible owner ultimately remains accountable for the realization of benefits on a program level, reliance on benefit owners is often necessary because, while performing these activities, they are often the "first line" resources closest to the business and program work. Such intimacy with the ongoing program enables benefits owners to detect and respond to issues and risks that may impact the realization of planned benefits more easily.

It is important to note that a single benefit owner could be responsible for the realization of more than one benefit. Especially in cases where benefits are tightly integrated, it may be appropriate for a single responsible individual to be responsible for multiple benefits. This may represent the best use of organizational resources. The appropriateness of a particular candidate to represent multiple benefits should be considered in the context of the guidance provided in the rest of this section.

## How Do Benefit Owners Fit within the Benefits Realization Management and Program Context?

As stated in Chapter 3, benefit owners are often considered to be supporting roles in the benefits realization management context. The role of benefit owner is listed as a supporting role primarily to distinguish it from the three "key" program management roles—program manager, senior responsible owner, and business change manager—defined in the program management literature. Certainly, clear ownership and accountability for realizing individual benefits is required for benefits realization management to be successful. The role of the benefit owner is critically important in this context.

In many programs, benefit owners support the program as members of the organizational change management team often reporting to the business change manager. While this alignment is not true for all programs, it is a sensible approach in many cases for several reasons:

- When benefits owners are part-time resources, direct alignment with the overall program management team is not appropriate
- As the work of the benefit owner is complementary to the work of the business change manager, alignment between them is appropriate
- As the program often includes multiple benefit owners, consolidating these owners within one team, aligned with organizational change management, provides opportunities for education and training on key organizational change management principles and supports peer collaboration and knowledge sharing

It is critically important that the role of the benefit manager is defined, formalized, and implemented within the benefits realization management context of the program. Leaving benefit owners to fend for themselves—without the active support of the program management team—is a tremendous mistake.

## Where Do Benefit Owners Come From?

Ideally, benefit owners are representatives of the organization undertaking business change and benefits realization. Benefit owners who are unconnected to the area where the benefit will be realized may have difficulty building credibility and understanding the complexities of the business environment. Similarly, it is generally not recommended that responsibility for benefit ownership reside in other roles within the program management team, unless the roles are complementary to the work being done. For example, on a small program, it could be appropriate for a business change manager to serve as a benefit owner, if he or she has the capacity to perform both roles and the required business alignment to successfully own the benefit. However, it would likely not be appropriate for a program manager to also serve in the capacity of a benefit owner, as he or she should maintain focus on overall management of the program. Similarly, it would generally not be appropriate for the senior responsible owner to share responsibility as a benefit owner. But in some instances, other members of the program management team, or other members of the business change management team within the program, may assume the benefit owner role in addition to their other duties.

When assigning benefit owners, strong consideration should be given to the candidate's alignment with the business organization in which the benefit will be realized as well as to his or her credibility and ability to support implementing change. Though enough seniority in the organization to establish credibility is desirable, a benefit owner need not represent any particular management level within the organization. Less senior employees with strong change orientation and a desire to improve the organization make more effective benefit owners than more senior employees who are not invested in the change, who view the benefit owner role as "one more thing to do," or who will attempt to delegate the work to a subordinate.

Other desirable characteristics include:

- A solid understanding of the business environment and culture of the business area(s) where change will be implemented
- A strong change orientation and desire to effect change within the business organization
- Understanding of (or ability to learn) basic principles and techniques of organizational change management
- Appropriate seniority within the organization to be able to effect change
- Appropriate time allocation to effectively undertake ownership of assigned benefit(s)

Additionally, key skills required to successfully execute the role of a benefit owner are described in the following section.

## What Skills Are Required?

A benefit owner must have a variety of skills to be successful in the role, and a strong training program to support benefit owners is often necessary, as some of the required skills are not formally developed in many training programs. Key skills for benefit owners include:

- Communication skills, especially the ability to communicate complex topics clearly

- Presentation skills, including the ability to effectively present to both management and employees
- Strong collaboration skills, particularly the ability to interface successfully with peers, management, and other stakeholders
- Background in organizational change management principles, including those related to communicating change and its impacts using appropriate frames of reference, communicating change benefits and impacts, surfacing and overcoming resistance, and organizational change management competencies
- Fundamental understanding of measurement as well as data gathering and reporting techniques

As all of these are practical business skills that apply to a wide range of business needs, their development in benefit owners supports the organization well beyond the tenure of the program. Investing in training in this area is worthwhile, and the opportunity to obtain training (and coaching and mentoring) in these important business skills may be a strong selling point when discussing the benefit owner role with candidates. Additionally, the program management team should work with corporate human resource or training staff in order to understand what existing training might already be available to support developing these skills. If readily available options exist, the program management team should investigate training options, after doing a skills inventory of benefit owners and other program team members to identify common training needs.

## How Can Benefit Owners Best Support Benefits Realization Management?

Benefit owners can best support realization of benefits through proactive engagement in the benefits realization management process, both within the business organization as well as through participation as a member of the program management team. Because benefit owners are often closest to the work, they are uniquely positioned to influence peers, to guide the program management team in case of risks and issues, to provide candid feedback as well as quantitative data (via measurement) regarding progress toward benefits realization, and for other important functions that would otherwise be difficult to discern and manage in a timely manner on the overall program level.

In this context, being proactive is key. While the benefit owner may not be a full-time resource to the program management team, he or she must use the limited capacity available to proactively steer the assigned benefits towards realization. This will require collaboration with all team members actively involved in capability creation to support benefits realization, with the business organization receiving the benefit, with other benefits management stakeholders, and potentially with external stakeholders to manage expectations, surface and manage resistance, and guide the benefits realization process on an individual benefit level.

## What Are Potential Traps to Avoid?

Benefit owners must balance the benefits realization needs of the organization, the requirements of the program, and the needs of their stakeholders in order to ensure that benefits are achieved with as few disbenefits as possible. This is not always easy. In fact, benefit owners will be, at one time or another, in situations where seemingly conflicting stakeholder needs lead to resistance to change, impacts to progress, or other undesirable consequences. Benefit owners must try to remain objective and considerate of the overall business goals. Thinking of the big picture may be difficult at times, but a reasonable degree of neutrality will help benefit owners to avoid the trap of getting pulled into "one side or the other" of a debate or discussion regarding benefits and the optimal way to achieve them.

Another potential trap that benefit owners may experience is a conflict between the requirements of the role of benefit owner and their other obligations to the organization. Put more simply, the benefit owner may find that his or her "regular" job reduces the available time for the benefit owner role. While it would be wonderful to assume that a particular time allocation to the benefit owner role could be assured, it is seldom the case. Benefit owners, however, must avoid situations in which their corporate obligations are not balanced with their benefit manager role obligations. If it does happen, it should be brought to the attention of the program management team so the impacts of allocation changes can be assessed, balancing the needs of the business with the needs of the program. Simply allowing the benefit ownership work to lapse or become a "time permitting" activity can negatively impact benefit realization and should not be permitted.

Unfortunately, expectations can be difficult to set and manage in this area, as there is no "right" amount of resource allocation for the benefit owner role. It would perhaps be easiest to have all benefit owners assigned full time to the benefit owner role, but that is largely impractical and potentially wastes organizational resources. A role assignment of 10% or less of someone's time makes little sense, as such assignments typically begin to approach zero percent. Beyond these extremes, the right allocation will largely depend upon the particular program and the type of benefit(s) the individual is to assume responsibility for. Based on my experience in resource allocation, a minimum allocation of 25% is appropriate for most programs. Beyond this guideline, the maximum allocation must be assessed by the benefit owner, together with appropriate members of the program management team, and agreed upon by the manager responsible for the assigned benefit owner.

# SENIOR RESPONSIBLE OWNER

This section addresses the role of the senior responsible owner. As the representative of the organization sponsoring the program, the senior responsible owner maintains accountability for ensuring that the program delivers the capabilities and benefits that have been elaborated as part of the program's business case and relevant chartering documents. This individual also serves as the senior leader responsible for resource allocation, ensuring that high-level issues and risks are addressed in a timely manner, acts as a liaison to the organization's senior management, and is the primary contact to the program steering committee or other governing body.

## What Does the Senior Responsible Owner Do?

The senior responsible owner provides leadership support to the program. While not directly a member of the program management team, the senior responsible owner interacts with the program management team, program steering committee or other governing body, senior organizational stakeholders, and others to support the program toward successful realization of planned benefits. The senior responsible owner often assumes this role in addition to numerous organizational responsibilities and seldom works full time as senior responsible owner.

The senior responsible owner assumes a variety of responsibilities related to leadership in program and benefits realization management, including:

- Representing the sponsoring group and providing leadership within it to support advancement of the program and realization of planned benefits
- Supporting the development of the benefits realization strategy and plan by providing key business input; supporting effective implementation of and compliance with the plans during the overall benefits realization management life cycle
- Leading benefits reviews and supporting validation of benefit realization with stakeholders
- Managing expectations within his or her sphere of influence and ensuring that the business organization maintains support for the program and the benefits goals
- Providing key input to significant program decisions that affect benefits delivery

This list of activities demonstrates the primary role of the senior responsible owner in supporting development of key program artifacts as well as serving as the senior representative of the sponsoring organization during important activities, such as benefits reviews, and at critical decision points during the program life cycle.

Specifically in the benefits realization management context, the senior responsible owner supports development of the benefits realization strategy as well as the benefits realization plan and maintains responsibility for reviewing benefits and validating achievement of benefits realization goals, together with other business stakeholders. As the senior responsible owner is ultimately accountable to the organization for achievement of benefits realization goals, he or she will be actively involved in activities, such as benefits reviews and risk or issue reviews, in order to ensure that the established objectives are being met. Similarly, the senior responsible owner will act as an escalation point for the program management team, ensuring that critical risks and issues are reviewed and addressed in a timely manner. This role gives the program management team a single point of contact for timely support when needed, which is unlikely to occur when a committee—such as a program steering committee, which may meet only every couple to few weeks—is tasked as a group with addressing issues and risks. While the senior responsible owner will serve as a key member of the program steering committee, program review board, or other governance board responsible for the program, he or she will make decisions when needed, using advice from these bodies but ultimately balancing the needs of all stakeholders.

## How Does the Senior Responsible Owner Fit within the Benefits Realization Management and Program Context?

In the benefits realization management context, the senior responsible owner plays a significant role in shaping the benefits landscape. Ultimately, the senior responsible owner is accountable for the delivery of the program's benefits. As such, the senior responsible owner will be involved in establishing benefits targets, developing the benefits realization strategy, reviewing benefit profiles and the benefits realization plan, reviewing benefits data and analysis, validating achievement of benefits through reviews, reviewing measurement data, and other activities that provide assurance that the program is well positioned to deliver the planned benefits. While this may appear to be a significant amount of work, the senior responsible owner relies heavily on the program management team to handle the majority of the detail associated with these activities, enabling the senior responsible owner to act in a management capacity to review, provide direction, support issue resolution, and liaise with organizational stakeholders to advance the program.

From an overall program standpoint, the senior responsible owner stands at the interface between the program and the business organization. While not directly a member of the program management team, the senior responsible owner will interact regularly with the program manager to assess program progress and to facilitate communication between the program and the business organization. Because the senior responsible owner is frequently a management representative, the senior responsible owner's role in the context of the program will include the required communication, negotiation, and consensus building activities to ensure that the appropriate business change is implemented in order to achieve the program's intended benefits.

## Where Does the Senior Responsible Owner Come From?

As a representative of the business organization sponsoring the program, the senior responsible owner is most frequently a member of the business organization's management team. He or she is often a mid- to senior-level manager within this team and is appointed by the business organization's senior leadership.

## What Skills Are Required?

The senior responsible owner, by virtue of his or her business experience and tenure as management within the organization, likely possesses a number of the critical skills required to effectively function in the senior responsible owner capacity. Important skills include:

- Strong understanding of the organization's business environment, strategy, objectives, and an ability to integrate these items into program and benefits realization strategies
- Effective negotiation and consensus building skills to influence diverse stakeholder groups
- Strong understanding of the organization's culture and politics and an ability to successfully navigate the cultural and political environment in order to advance program and benefits realization goals
- An understanding of benefits realization management principles and the ability to understand benefits-related data and analysis
- An understanding of organizational change management principles and how to effectively support changes in a complex business environment
- Experience leading business reviews in order to effectively facilitate program steering committee and other governance meetings
- An understanding of financial management principles, forecasting, and analysis to support establishing financial KPIs

In many cases, the program management team will need to provide education and training, primarily in benefits realization management principles and organizational change management principles, which may be components of a larger overview of the organization's program management processes. This acclimation to the organization's ways of working, as they relate to benefits realization, is especially important for a manager who has not previously served as a senior responsible owner. This training should be customized to the needs of the senior responsible owner, focusing the key principles, tools, and techniques the organization uses to manage benefits realization and on the types of expected reviews, data, and reporting the senior responsible owner will receive on a regular basis. This training also provides an opportunity for the program management team to manage expectations regarding the types of interactions the senior responsible owner will have with the program team, the types of responsibilities the senior responsible owner will be expected to undertake, and the ways of working to effectively leverage the senior responsible owner to advance the program's goals.

## How Can the Senior Responsible Owner Best Support Benefits Realization Management?

The senior responsible owner supports benefits realization management in three primary ways. The first way is through ensuring continued alignment of the program and benefits goals with organizational needs. While the program management team will facilitate alignment of the work with program goals, it is not always possible for the program manager and the program management team to see into the greater goals of the organization or how the organization's strategies and objectives are being influenced—and potentially reshaped—by factors internal and external to the organization. The senior responsible owner can play an important role by having visibility into the broader business environment, both within and beyond the organization, considering the program and its goals, and assessing potential impacts to benefits realization that may result from changes in the business context. Assessing and determining responses to these changes early is critical for benefits realization success, as factors that may limit benefits realization, or opportunities to enhance benefits realization, must be brought to light as quickly as possible for analysis and decision-making. As the senior responsible owner interacts with a variety of business stakeholders and participates in a variety of objective-setting and review exercises within the organization, he or she is typically well positioned to understand the program in the context of the broader business environment. When factors that may affect benefits realization are noted, the senior responsible owner can work with business stakeholders and the program management team to plan and execute appropriate responses.

Second, the senior responsible owner supports benefits realization management through assisting in managing stakeholder expectations. As issues, risks, and other factors impact the dynamics of the program, as business change activities begin to affect program stakeholders, and as the business environment influences benefits realization, the senior responsible owner can provide support to socialize change with stakeholders, agree upon courses of action to overcome obstacles, diminish resistance to approved change, and perform other duties as required to ensure that obstacles to benefits realization are removed. The senior responsible owner may primarily act in an escalation management role in this capacity, influencing in the described areas only when the program management team is unable to achieve an acceptable result on its own. This is the desirable way, ensuring that a large percentage of such stakeholder management issues are resolved by the program management team, while ensuring that the senior responsible owner is available and able to provide support as needed for greater difficulties, such as matters that require resolution, decisions, influence, and negotiation with more senior management of the organization.

Finally, the senior responsible owner provides specific support to the program's benefits realization goals in the areas of review and validation. In this regard, other important benefits management roles, such as benefit owners and the business change manager, will be instrumental as well, but the senior responsible owner, as the individual ultimately accountable for benefits realization, must ensure that benefits claimed to be realized are in fact, realized. This is both a review exercise and a validation exercise, supported by data collected in measurement to support claims that benefits have been realized. As noted previously, not all benefits will be realized during the program. As such, the senior responsible owner may assume responsibility for program-related benefits validation as well as for ongoing benefits validation, when benefits are planned to be achieved after the program is concluded. The senior responsible owner must be able to effectively analyze and scrutinize data, appropriately question benefits realization claims, and proactively validate that business change management activities were successful in embedding change in the organization in a sustainable way. Education and training may be required in order to ensure that the senior responsible owner understands the organization's processes for benefits review and validation as well as his or her role in this process. This training should be provided as early as possible—certainly prior to significant benefits realization management activities.

## What Are Potential Traps to Avoid?

To be sure, the senior responsible owner's job is not easy, as programs seldom proceed exactly according to plan. And, given the importance of benefits realization, changes in factors that will affect it often come to the senior responsible owner to resolve, when the impact is significant or the situation cannot be resolved on the program level. Thus, the senior responsible owner is involved in the "tough" decisions of the program. Some practical guidance to help senior responsible owners effectively support benefits realization management is provided in this section.

First and foremost, it is incumbent upon the senior responsible owner to take time to understand the processes, tools, and techniques used within the organization to manage benefits realization. The program management team will rely on standard ways of working, reports, software tools, and other items to deliver the program and its benefits. The senior responsible owner will come into contact with these processes and associated deliverables and will need to understand how the processes work, the types of data contained within reports and their meaning, the types of data collected by software tools and processes, and so forth. While the senior responsible owner will not need to be an expert in these topics, familiarity will provide an understanding of what types of information he or she will receive, how issues will be escalated to him or her, his or her role in various meetings, how to obtain supporting data, and so forth. To the extent possible, the senior responsible owner should plan to operate within these processes. Requesting out of process reports, expecting special briefings beyond established meetings and reviews, and similar exceptions to the organization's standard ways of working create extra work for the already busy program management team and rarely yield significant benefits.

Secondly, it is incumbent upon the senior responsible owner to avoid the phenomenon of "analysis paralysis," in which he or she invests significant time in analyzing the dynamics of a decision to be made but never commits to a decision. The role of the senior responsible owner, in part, is to ensure that good decisions are made and that these decisions are made in a timely manner. A situation that plagues many project and program managers is the "management by committee" mentality, in which decisions are deferred to groups of people rather than being made by a single responsible individual with clear accountability for the decision. As an example, some organizations require a meeting of a steering committee or governing body in order to decide project-level issues that cannot be resolved by the project manager and/or team. These bodies, while well intentioned, are often not flexible enough to respond quickly when required. In the program management environment, this can be disastrous. When opportunities to take advantage of emergent benefits arise, when critical benefits realization issues become apparent, or when organizational roadblocks prevent progress, the program management team must be able to rely on the senior responsible owner to review relevant facts, assess options, and make a binding decision on behalf of the organization. This does not always make the senior responsible owner (or the program management team for that matter) popular, but such empowerment is absolutely necessary in a dynamic environment. There are often opportunities for more data analysis, to consult more experts, to involve more stakeholders, or otherwise to gather more information, but this must always be balanced with the current, often pressing need to come to agreement on a decision and move on. While we certainly do not desire rash or unreasoned decisions, it must always be remembered that time is of the essence in the program management environment.

Additionally, the senior responsible owner must avoid the trap of trying to be everything to everyone. In benefits realization management, there may be winners and losers. Sometimes, losses come in the form of disbenefits that affect organizational stakeholders, sometimes losses come in required process change to support benefits realization, sometimes losses come in making hard decisions to balance risk and reward in a dynamic program environment. Attempting to please everyone is seldom the formula for success. In reality, this approach often robs the organization of potential benefits realization, while still not making everyone happy. While I certainly do not advocate that anyone be outright obstinate, it is incumbent upon the senior responsible owner to be firm when necessary and to make the "hard calls" that are occasionally required. The politics and culture of the organization will influence how this is approached, but the senior responsible owner, as a supporter of change, should be willing to ensure that appropriate decisions are made and communicated in a timely manner, and that resistance is managed in the best way possible while still preserving the best resolution for involved stakeholders and the program's benefits goals.

## BUSINESS CHANGE MANAGER

This section addresses the role of the business change manager, who is critical to successful delivery of benefits. The business change manager maintains responsibility for ensuring that stakeholders impacted by business change, created during capability delivery and benefits realization, are prepared for change, that integration of new capabilities and realization of anticipated benefits is managed in a way that minimizes disruption, and among other duties, that stakeholders are managed in such a way as to ensure continued alignment with program goals. This role is often one of the most difficult benefits realization management positions to staff. Ideally, the business change manager possesses a deep understanding of the organization and its business processes, understands organizational change and benefits realization management principles, and is a credible leader within the business organization implementing change.

### What Does the Business Change Manager Do?

The business change manager role encompasses a broad scope of activities to effectively manage change within the program. While many of these activities impact benefits realization, the business change manager additionally supports the broader program through ensuring appropriate business change management in support of program planning, execution, capability delivery, and benefits realization. Common activities undertaken by the business change manager that directly relate to benefits realization management include:

- Facilitating identification and quantification of program benefits, engaging the business stakeholder community to establish consensus and alignment
- Effecting business change to support benefits realization through sound organizational change management practices
- Proactively monitoring the business environment for changing business conditions, resistance, or other factors that may influence realization of benefits
- Supporting the creation of the benefits realization plan, ensuring that the required business change activities and processes are represented within the plan
- Developing and maintaining key benefits realization management artifacts, including benefit profiles
- Supporting ongoing sustainment of benefits

As this list demonstrates, a business change manager is required from early in the benefits realization management life cycle, to support activities related to identification of benefits, through late in the benefits realization management life cycle, to support benefits sustainment.

The second item in the list is worthy of special mention, as it is the only activity not directly related to benefits realization management. Organizational change management is not specific to benefits realization but is critically important for its success. Because of its importance, Chapter 11 provides an overview of key activities in organizational change management and of the relationship between organizational change management and benefits realization management. It is likely that the business change manager will spend a significant amount of time focused on organizational change management, using these activities to support the realization of benefits.

The other listed activities recognize the key role of the business change manager in supporting the processes associated with identifying and quantifying benefits, creating the benefits realization plan, monitoring the business environment, and maintaining important artifacts. Because the business change manager should have a deep understanding of the organization and its ways of working (or the capability to quickly develop this understanding) and will be responsible for driving the changes to be implemented, it is important that he or she play a key role in development of benefits realization plans. This is important for two reasons. First, early engagement ensures that the business change manager's understanding of the organization and of business change management principles can be leveraged—from the start—to develop sound plans for effective benefits realization. Second, the business change manager, in his or her capacity as a business representative, will build credibility with the organization, since he or she actively supports plans for change that will impact the organization in which the business change manager resides. This credibility will be important as the program progresses, as the business change manager will be a key resource championing business change and working to overcome resistance in order to advance the program's benefits realization objectives.

## How Does the Business Change Manager Fit within the Benefits Realization Management and Program Context?

The business change manager provides direct support to the program management team to enable benefits realization. As such, the business change manager represents one of the key roles in benefits realization management and will likely develop a team to support the changes necessary to enable effective benefits realization. This team should include representatives from business areas affected by business change, who serve as change agents within their respective business areas, as well as support resources who assist with producing documentation, support training, support communication, or other support activities required to ensure that business change management activities for benefits realization are effectively executed. Additionally, the benefit owners are typically included within the scope of the business change manager's team in order to ensure close coordination between the benefit owners, who are often heavily involved in the required business change to support their respective benefits, and the business change manager, who has responsibility for overall business change management to support benefits realization on the broader program level.

Overall, the business change manager, together with the program manager and senior responsible owner, represent the three central roles within the program. The business change manager is included among these roles to represent the critical importance of business change management to program success. Additionally, ensuring close alignment between the business change manager, the program manager, and the senior responsible owner ensures that issues affecting business change can be quickly escalated to the program or business change manager—should it not be able to be resolved within the business change management team. It is strongly recommended that organizations implementing benefits realization management ensure close alignment between the benefits realization management work and the program management team, including the business change manager as a formal member of the program management core team. Relegating business change management and the role of the business change manager to a support function within the program, rather than a central role, is occasionally attempted but rarely successful.

It is important to note that the business change manager should be allocated on a full-time basis in the vast majority of cases. The work required to effectively drive organizational change and benefits realization is often underestimated. Until organizational history is established to justify a lesser resource allocation, the organization will be best served by erring on the side of caution and appointing this critical role on a full-time basis to ensure appropriate focus on the activities required to successfully implement change in the organization for realizing the desired benefits.

## Where Does the Business Change Manager Come From?

Ideally, the business change manager is a representative of the receiving business organization itself. This will be advantageous, especially if the business change manager comes from a business area being impacted by the program change and expected benefits (or potentially disbenefits). The primary advantage of this approach is the business change manager's credibility within an affected area will be known to many of the stakeholders affected by change and will be more readily able to drive change because those affected see him or her as a knowledgeable peer. He or she will be able to speak the language of the business, understand current challenges, navigate the politics and organizational culture, and better present change to the affected stakeholders than will an individual with limited experience and credibility within the organization. An additional advantage is that business change managers sourced from the business typically require less ramp-up time before effectively contributing to the program efforts. Finally, they are typically better positioned to support development of key benefits realization management artifacts, such as the benefits realization plan, because they understand "what works" in the organization—referring to their ability to develop business change management and benefits realization plans that will be likely to succeed, given the organizational environment, culture, and other factors.

As noted, the business change manager role should be allocated on a full-time basis. Often, this causes concern for organizational leaders, as such an allocation requires removing a capable business resource from his or her role for an extended period of time. This concern may extend to the candidate as well, fearing that by taking on the business change manager role, he or she may not have a role to come back to—once the business change manager role concludes. Balancing the needs of the organization with those of the individual is critically important, and organizations should position the business change manager role as an opportunity for a motivated employee to extend his or her business knowledge and skills by taking on a new challenge. To sell the business change manager role, the organization should assign the employee to a critical initiative that provides an opportunity to be "in the spotlight," developing and using skills that are broadly applicable and will make him or her more valuable to the organization. Additionally, it is important to ensure the employee that he or she will still have a place after the role concludes. While such things are seldom guaranteed, business leaders should recognize the value that trained business change managers bring to the organization and further recognize that this experience will be helpful when benefits sustainment activities commence at the conclusion of the program and when the organization undertakes business change efforts in the future. It is seldom the case that businesses stop changing and evolving and for this reason, maintaining business change management capability within the organization is desirable.

Some organizations however, are unwilling or unable to provide their own business change manager. This leaves the organization with two potential sources for the role. The first involves utilizing a project or program management resource to fill the role. The advantage of this approach is that project and program managers often possess the discipline and organizational understanding to effectively develop plans to drive change and to manage these plans successfully, relying on project and program management expertise. The disadvantages to this approach could include the resource not having sufficient business background to effectively understand the impacts of change and benefits on the organization (potentially overcome by training and mentoring), a lack of understanding of organizational change management principles (potentially overcome by training), and a lack of credibility with the business organization itself. If a project or program management resource is utilized, it is strongly suggested that this resource be partnered with a business representative who, usually on a part-time basis, provides insider perspective and support to the business change manager to ensure successful change integration within the business itself.

The second option is to hire a third party contractor or consultant. The advantage of this approach is that organizational human resources are not consumed directly and in many cases, external consultants and contractors can be found that have significant background and experience in organizational change and benefits realization management principles. This expertise can enable the organization to quickly realize benefits—with qualified personnel participating in the development of plans, such as the benefits realization plan and organizational change management plan, and the external consultant or contractor being able to leverage expertise gained from experiences with a variety of organizations. This external perspective can be valuable, especially when the business organization has limited formal experience with driving business change.

The consultant or contractor approach comes with its own potential drawbacks as well. First and foremost, external parties initially lack credibility with the business and will need to build an understanding of the unique business environment they are expected to drive change in. While this is not an insurmountable obstacle, it is worth noting that the time required to build this expertise will come at a cost to the organization, both in money and in time—because organizational human resources must assist the external party with what he or she needs to understand in order to be successful.

An additional challenge is the fact that when utilizing external resources, the knowledge and expertise these resources gain is a lost organizational asset when the resource leaves, unless an investment is made in appropriate documentation, knowledge transition, and other activities that codify that knowledge for the organization. Even with these efforts, some implicit knowledge will ultimately leave with the external resource. This is not an insurmountable challenge, but it does require the organization to invest some resource to "shadow" the external contractor and gain training and mentoring in principles and practices related to managing organizational change and benefits realization. This training and mentoring builds these key skills into the organization, which will be valuable when it undertakes such efforts in the future.

## What Skills Are Required?

Successful business change managers are able to effectively integrate their business knowledge and acumen with formal knowledge of proven techniques in organizational change management. Additionally, successful business change managers effectively utilize sound communication and collaboration skills in order to lead change. Specific skills that are assets in business change managers include:

- Strong understanding of the organization's business environment, including organizational strategies, ways of working, cultural aspects, and political aspects
- Ability to effectively understand the relationship between organizational strategies and goals and expected benefits with a focus on understanding how stakeholders will be impacted by the changes from planned benefits realization
- Strong communication skills and an ability to speak the language of intended recipients
- Effective consensus-building and negotiation skills to successfully balance stakeholder needs across potentially diverse groups
- Ability to say "no" when required and to balance the organization's interests with individual stakeholder interests

- Knowledge of and training in organizational change management principles and methodologies
- Knowledge of and training in benefits realization management principles and methodologies, including standard organizational processes
- Knowledge of project management methodologies, including a basic understanding of scheduling, budgeting, risk management, and related disciplines

A key focus of professional development for the business change manager should be gaining knowledge and experience in methodologies related to business change management and benefits realization management, utilizing external training when necessary in order to gain perspective into proven methodologies for effectively managing change in a business environment—if internal processes and tools are not available to support this work. There should be little need for the business change manager to individually create processes for successful business change management although some customization of standard tools may be necessary for adapting to the unique environment of a particular business organization. If an organization is implementing organizational change management methodologies for the first time, it may be necessary to do more customization, but these customized artifacts should become reusable assets that the business can include as part of its program management methodology.

Additionally, the business change manager will benefit from a fundamental understanding of project management principles, enabling him or her to plan and execute business change management activities as a project. This is important for ensuring that these activities are proactively formalized via plans, issues and risks that may impact success of business change management activities are tracked and managed, and the business change management team's expectations reflect that the required activities will be managed in a coordinated way.

## How Can the Business Change Manager Best Support Benefits Realization Management?

This question is actually quite simple to answer. The business change manager, as the resource primarily responsible for ensuring successful business change toward benefits realization, can support benefits realization management by effectively leveraging his or her knowledge and experience in the business environment and in organizational change management, along with the collective experience of his or her team, to proactively effect change in the business organization in a way that ensures the successful delivery of benefits. The words *effectively* and *proactively* are most critical here. Effective implementation refers to doing the right things to achieve the right end goals, not simply doing work for the sake of work. It is somewhat surprising, when reviewing failed programs, that a common cause of failure relates to organizational change management, in the sense of doing organizational change management activities to "put a check in the box" that certain deliverables were created, trainings held, and so forth, rather than understanding at a detailed level the types of deliverables, trainings, communication vehicles, and other artifacts and activities that are appropriate for the business organization and will be effective in supporting business change. Doing the right things is critical. Simply doing things is not effective.

In this context, being proactive refers to managing the benefits realization plan, managing the organizational change management plan and associated artifacts, managing stakeholder expectations and responding to stakeholder needs, and otherwise ensuring that management of change occurs *before* issues arise. Simply responding to the business environment is a formula for failure. Often, by the time issues become apparent, their effects are already being felt. And, while it is impossible to effectively anticipate every potential issue that might occur or risk that might be realized, it is incumbent upon the business change manager and his or her team to regularly survey the business environment, to regularly communicate with and seek feedback from stakeholders, and to regularly communicate with other members of the program management team to identify potential issues and risks to be managed. These activities should be formalized in the organizational change management plan.

## What Are Potential Traps to Avoid?

To be sure, business change management is not easy work. The business change manager will be faced with many situations in which competing stakeholder needs must be balanced against the benefits realization goals for the program. Navigating this environment is not easy, but success begins with a firm plan. A common trap in business change management is believing that change will happen through the mere will of the organization, enforcement of rules and policies, and other "strong" tactics designed to force business change. While some of these strong tactics may be appropriate, they should not form the sole basis of the business change management plan. Successful business change managers understand how to develop plans that guide people through an orderly transition, from their current ways of working to new ways of working. This planning begins long before capabilities are delivered and must be formalized and run like a project. Successful business change managers formalize their plans, communicate them, and manage them in ways that enable them to track progress and proactively identify issues and risks that may impact business change success. Establishing a project mindset early is critically important.

Additionally, the business change manager may fall into the same trap as the senior responsible owner, if he or she attempts to manage organizational change with the goal of making all stakeholders happy. While managing disbenefits to minimize impacts and proactively working to overcome resistance to change and create a positive change environment are important activities the business change manager will undertake, there will probably still be pockets of dissatisfaction, resistance, or unwillingness to support change within the organization. While it may be tempting to focus on these pockets of resistance, the business change manager must recognize the overall benefits realization goals of the organization and focus on activities that support those goals. Over-managing resistance is a trap to avoid. Under-managing resistance is not desirable either, but the business change manager must maintain focus on building support for the change-ready organization and leveraging this organization to advance benefits realization goals. A primary focus must be on leveraging supporters to advance benefits realization goals. Management of detractors should focus on ensuring that relevant issues are addressed, but attempting to "win over" all stakeholders is unlikely to be successful.

## SUMMARY

This chapter addressed important considerations in defining the role of, and selecting staff for, the critical roles required to effectively support benefits realization management. Organizations implementing benefits realization management should focus on identifying qualified staff to fill these roles, and providing training, coaching, and mentoring to ensure that staff develops the skills required to be successful. While some reliance on external parties may initially be required, organizations are best served by developing internal capabilities, which enables them to effectively manage the benefits realization management life cycle with well-qualified internal team members who can provide education, coaching, and mentoring to the organization to build additional competency over time. This important concept will be discussed in more detail in Chapter 16.

# 11

# ORGANIZATIONAL CHANGE MANAGEMENT IN THE BENEFITS REALIZATION MANAGEMENT CONTEXT

## INTRODUCTION

This chapter provides a practical introduction to organizational change management. The general field of organizational change management addresses the entire life cycle of planning for, implementing, monitoring, controlling, and sustaining organizational change initiatives. It is relevant for all organizations since they must undertake some change in order to survive in a changing business and global environment. Unfortunately, the degree of implementation and acceptance of organizational change management principles, as standard ways of managing change, varies widely. In some organizations, change is managed in a structured way, relying on methodologies (either externally acquired or internally developed) to guide its implementation. In other organizations, change is handled less formally, often relying primarily on brute force or informal communication. Typically, organizations applying less formal approaches encounter lower overall success rates and higher internal resistance than those that use more formal approaches. While there are certainly exceptions to this general rule, more often than not, the lack of formality creates unnecessary organizational stress, resistance, and effort investment during the change life cycle. For more critical organizational efforts, these impacts can lead to significant consequences—up to, and including, failure of change initiatives.

Recognizing that many of the organization's critical change efforts will be (or should be) managed with program management principles—and correspondingly, with embedded benefits realization management principles—the relationship between execution of program work, realizing benefits, and managing organizational change should be clear. Yet, more often than should be the case, organizational change management efforts are among the least developed in program plans and among the least closely managed in program execution. Some programs relegate organizational change management to the business organization with little coupling to the program; some relegate organizational change management to the constituent project level, relying on project managers to plan for and execute change; still others implement change planning, only to ignore the planning when the program encounters trouble, choosing to focus on capability creation rather than on organizational change. All of these approaches have serious limitations. Successful benefits realization via programs requires an appropriate focus on organizational change management throughout the program life cycle, beginning with early change planning and continuing through benefits sustainment. This important component of the program is formalized, to some extent, by the business change manager who must be more than simply a person with a title. Formal organizational change management must be an integral part of both program planning and execution as well as benefits realization management.

This chapter will not provide you with expertise in organizational change management. Rather, its purposes are to provide an overview of key principles of organizational change management and to discuss the linkages between these principles and benefits realization management. There are a number of excellent organizational change management methodologies available in the marketplace, many good books that cover the subject, and many competent consultants who can provide expertise to organizations in this domain. An investment in methodology, training, and if appropriate, consulting can assist an organization in building an appropriate methodology and set of corresponding artifacts to support managing organizational change within its unique business (as some tailoring of standard methodologies is often appropriate), forming the basis for a repeatable process that will be useful across multiple change initiatives. Alternatively, program management teams may be able to leverage existing methodologies in the organization (perhaps residing in business functions, such as human resource departments) as a basis for program work. The key is to avoid "reinventing the wheel." Organizations that execute programs to drive benefits realization should build repeatable capability for organizational change management in order to equip business change managers and program management teams with the foundational tools necessary to successfully achieve planned benefits through change.

## THE FUNDAMENTAL CONCEPT OF ORGANIZATIONAL CHANGE MANAGEMENT

At a fundamental level, organizational change management is not particularly difficult to understand. Organizational change management exists as a process to move people (in the form of divisions, groups, individuals, companies, etc.) in an orderly way, from a current state (of operation, ways of working, organizational alignment, etc.) to a new state, in a way that minimizes disruption (to the organization, its customers, affected individuals, etc.) and maximizes benefits from the change. It is worth making a few comments about each of these essential components.

### The Notion of Movement

"Moving people" is a multi-faceted concept. At its simplest, one could view this in the context of moving people physically (perhaps in the case of an office relocation program) or moving people within the organizational context (such as aligning people to new positions within an organizational structure). However, more interesting in the organizational change management context is the idea of moving people from the perspective of mindset. We often use organizational change management to manage the psychological impacts of change. Many people experience some amount of doubt, resistance, anxiety, or fear when external forces bring change that impacts them personally. Business change programs often do just this. Realizing benefits through change often requires us to change ways of working, to realign organizations, to reduce staff or change staff roles, or to perform other actions that personally impact stakeholders. This psychological movement, from a comfortable current state to an initially less comfortable future state, is not always easy and in the organizational change management context, must be managed.

### Who Are We Impacting?

The use of the word "people" is meant to be broad, recognizing that the impacts of business change can be far-reaching. While organizational change management is often initially implemented in organizations as a way to manage internal change, it is clear that stakeholder diversity in many programs will extend beyond organizational boundaries. Suppliers, partners, customers, governments, and other stakeholders may all be impacted by change programs. As such, organizational change management efforts must broadly consider the needs of these stakeholders, which may be different, and consider these needs *in addition to* the needs of internal stakeholders. This dynamic can be difficult to manage, as it may not be possible to exert the same influence over external stakeholders as can be exerted over internal parties.

## How Do We Manage Change?

The key here is "orderly" management of change. It is quite possible to affect change in an organization by brute force. Managers, by virtue of their positions in the organization, can dictate changes in ways of working, mandate reorganization, or take any other actions within their authority. Memoranda can be created, town hall meetings can be held, e-mails can be sent, and other forms of communication can be used to tell stakeholders what is changing and require them to begin operating according to management's wishes. Unfortunately, the brute force approach has undesirable consequences, such as increased employee attrition, decreased employee morale, and other consequences from being bossed around. A change management approach that focuses on achieving the desired benefits associated with change but in a way that prepares affected stakeholders for change—proactively seeking input regarding the change, managing resistance, and adapting where possible to the unique culture of the organization—is typically much more successful. As such, organizations seek to establish an orderly approach to change in order to guide people through the process in a way that helps to build comfort and minimize stress on its people. Appropriate planning and management of organizational change is crucial. Thankfully, principles from organizational change management, program management, project management, and benefits realization management can be leveraged to create order and ensure that activities are coordinated in a way that achieves the most beneficial outcomes, both for affected stakeholders and for the organization.

## Minimizing Disruption

Have you ever experienced a change in your professional or personal life that created some degree of chaos? Most people have. And while chaos is unavoidable in some situations, there are many cases of organizations making change harder than it needs to be (for both the affected stakeholders and the organization), through insufficient understanding of the potential disruption change can create. It is somewhat amazing how "relatively small" changes can result in significant disruption to a business, isn't it? Really, it's not surprising. In many organizations, things have been done in the same way for a long time. Even small changes to entrenched processes can cause significant confusion and disruption. The imperative of organizational change management is to ensure that disruption is minimized, to the extent possible, as change is implemented. This is especially important from a benefits realization management perspective, as unnecessary disruption in business operations often causes reduced benefits realization. While these effects can be corrected over time, an opportunity cost always results, which is certainly relevant in the benefits realization management context.

### Maximizing Benefits

It is a clear imperative for organizational change management to support the realization of benefits. Proactively managing change supports achievement of benefits realization management goals by minimizing disruption to the organization, supporting effective benefits transition and sustainment, equipping stakeholders with the skills, knowledge, and experience necessary to support benefits realization, managing resistance to change, and identifying potential risks and issues that may affect benefits realization. The important relationship between benefits realization management and organizational change management is, unfortunately, not appreciated in some organizations. I have seen organizations begin to implement benefits realization management without a corresponding focus on organizational change management. The consequence of this approach, in many cases, is that benefits realization management implementation does an excellent job of helping organizations capture data telling them they're not meeting their benefits objectives. While this is nice, from a data management and information analysis perspective, it certainly does not help to move the business forward. Therefore, I strongly recommend that a focus on benefits realization management come with a corresponding focus on organizational change management, if organizational change management practices are not already established and effective within the organization. Doing so will allow the benefits realization management team to develop methodologies, tools, templates, and other artifacts that integrate the required benefits realization management and organizational change management work into a cohesive process. Integration of these processes is strongly desirable where possible but, recognizing that ownership for organizational change management practices may be outside the control of the organization responsible for ownership of benefits realization management practices, it is not always possible to achieve perfect integration.

## CHANGE MANAGEMENT ROLES

Several key roles are integral to successful management of change. While the roles described here are not exhaustive of all potential roles within the scope of change management, they are meant to highlight primary roles that most organizations undertaking organizational change management activities in the program and benefits realization management contexts are likely to staff.

## Business Change Manager

The role of the business change manager was described in detail in Chapter 10. In the organizational change management context, the business change manager should serve as the overall leader of the organizational change management team and should maintain responsibility for coordination of all activities within the scope of organizational change management, delegating responsibilities to members of the organizational change management team and other parties to ensure effective and efficient management of the work.

## Benefit Owners

The role of benefit owners has also been described in the context of benefits realization management. In the organizational change management context, benefit owners play an important role in helping to craft the required change management activities to support their particular benefits. As experts on the individual benefits to be achieved, benefit owners are best positioned to help the organizational change management team define, plan, and implement appropriate change management actions for successful benefits realization. It is important for the organizational change management team to understand the dynamics of each planned benefit, as well as the relationship between benefits and between benefits and capability delivery (inclusive of relevant interdependencies), in order to ensure that the right change management activities are planned at the right times to support capability delivery and benefit realization.

## Change Agents

Change agents represent a broad category of resources that support the change management team within their respective spheres of influence. Change agents are often the "grassroots" drivers of change: they believe in the change and are willing to devote their time to advancing it. Often part-time and extended members of the core change management team, these resources are powerful allies to the core change management team and should be leveraged throughout the change life cycle to provide feedback to the change management team, as well as to provide coaching, mentoring, training, and communication support within their respective business areas. Change agents may lack significant formal influence but are often exceptionally positioned to informally influence peers, manage resistance to change, and support peer communication regarding change. The change agent role should be appropriately recognized and rewarded by the organization.

## Champions

Champions are individuals within the organization who are strong supporters of the planned changes and have appropriate influence within the organization to drive change. Often, champions are sourced from middle management, between the program sponsors and steering committee, and are primary change agents within the organization. Their formal position within the organization enables them to influence the organization by directing change as needed, but more importantly, their visible support for the change within their respective spheres of influence provides reinforcement for the change, assists with minimizing fear of and resistance to change, and provides a feedback mechanism for members of the organization to voice their concerns. Champions should be regularly utilized to assist with key communications and reinforcing messaging, as well as for gathering important feedback. There will likely be significantly fewer champions than change agents; therefore, regular significant engagement in meetings, one-on-one discussions, and other opportunities to keep champions involved and supporting the change should be a high priority for the change management team.

## Management

Management plays a critical role in organizational change management success. In addition to setting business priorities and authorizing work, management must be visible, proactive, positive supporters of change. It is well established that change initiatives with a low degree of visible management support are often doomed from the start. Support starts at the development of the business case and must continue through benefits sustainment after the program concludes. It is incumbent upon the business change manager to educate management on the importance of visibly supporting the program, to include relevant management actions in the organizational change management plan, and to equip management with the tools to effectively support the change. Formal, proactive support for change in the context of organizational change management may be new to some (perhaps all) management, and a focus on education and training to help managers understand *why* their participation is important and *how* to best provide support is crucial. Some organizations I have encountered developed specialized training or specific "toolkits" for managers to help them effectively support change. While these can be effective, they must be accompanied by clear expectations about the type of support, frequency of support, and so on. The organizational change management plan offers an important tool for documenting plans, actions, and tracking progress.

## Relationships between Roles

The various roles involved in organizational change management are shown in Figure 11.1.

Figure 11.1 depicts a hierarchy of roles, with the foundation being the change agents, who typically represent the largest group and who typically provide the most direct, grassroots support for business change. Above the change agents are the champions, who may represent influential stakeholders who are supportive of the planned business change, or who may represent change agents who provide additional, dedicated support to driving change. Above the champions are the benefit owners, who will interface with change agents and champions, as well as with the business change manager, to ensure appropriate focus on benefits realization for their assigned benefits. The business change manager sits between the benefit owners and the business management, which may represent the sponsoring group—or other management within the organization—that is affected

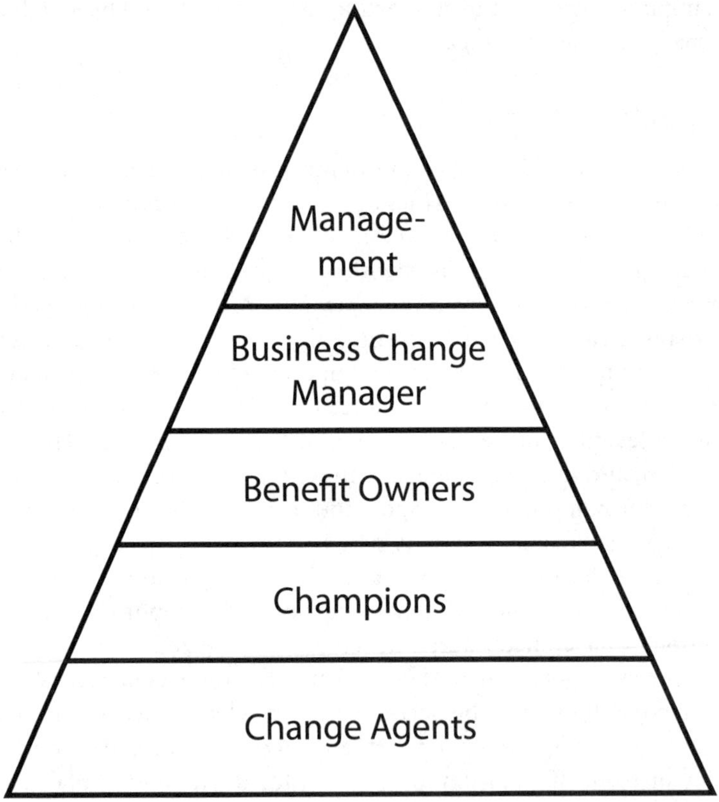


**Figure 11.1** Organizational change management role relationships

by business change. The business change manager will navigate across the entire pyramid, with support from the program management team as needed, to ensure appropriate organizational change management work is undertaken to support change. While variations on this hierarchy exist, the importance is not in the structure and names as much as ensuring that there is consistent support—from the lower levels of the organization to upper management. Organizational change management cannot be driven by the business change manager or program management team alone, and building a network of support is important for overall change success.

## AN ORGANIZATIONAL CHANGE MANAGEMENT LIFE CYCLE

This section is specifically titled *an* organizational change management life cycle, as opposed to *the* organizational change management life cycle, in recognition that no single authoritative model is the universal standard in this area. Many organizations, consultancies, consensus bodies, and others have proposed models for managing organizational change. Each has its own scope of applicability (e.g., some are industry specific), benefits, and drawbacks. Organizations seeking to establish organizational change management capability will likely need to review several reference methodologies to find one most appropriate for them. This section describes a general model that contains elements common to many available reference models. It is reasonably expected that organizations could take this generalized model and adapt it to their own needs, perhaps adding phases or processes as needed or augmenting this information with additional detail or elements from other reference models in order to build a complete methodology for the organization. Of course, this approach requires prior experience in organizational change management. Without such experience, the generalized model described here can be implemented as a starting point and evolved over time, as lessons learned from its use are leveraged to create better processes, artifacts, and other assets to support organizational change management activities.

The diagram in Figure 11.2 illustrates the basic life cycle that will be referenced in this chapter.

Each of the phases in the life cycle is briefly described here for reference. Additional detail may be found in the subsequent sections of this chapter. These phases include:

- **Define Change Drivers**—the activities required to define *why* change is needed, to assess readiness for it, and to document specific change drivers as inputs to its definition

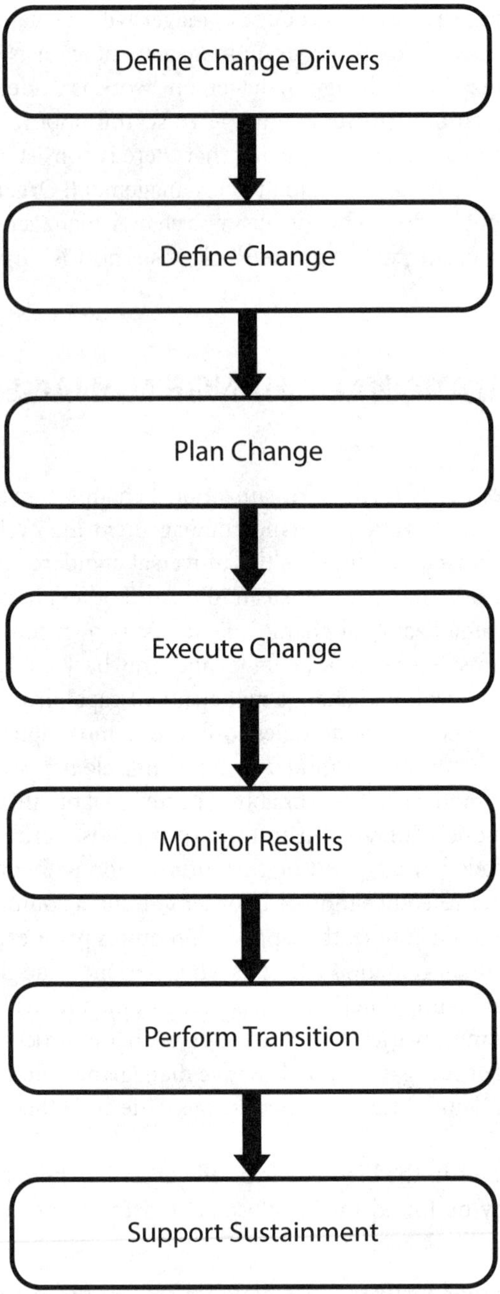


**Figure 11.2** Organizational change management life cycle

- **Define Change**—the activities required to define the specific change as well as its corresponding potential benefits and impacts
- **Plan Change**—the activities required to plan for the proactive, orderly management of change as well as to integrate organizational change management work into overall program plans, manage risk and issues, and track and report progress
- **Execute Change**—the activities required to execute organizational change management activities according to plans
- **Monitor Results**—the activities required to respond to issues and risks, take corrective actions, report progress, and ensure successful achievement of associated benefits realization goals
- **Perform Transition**—the activities required to validate change success and to ensure its successful transition into business operations
- **Support Sustainment**—the activities required to ensure the continued success of organizational change management activities as well as the ongoing realization of associated benefits

It is important to note that Figure 11.2 can be represented as a cyclical process. This is because organizational change management activities often occur continuously in organizations. The successful sustainment of change for some period of time may inevitably lead to the need to define new change drivers, to impact that change or to create other beneficial change in the organization. This work may mean chartering new programs to implement new capabilities, requiring organizational change management in order to successfully manage change to realize benefits.

In the following sections, each phase in the organizational change management life cycle is described in further detail. It is not possible within the scope of this book to provide detailed organizational change management implementation guidance. However, in addition to further detail regarding each phase, guidance specific to the relationship between the phase and activities associated with benefits realization management will be discussed to show how benefits realization management is influenced by work that takes place within the phase. For further detailed guidance regarding implementation of organizational change management, refer to Internet resources or literature.

## Define Change Drivers

Defining change drivers is presented as the first phase in the organizational change management life cycle in recognition of the need to first ensure that the specific needs and expectations of the organization are clarified *before* change is undertaken. Often, the organization's strategic plan is the starting point for the development of a portfolio of work to be undertaken to realize the elements within the strategic plan. From this portfolio, specific initiatives (often in the form of programs) are defined to realize the objectives necessary to implement the strategies. The starting point for defining change drivers comes from the portfolio level, as the translation of strategies into more granular objectives necessitates considering and elaborating the need for change and the relevant high level activities (which are often included as part of relevant business cases that support the portfolio). This translation allows the rationale for each constituent program or other component to be understood and documented. Thus, there should be relative clarity on the portfolio level about how each element contributes to the relevant strategic objectives as well as to, at a high level, the relevant business change required to accomplish each portfolio element.

While the portfolio elements and their corresponding high-level change drivers and activities may be clear on the portfolio level, diverse stakeholder interests will be associated with each initiative. These stakeholder interests must be understood before any change definition is undertaken in order to ensure clarity regarding the needs and expectations of various stakeholders as well as to confirm the alignment of the change program with stakeholder needs. It is often the case that portfolio development includes input from only a subset of potential stakeholders; therefore, an important first step in defining change drivers is to conduct stakeholder analysis, which identifies relevant stakeholders and assesses their high level needs and attitudes. A stakeholder map is a common tool for this important first step, an example of which appears in Figure 11.3.

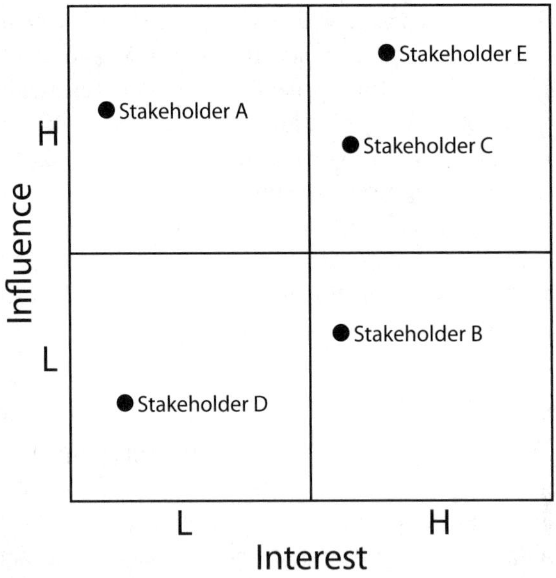


**Figure 11.3** Stakeholder Map

The stakeholder map format is relatively standard and considers stakeholders in terms of influence and interest. While it is likely that the stakeholder map will change over the life of the program, as organizational change management activities are undertaken, it is important to develop the stakeholder map early in order to perform an initial inventory of stakeholders. Assessment of influence and interest may be modified, as more detailed discussions with stakeholders are undertaken; at this stage, it is important to ensure that the stakeholder map is *complete*, including relevant stakeholders, as opposed to *perfect*—assessing their influence and interest.

With the stakeholder map complete, discussions with stakeholders can be undertaken to understand specific change expectations, issues that may be on their minds, and benefits they expect to receive from the change. It is likely that these discussions will reveal diverse, potentially conflicting, stakeholder needs and interests as well as numerous opinions on how best to achieve the desired business benefits. For the purposes of defining change drivers, the key outputs from these discussions are the specific stakeholder expectations for business change and any issues that are brought to light. These two critical outputs form the basis for documenting change drivers as well as for managing stakeholder expectations, bearing in mind that it is difficult to manage expectations that you are not aware of.

In addition to stakeholder analysis, it is important to assess the readiness of the organization for change. While this may seem disconnected from defining change drivers, the point of this exercise is to make a high-level assessment to determine whether the relevant change drivers are achievable within the organization. If specific change drivers or expected benefits from change are elaborated by stakeholders but are not likely to be achievable, from a lack of organizational readiness for change, then these factors must be considered and addressed before detailed change planning takes place. It makes little sense to plan for change that is not likely to succeed, even with appropriate organizational change management activities. If nothing else, performing this exercise now provides the organizational change management team with valuable insights into potential resistance, areas where organizational change management activities should be concentrated, and other useful information for change management planning. In extreme cases, this information may be useful for discussing the likelihood of change success with change sponsors, reevaluating existing business cases, or even canceling planned initiatives.

### Benefits Realization Management Considerations

There is a strong correlation between organizational change management and benefits realization management. The process of defining change drivers supports the initial identification of benefits from change for a reason, and the reasons for change are often closely related to expected benefits. While initial definition of change drivers will likely precede formal benefits identification, the effort undertaken here can support ensuring that anticipated benefits are clarified and understood, that change issues are viewed in the context of potential impacts on benefits realization, and that any disconnects between change activities and benefits realization expectations—on the portfolio level, within relevant business plans, or in other forms—are addressed early in the program life cycle, ensuring that resolutions are achieved in a timely manner for appropriate change planning and benefits definition.

It is sometimes appropriate to link the activities related to identifying change drivers with early efforts to identify benefits. Change drivers are often formally presented in organizational change management documentation; similarly, benefits are formally documented in the benefits register. The stakeholders of interest, in both identification of change drivers and identification of benefits, are often similar. Both activities occur early in the program life cycle. And perhaps most importantly, the business change manager will be an integral participant in both exercises. There may be situations in which uncoupling these activities makes sense; however, for organizations beginning to implement benefits realization management, it is often appropriate to link these efforts together and address stakeholders *once* to gain information that satisfies both needs.

## Define Change

With an understanding of the relevant change drivers, it is then possible to elaborate additional detail, providing specific change definition that enables validation of the required change elements and supports more detailed change planning. These activities require elaborating the specific change drivers further, by defining specific changes to be undertaken, determining appropriate measures of change success, and validating the specific capabilities required to achieve the desired objectives. These activities, summarized together in a single document, provide the necessary detail to support more detailed change planning in the next phase. Each of these critical activities is briefly described below.

### *Defining Changes*

The primary activity at this stage is the translation of change drivers into a small set of high-level changes that are required to meet the defined strategic objectives. Significant detail, in the form of change plans, is not the goal. Rather, the goal is to create the high-level picture of change, so organizational stakeholders can:

- Validate change scope
- Prioritize benefits (which in turn, drives resource allocation)
- Identify issues and risks

- Define a basis for developing success criteria, or key performance indicators (KPIs)

There are a number of tools available to support this activity. For organizations that are beginning to implement organizational change management in support of benefits realization management, it is best to leverage a tool that has already been discussed—the benefits map. The benefits map provides a visual representation of high-level objectives, outcomes, and benefits, which can serve as a basis for understanding both *what* change is required and *why* change is required. Developing a benefits map with relevant stakeholders supports creating a picture of the change that:

- Includes all major change elements—but not to the degree that one becomes lost in the details
- Considers both the required changes and the associated expected benefits
- Demonstrates the relationships between change activities and benefits
- Provides a starting point for developing relevant measures

Some organizations prefer a variation on the benefits map called a benefits breakdown structure. An example of the benefits breakdown structure can be seen in Figure 11.4.

The benefits breakdown structure follows a logical flow, from overall organizational objective to required capabilities, elaborating the specific benefits, outcomes, and results that link the organization's desired change objectives to the specific capabilities required to achieve them. The example is relatively simple to show its basic format. Certainly, an elaborated benefits breakdown structure could consider multiple outcomes required to achieve a single benefit, multiple capabilities required to achieve a specific result, and so forth. While it may be tempting to develop highly detailed benefits maps or benefits breakdown structures, it is worth remembering the purpose of the exercise which is to enable stakeholder understanding and alignment with prioritization and resource allocation. An overly complex picture will be extremely difficult to navigate. As such, the number of elaborated benefits should be limited to the six to twelve most critical, recognizing that other benefits may be within reach.

Review of the benefits map or benefits breakdown structure with stakeholders is critical. This review should focus on ensuring alignment, identifying issues, and prioritizing benefits. In the context of prioritization, organizational change

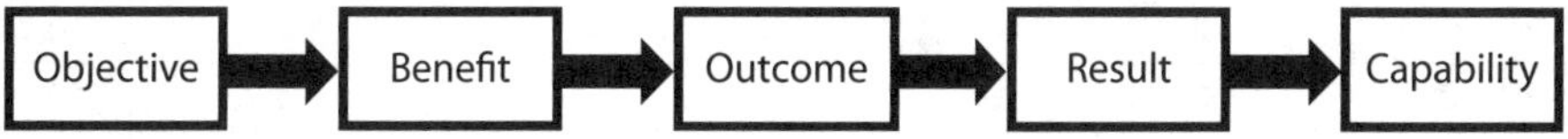


**Figure 11.4** Benefits breakdown structure

management focuses on ensuring that resources are allocated to the necessary change components for realizing the most critical stakeholder benefits. Complex models, comparison methods, and other quantitative techniques could be used to accomplish this objective. However, for organizations beginning to implement benefits realization management, a simpler approach is more appropriate.

The easiest method of initial prioritization (both to administer and for stakeholders to understand) is to use a simple ranking scale from one to *n*, where *n* is the number of elaborated benefits to be ranked. Each relevant stakeholder will rank the benefits, from most important to least important, and the priority order of the benefits can be determined according to accumulated points. Table 11.1 provides an example.

In this simplified example, Benefit D has been identified as the most critical benefit, scoring the least points from two stakeholders (Stakeholder A and Stakeholder B). Variations of this model, such as multi-voting techniques, may be used as well. Over time, as an organization becomes more sophisticated in its benefits realization management efforts, more sophisticated techniques may be used. Simplicity is an excellent starting point, since simple methods engage stakeholders without overwhelming them with process or details and yield reasonably accurate—though perhaps imperfect—data for initial prioritization.

The outputs of this prioritization exercise are valuable for making resource trade-offs during change and program planning as well as for helping relevant steering committees or governance boards understand areas of focus before detailed planning is undertaken. Early stakeholder involvement and active stakeholder engagement is essential to success.

## Defining Measures

In organizations employing benefits realization management as a process, defining the measures for change success relies on the measurement development process of benefits realization management. As such, an extensive discussion of measurement development is not provided here. Refer to Chapter 6 for a fundamental understanding of measurement development.

In the organizational change management context, the important topic is to ensure that stakeholders agree upon the relevant measures. The business change

**Table 11.1** Initial benefits prioritization ranking

| | Stakeholder A | Stakeholder B | Stakeholder C | Stakeholder D | Total |
|---|---|---|---|---|---|
| Benefit A | 2 | 3 | 4 | 1 | 10 |
| Benefit B | 3 | 4 | 2 | 3 | 12 |
| Benefit C | 4 | 2 | 1 | 4 | 11 |
| Benefit D | 1 | 1 | 3 | 2 | 7 |

manager plays an important role in ensuring this alignment, with support from the senior responsible owner as needed. It is critical that change stakeholders buy in to the measures for gauging success, so there are no unnecessary debates later in the change program life cycle about whether implemented change was successful.

### *Capability Validation*

Initial definition of required capabilities is accomplished by completing a benefits map or benefits breakdown structure. With further work done to prioritize benefits and define appropriate measures, the basis for confirming that the correct capabilities have been elaborated is established. As a final step in defining the change, it is appropriate to review the elaborated capabilities, from the benefits map or benefits breakdown structure, in the context of benefit prioritization decisions that have been made, in order to ensure that the appropriate capabilities are elaborated to support the prioritized benefit goals. This validation represents the final "sign-off" activity with stakeholders, producing a benefits map or benefits breakdown structure that can be used for further planning. While it is possible that the benefits map or benefits breakdown structure will evolve over time—as business priorities change, emergent benefits come to light, or other factors influence change—this initial version, in its final and agreed-upon form, is important to ensure that planning is undertaken with the right goals in mind.

At this stage, an initial benefits register is often created to elaborate detail from the exercise described in this phase, and an initial benefits roadmap is elaborated according to the defined benefits map or benefits breakdown structure. These artifacts are critically important in benefits realization planning—specifically in the development of the benefits realization plan—and are additionally helpful to the business change manager, as he or she begins detailed business change planning to support the program goals.

## Plan Change

Change planning involves the activities undertaken to define specific actions required to successfully execute change management activities, to build those activities into a plan, and to integrate change management plans into the overall program delivery plan. These plans will consider the entire benefits realization management life cycle, through transition and preparation for sustainment, and therefore must be tightly integrated into overall program plans to ensure a single integrated plan that considers the program work, the required change management work, and the associated benefits realization management work. This integration exercise is undertaken by the program management team as part of overall program planning, with significant input from the business change manager who identifies requirements from the organizational change management and benefits realization management perspectives.

### *The Organizational Change Management Plan*

A key component of change planning is the development of an organizational change management plan. There are numerous formats for such plans, including proprietary methodologies with their own variations. However, in general, the organizational change management plan includes activities focused on:

- Stakeholder expectation management
- Communications management
- Readiness assessment
- Training, coaching, and mentoring
- Managing resistance
- Transition management

It is not possible to describe the many tools, techniques, and methodologies associated with these components in this book. However, each component is described below, together with examples illustrating how these important components of the change management plan impact benefits realization.

**Stakeholder Expectation Management** The stakeholder expectation management section of the organizational change management plan focuses on ways to manage stakeholder expectations throughout the change management life cycle. These include actions required to build and maintain stakeholder support for the program and associated change, as well as activities required to recognize when new stakeholders are of interest or particular stakeholders are no longer of interest. A starting point for elaborating this section of the organizational change management plan is to review the stakeholder map to understand the specific stakeholders of interest and their current attitudes and influence. The stakeholder map shown in Figure 11.3 has been redrawn in Figure 11.5 with additional detail.

The focus in stakeholder expectation management planning is on the actions required to address stakeholder needs according to their interests in and influence upon the program. In general, four general categories of stakeholder actions are described:

- **Support**—stakeholders with low influence and low interest are generally supported, through regular communication and opportunities to ask questions and provide input, but are managed the least closely
- **Maintain**—stakeholders with high influence but low interest should have their specific expectations understood and managed with the goal

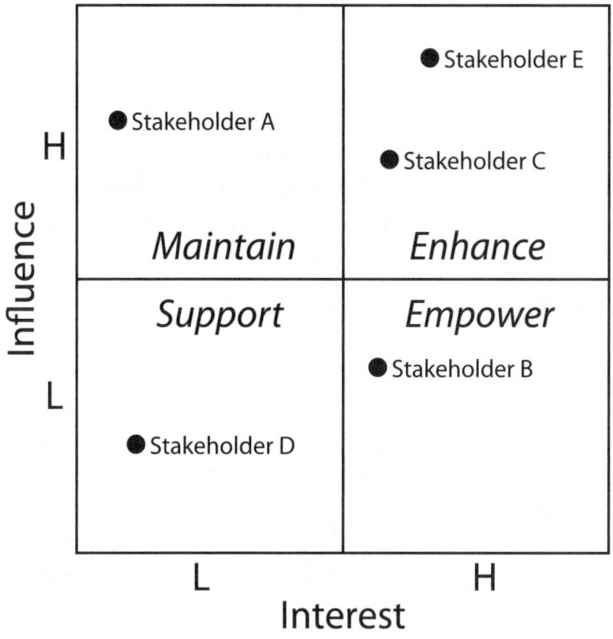


**Figure 11.5** Enhanced stakeholder map

of ensuring their continued satisfaction with the program and specific changes and benefits that interest them

- **Empower**—stakeholders with low influence but high interest should be empowered, to the extent possible, to support the change as grassroots change agents who work within their specific spheres of influence to build interest in the change, manage resistance, and impact their specific workgroups or organizations. While these individuals or groups may not have much direct influence over the program, numerous examples in the literature and elsewhere demonstrate the power of grassroots efforts to positively effect change.
- **Enhance**—stakeholders with high influence and high interest should be managed the most closely with a strong focus on enhancing their commitment to the change and leveraging their influence within the organization to advance the program. These individuals are often the "champions," from whom the program management team regularly seeks feedback and asks for assistance in advancing the program's goals within their respective spheres of influence.

The stakeholder expectation management section of the overall organizational change management plan should focus on the activities required to support, maintain, empower, and enhance, as well as the activities required to monitor for changes in stakeholder influence and interest—specifically, to understand when new stakeholders are of interest or existing stakeholders are no longer of interest.

Finally, the specific stakeholder expectation management efforts to be undertaken should be formalized, along with stakeholder information, in a stakeholder log or similar document that identifies stakeholders, their needs, and the ways to manage their expectations. Numerous formats exist, but the stakeholder log should generally contain information related to:

- **Identity**—name, contact information, and related details
- **Interest**—specific benefits of interest, specific capabilities expected, and specific organizational challenges to be addressed through change delivery and benefits realization
- **Influence**—primary groups the stakeholder can directly influence and secondary groups the stakeholder can indirectly influence
- **Relationship**—key relationship between the stakeholder and the program, identification of a specific contact person within the program team to manage stakeholder expectations, and results of formal surveys or other measures of satisfaction with the program
- **Communications**—specific communications vehicles used to communicate with the stakeholder (often a subset of common communications vehicles defined in the communications management plan), relevant informal communications vehicles, and frequency and format of communications, if nonstandard. Communication often includes formal reports or other formal status communications, including review meetings and the like.
- **Training**—specific training or other educational opportunities the stakeholder needs
- **Issues, risks, and challenges**—specific stakeholder issues, risks to stakeholder support for the program, and specific challenges to managing stakeholder expectations, along with relevant plans to address these issues, risks, and challenges

The stakeholder log is maintained by the business change manager or a representative of his or her team, reviewed regularly as a change management team activity, and updated to capture changing stakeholder dynamics within the program.

**Communications Management** The communications management section of the organizational change management plan focuses on specific communications vehicles to be implemented, as well as the associated detail required to elaborate the communication purpose, audience, and other information. In general, communications management requires a focus on reporting, meetings, informational written communications, personal (one-on-one) communications (often part of stakeholder expectation management), and other necessary communication types.

A communications management plan is typically developed to formalize the communications vehicles and associated information. The communication management plan often includes details including:

- The specific communication vehicle (e.g., a status report, a newsletter, a town hall meeting)
- Intended audience (e.g., a specific stakeholder, a specific business unit, all stakeholders)
- Communication purposes (e.g., Why is this communication important? How does it support change management goals?)
- Format (e.g., a newsletter, a meeting, an e-mail)
- Frequency (e.g., weekly, monthly, ad hoc)
- Owner—the specific person responsible for ensuring the communication is managed according to the plan
- Comments—relevant comments regarding the communication

An important check when developing the communications management plan is to validate that a clear relationship between the communications vehicles and the identified stakeholders exists, and that the communications management plan appropriately addresses program needs to manage stakeholder expectations effectively. In some cases, portions of the communications management plan may include specific activities directed at individual stakeholders, while others may address broad communications needed for multiple stakeholders. Striking a balance is important. While there is often a temptation to over-communicate (or—perhaps worse—to use trite phrases such as, "you can never communicate enough"), the reality is that the communications management plan must focus on the *quality* and *effectiveness* of communications and not on the *quantity* and *frequency* of communication. To be sure, the organizational change management team will be very busy. And while communication is essential for effective management of change, spending time on ineffective or excessive communication needlessly robs the organization of the capacity to do other important work.

**Readiness Assessment** An important component of the organizational change management plan is the process by which change readiness is assessed. In order to support successfully embedding change in the organization and realizing the associated benefits, it is necessary to check that the receiving business organization is prepared for change. Readiness assessment provides a formal process to identify whether appropriate change management activities—including communication, training, mentoring, or other activities—have been performed and the receiving business organization is prepared for change. Typically, two key artifacts are created to support change readiness—the readiness checklist and a readiness-tracking log.

The purposes of a readiness checklist are to document the required readiness activities associated with a particular change and to formalize their achievement via the checklist. The readiness checklist supports two essential functions. First, by formalizing readiness activities, both the change management team and the receiving organization are clear about what is expected for change readiness. By formalizing this early in the program, expectations are set, and the receiving business organization can begin to plan, so that sufficient capacity is available to support readiness activities, so that expectations can be communicated to stakeholders within the receiving business organization, and so that formalized processes to check readiness and report on change readiness can be incorporated into program plans. Second, the readiness checklist provides an easy way for the business change manager and members of the team to assess readiness gaps, to identify potential issues and risks to change readiness, and to address other similar concerns.

It is important to note that while the format of the readiness checklist should be standardized, the readiness activities in the checklist will likely be tailored to the affected organization and change. For example, within a single program, there may be a number of anticipated business changes that must be implemented together in order to realize planned benefits. These changes may affect different stakeholder groups in different ways—some business changes may be unique to particular stakeholder groups, and so forth. Understanding the particular change impacts on various areas of the organization and stakeholder groups is an important organizational change management activity, and developing the readiness checklist supports validation of this work by enabling the business change manager and members of the organizational change management team to cross-check readiness activities against planned change and to identify any gaps. An example readiness checklist appears in Table 11.2.

The readiness checklist in Table 11.2 is fairly straightforward. The specific readiness activity is detailed, along with a clear owner for the activity, a due date,

**Table 11.2** Sample readiness checklist

| Number | Activity | Owner | Due Date | Complete |
|---|---|---|---|---|
| 1 | Names of all users requiring data migration submitted | B. Smith | December 15, 2013 | ☑ |
| 2 | Job role redesign actions complete | T. Jones | January 15, 2014 | ☑ |
| 3 | Data migration template validated by business owner | B. Smith | January 15, 2014 | ☑ |

and a place to indicate completion. As a note, the completion indicator may be replaced with a percentage complete indicator for more detailed tracking. In most cases, however, this percentage complete is a best guess rather than a quantitatively derived value, so its usefulness may be questionable. Additionally, it is important to note that the readiness activity owner must be a single individual. It is tempting to indicate a group (e.g., "the data management team"), but—in order to ensure accountability for getting the work done and to enable the business change management team to have a single point of contact for each activity—it is required that a single individual be assigned.

In order to support consolidated reporting of readiness activities, the readiness checklists are often consolidated into a readiness-tracking log, used for tracking readiness across the landscape of required business changes. This log most frequently rolls up the individual readiness assessment checklists, indicating where readiness is not on target and providing summary data across the various stakeholder groups impacted by change. The format of the log, however, will vary—depending upon the commonality of change across stakeholder groups. If the degree of commonality is relatively high, a format similar to Table 11.3 is appropriate.

The example in Table 11.3 provides an easy format for reviewing data and identifying gaps between actual readiness and planned readiness. The business change manager approves the release of updates to this tracking spreadsheet, which should be performed regularly, in order to ensure that a fair representation of readiness versus plan is provided. The readiness tracking spreadsheet, or a further summarized version of it, should be included in regular updates from the business change manager to key stakeholders, the program steering committee, and other bodies. For simplicity, these updates may be summarized, as in Table 11.4.

The example in Table 11.4 provides an opportunity to present quantitative data regarding completion of planned readiness activities by comparing target dates and actual completion status to derive the numbers in the first two columns. In-progress activities, both on track and behind schedule, are indicated in the next two columns, followed by activities not started in the following column. This information assists those reviewing the data to understand the relative amount of work in progress, in progress but not yet being realized according to plan, and work left to do. While it may be difficult to understand the true magnitude of work, based simply on activities without corresponding data on the amount of work required to complete any particular activity, the goal of this report is simplicity; therefore, more detailed analysis of the hours of work needed to complete in-progress activities, bring behind schedule activities back on track, and so forth, is purposely not included but may be underpinned by other reporting. Finally, the last column provides a qualitative assessment of overall change readiness. This is a subjective opinion of the change management team and should be validated

**Table 11.3** Sample readiness-tracking log

| | **Organization A** | **Organization B** | **Organization C** | **Organization D** | **Organization E** | **Organization F** |
|---|---|---|---|---|---|---|
| Minimum of 75% of Users Trained | | | | | | |
| Training Complete | G | G | G | A | NS | NS |
| Data Validation 100% Signed Off | | | | | | |
| Data Migration Template Validation | A | G | G | R | G | NS |
| Overall Assessment | | | | | | |
| Overall Readiness | **G** | **G** | **G** | **A** | **G** | **NS** |

G = On Track A = Behind R = Critical Issues NS = Not Planned to Start

**Table 11.4** Change readiness summary report

| **Organization** | **Change Activities Planned to be Completed** | **Change Activities Actually Complete** | **Change Activities on Schedule** | **Change Activities Behind Schedule** | **Change Activities Not Planned to Start** | **Overall Assessment** |
|---|---|---|---|---|---|---|
| Organization A | 5 | 5 | 3 | 0 | 4 | GREEN |
| Organization B | 4 | 2 | 4 | 2 | 3 | AMBER |
| Organization C | 6 | 6 | 3 | 0 | 4 | GREEN |

by the business change manager prior to its release. It is important to note that it may be possible to create a mathematical formula for deriving the green, amber, and red indicator—based on the number of activities behind, number of planned activities still to be completed, and so forth—but, again for simplicity, a subjective assessment of readiness from the organizational change management team is often more accurate and faster to produce than a mathematical model.

The readiness assessment tools described in this section are important communications tools for use with organizational stakeholders, important management tools for the business change management and program management teams, and important data points for assessing overall change readiness. As such, a focused effort to track and manage readiness must be part of the overall organizational change management plan. The business change manager, benefit owners, and stakeholders within the business organization—all of whom are responsible for readiness activities—must work together to ensure business readiness.

**Training, Coaching, and Mentoring** Another important component of change planning is planning for training, coaching, and mentoring activities that support change readiness, transition, and benefits realization. A clear necessity for change success is successfully training affected stakeholders on new products, new services, new ways of working, changes to existing ways of working, and other changes that impact them. For large change programs, this can represent quite a lot of work. In fact, in many large change programs (and even many smaller ones), training is identified as one of the critical few areas that must be implemented consistently and successfully in order to ensure change success. As such, many organizations place a high priority on training within the overall organizational change management plan. To support this, a training plan is often developed that addresses the activities required to:

- Assess stakeholders' training needs and develop training plans
- Prepare the business organization for change through training activities
- Assist stakeholders to understand the impacts of change in their frames of reference
- Provide direct training on new products, services, or other components to be implemented in the program
- Monitor training effectiveness and identify remaining skill gaps after training has been completed
- Integrate coaching and mentoring activities into overall change management plans

Organizations should rely on the skills and expertise of their training departments or human resources functions to assist with development and implementation of training plans. Utilizing experts who focus on training for the broader organization has many benefits, including leveraging expertise, software, or other technology implemented in the organization to support training delivery and tracking; and reusing existing organizational training assets to support training needs. Ideally, a representative of the organization's training or human resources department is assigned to the business change management team and provides overall coordination of these efforts. If this is not possible, identifying a single point of contact within one of these departments to provide access to existing tools, templates, methodologies, software, and other related items is desirable.

While the training plan may be well formalized and supported by specific resources with expertise in training and development, less formal means of providing support for change are coaching and mentoring. Coaches are often trained as subject matter experts, or "super users," who provide knowledgeable support to stakeholders during execution, transition, and sustainment of change. Mentors may be less formally appointed and trained than coaches but play an important role in providing peer support for change within the business community. Coaching and mentoring activities provide opportunities for peer learning, peer knowledge sharing, and related activities that provide "grassroots" support for change. Change planning activities to support coaching and mentoring often involve:

- Identifying potential coaches and mentors within the business organization
- Determining which change initiative(s) would benefit most from coaching and mentoring
- Developing (or enhancing) a coaching and mentoring framework, including standard ways of working, tools to assist mentors and coaches, and training and development opportunities for coaches and mentors
- Integrating coaching and mentoring activities into overall change management plans

In some organizations, coaching and mentoring is a standard business practice that is supported by organizational development, training, or human resource functions. In these organizations, frameworks for assignment of coaches and mentors, processes for effectively implementing coaching and mentoring, training for coaches and mentors, and similar services may exist. If so, they should be leveraged to the extent possible. If such capabilities do not exist, the business change manager will need to weigh the costs and benefits of implementing formal coaching and mentoring into the overall change management program. While informal coaching and mentoring often occurs in organizations, some investment in development and deployment of a framework and basic support model for coaches and mentors should be developed, if coaching and mentoring are to be included in the overall change management plan. While informality is not necessarily bad, it is difficult to assure the effectiveness of coaching and mentoring activities when there is no basic framework describing the relationship between coaches, mentors, and the overall program and providing mechanisms for coach and mentor feedback as well as for the business change management team to inform and train coaches and mentors.

**Managing Resistance** Some resistance to change is inevitable in all change programs. As such, it is incumbent upon change management teams to develop plans to surface, understand, and respond to resistance from stakeholders throughout the entire program life cycle. There are many reasons for resistance, including, but not limited to:

- Fear of the unknown
- Lack of understanding of the change
- Insufficient or ineffective training
- Comfort with current ways of working
- Discomfort with organizational change, restructuring, or job role redesign
- Lack of time to understand and prepare for change
- Insufficient or ineffective communication
- Lack of sponsor involvement to reinforce the importance of the change

From the standpoint of planning change, activities the business change manager should consider include:

- Assessing likelihood of resistance, given the organization's culture, politics, appetite for change, and the unique dynamics of the change
- Assessing stakeholder attitudes and potential areas of resistance through stakeholder analysis—both that are already performed and that are required as the program continues
- Identifying key areas of potential resistance (especially in the context of disbenefits) and developing proactive plans to address it
- Defining processes by which identified resistance can be understood, assessed, and managed

These activities assist the change management team in proactively understanding potential areas of resistance and in developing plans to address it during planning. The integration of these activities into the overall change management plan and correspondingly into the overall program plan is important. However, while it is possible to plan to address known areas of resistance, there will certainly be some resistance that does not become apparent until well after change planning is complete. Proactively managing this emergent resistance is especially important, as such resistance can quickly become a source of concern for the business change management team if it is not effectively managed. It is not unusual for issues (real or otherwise) to be exaggerated by concerned stakeholders in an effort to derail change. These situations are serious, as they create unnecessary distractions and require focus from the business change management team that could be spent on other important change management activities. Separating real issues from perceived issues and managing stakeholder expectations are critical components of effective management of emergent resistance. Techniques for managing resistance include:

- Clarifying issues and responding to concerns with additional or enhanced communication
- Actively engaging managers, coaches, and mentors to clarify issues and respond to concerns
- Involving corporate functions, such as human resource and organizational development functions, to reassure employees concerned about job security, job roles, or other factors
- Working with the senior responsible owner and other senior leaders to provide visible support for the program and address stakeholder concerns
- Enhancing or adjusting training plans to reinforce key change messages as well as to ensure comfort with new or enhanced products, services, or results delivered by the program
- Establishing communities of practice or other mechanisms to allow stakeholders to navigate change together, limiting the "islands of isolation" effect that may accompany change

Realistically, a certain amount of resistance management will be reactive, rather than proactive. Two keys for success for the business change manager and the change management team are to regularly assess the business environment to identify and to understand resistance and to take a proactive approach to managing resistance once they become aware of it. The first activity, identifying resistance and its sources, is not necessarily easy, as resistance is often passive and not immediately apparent. However, in many cases, this passive resistance comes from factors—such as fear of consequences if resistance is voiced, worry that "I'm the only one" who is concerned, or other factors—that cause individuals to hesitate to openly voice resistance or concerns. Many organizations have recognized the need to provide opportunities for anonymous feedback to the change management team, enabling parties to provide feedback in a way that is more comfortable.

Anonymous feedback can be gathered in a number of ways. In some organizations, surveys are used to enable employees to provide feedback regarding change readiness and other matters in an anonymous way. In other organizations, online suggestion boxes or other mechanisms are used to enable stakeholders to submit observations, issues, and concerns. Anonymous online chat forums or similar mechanisms have been used successfully in still other organizations. Regardless of the specific method employed, a key to success is letting the individuals who submit feedback know that they've been heard and that their feedback did not go into a black hole, never to escape. With the identity of the individual unknown, the change management team must rely on broad communications mechanisms to respond to feedback. These mechanisms may include:

- Giving answers to "frequently asked questions" in newsletters or other broad communications
- Establishing online forums or message boards for two-way change communication
- Facilitating small group or larger town hall meetings to provide proactive communication, clarify issues, and respond to feedback
- Providing information to coaches and mentors that is informally cascaded to stakeholders

Many other mechanisms may be established as well, and the change management team must consider the appropriateness of each. Additionally, a balance must be struck between managing resistance and advancing the goals of the program. In this context, some resistance may not be able to be managed. Put more plainly, some people will never be happy. While we seek to minimize resistance, in much the same way as we seek to minimize disbenefits, some resistance will remain. The business change manager and his or her team must prioritize their limited resources to proactively manage the most critical change management issues, employing the "80/20 rule" where appropriate to ensure that focus is placed where it can be most effective.

**Transition Management** Transition management has already been discussed in the benefits realization management context (Chapter 8). There, the clear need to integrate transition management into benefits realization management within the broader context of program transition was elaborated. Similarly here, change management activities to support change transition must be integrated into the overall program plans. The primary challenge to this integration is the contrast between formality and reality. As project and program managers, we appreciate the value that plans bring, in the sense that they provide a basis and stability for getting work done. We seldom begin a program without a reasonably solid plan, for at least the first critical tranches of work. We do, however, recognize that even the best plans may change as the dynamics of the business environment exert themselves on the program. When this happens, we must make appropriate adjustments. In the context of organizational change management, the dynamics of the business environment, stakeholder expectations, program plans, and other factors virtually ensure that adjustments will need to be made to change management activities to support transition management, which is elaborated during change planning.

We do, however, understand in general how to respond to this situation. We respond by not doing too much. This does not imply that we don't care too much, but rather that we recognize that robust organizational change management planning to support transition planning during the planning stages is often premature. We prefer to operate in a more flexible way and lay out a high-level framework for organizational change management to support transition management, and then rely on the organizational change management team to derive the necessary additional detail to put the plan into action as the transition draws closer. This approach enables several important benefits, including:

- Being responsive to a changing business and stakeholder landscape by more closely aligning detailed planning with the realities of the program and change environment at the time of transition
- Developing specific plans to respond to emergent resistance and changing stakeholder attitudes and influences
- Enabling change agents, benefit owners, and other important program stakeholders to "own the change" and providing the best change management approach for their particular circumstances through less prescriptive formal transition change planning
- Reducing time spent on change planning for transition activities, knowing that plans and approaches will likely need to be adjusted

Some suggest that an "agile" approach is best utilized to accomplish these goals. For organizations that have made an investment in agile methodology and have agile practitioners available as resources to the organizational change management team, this approach may be perfectly acceptable. However, I caution against using organizational change management initiatives (and more broadly, programs) as the place to make first attempts at agile approaches. It is better to learn lessons on smaller, less critical, initiatives and then to scale efforts up, as the organization learns how to best leverage agile—as opposed to taking a "one size fits all" approach that treats agile as a method for handling all things for all people. In the case of transition management, flexibility is the key. If agility, via formal agile approaches, is an option, it may or may not be appropriate in these circumstances. The business change manager, program manager, and senior responsible owner, in consultation with key business stakeholders, should assess the applicability of agile approaches and make an informed decision about applying agile, if at all.

Agile techniques aside, the focus in transition planning should be on the high-level framework that defines how change will be supported during transition. This framework includes elements already developed (e.g., training and managing resistance plans) as well as a specific focus on ensuring successful transition and benefits realization. These plans must tightly integrate overall program planning, components of the benefits realization plan, and the necessary change management aspects for successful transition and preparation for ongoing change sustainment.

A final important point relates to planning for measures to validate the success of change after transition. These measures will closely align with the relevant measures developed in benefits realization planning. The focus of the organizational change management team should be on developing a relevant set of measures that can be used to validate that the desired business outcomes from change are achieved. The business change manager plays a key role in developing the relevant metrics and measurement system for benefits realization and as such, is well positioned to assess whether these measures are sufficient or additional measures are needed to specifically address successful change integration. Because change integration and benefits realization are related topics, some of the work required here is probably already in the benefits realization measurement plan. The organizational change management plan should address how these measures and any added measures will be managed (relying on the benefits realization plan to ensure that duplicate work is not undertaken) during transition, including information regarding:

- Parties responsible for collecting and analyzing data, including specific roles, responsibilities, and named parties
- Methods by which data will be collected
- Methods by which data will be analyzed
- Processes for addressing gaps between actual results and plans

The business change manager and benefit owners are excellent resources to start with when addressing these topics, involving additional business stakeholders as appropriate to ensure completeness. Additional information regarding this process will be discussed in the perform transition section of this chapter.

### *Summary*

A significant amount of work is required for appropriate change planning, and this section provided an overview of the key elements of successful change planning, as well as some representative tools and techniques for successful change planning. The end result of the planning process should be a comprehensive organizational change management plan that guides the change management team as they work to realize change. This plan is owned by the business change manager and reviewed and updated as necessary to reflect the current needs of the program. While significant rewrites will likely not be required, it is anticipated that elements of the change management plan will need adjustment in order to ensure that the plan supports successful realization of change and benefits.

## Execute Change and Monitor Results

During program execution, change management activities are undertaken in order to realize change and benefits realization within the organization. This section focuses on several key aspects of organizational change management in change execution, including activities required to:

- Prepare the organization for change and execute change management activities required to successfully realize change
- Mobilize stakeholders to realize change, including change recipients, change agents, senior organizational leaders, and others
- Monitor the results of change management activities in the context of transition and benefits realization
- Proactively respond to issues, risks, resistance, and other situations that affect successful delivery of change

### *Execute Change Management Activities*

It is important to execute the agreed-upon change management plans. During capability delivery and integration of capabilities into the business, it is necessary to ensure that the change management activities, defined and agreed upon in the organizational change management plan, are put into practice. Specifically, readiness should be assessed by reviewing change readiness checklists, resistance should be monitored to identify and manage risks and issues, and transition change management support for benefits realization should be considered. At this stage, it is critical to closely monitor the environment, as—even with appropriate readiness activities undertaken—issues may still arise. Some issues may relate to the inevitable "learning curve" as change is introduced into practice. Mistakes may be made, confusion may exist, and other issues may temporarily manifest themselves. The change management team must be prepared to handle these situations and should have the appropriate communications processes in place to enable the team to become aware of issues, as well as the appropriate processes to respond to them, both individually as well as on a broader basis, according to the number of stakeholders affected.

To the extent possible, the organizational change management team should plan to leverage the network of change owners, benefit owners, coaches, mentors, key users, and other parties who regularly interface with the change management team to assist with managing issues, resistance, and situations that may limit change success. It is simply not possible for the business change manager and the change management team to be everywhere at once; therefore, a network of change agents represents the best opportunity to manage issues on the individual level as well as to escalate issues, which cannot be resolved through the change agent network, to the change management team.

### Mobilize Stakeholders

An important component of executing change is ensuring that all stakeholders, from sponsors to change agents to change recipients, are mobilized to support the change. The keys to success are having a plan to communicate with these parties and providing regular communication and opportunities for feedback during change execution. The planning elements will ideally be present from work already undertaken, specifically in the forms of the stakeholder management plan (which includes stakeholder communication needs) and the program communications management plan (which should identify specific program communications processes to be undertaken during program execution). These plans must be executed with the support of the program management team and members of the change management team's distributed network.

### Monitor Results

Monitoring results of change management activities is not something that occurs only during change execution. An important part of readiness activities (and additional change management activities) is monitoring to ensure that the required readiness activities are complete. In this context, the primary concern is monitoring the implementation of the change, with a focus on:

- Ensuring that delivered capabilities meet stakeholder needs
- Ensuring that resistance to change is managed and that issues impacting change acceptance are resolved
- Ensuring that implemented change appropriately supports planned benefits realization
- Ensuring that stakeholders remain committed to the change and that changes in stakeholder expectations are understood and addressed

The business change manager should work together with the change management team, benefit owners, change agents, and other parties to perform the required monitoring activities. Results of monitoring should be formalized, via updates to relevant artifacts (e.g., readiness checklists, benefits realization reports, stakeholder management plans), and reviewed both in regular change management team meetings as well as in formal program reviews with the steering committee and other governance bodies.

An important component of monitoring is the process of ensuring that delivered business change supports planned benefits realization. While it is not always possible to validate achievement of benefits immediately, it is important to validate that benefits planned to be delivered in the near-term are positioned for realization as well as to ensure that benefits planned for realization on a longer-term horizon are considered as well. The links between change and benefits realization must be understood, so there is a clear validation that the readiness supports both successful implementation of the change and successful integration for benefits realization, as readiness activities complete and implementation of change commences.

### Manage Stakeholder Expectations

Managing stakeholder expectations occurs across the program's full life cycle. However, it is worth noting that some issues and resistance will not come to bear until change is being implemented. For this reason, it is especially important that the change management team proactively manage stakeholder expectations during this critical phase. Specific activities to be undertaken to support managing stakeholder expectations during change execution include:

- An enhanced focus on communication to keep stakeholders informed of change progress
- An enhanced focus on seeking stakeholder feedback and analyzing perceptions of change success
- An enhanced focus on issue and risk management, especially with timely prioritization and resolution of stakeholder issues and proactive management of risks
- Monitoring for changes in stakeholder influence and understanding the impacts of those changes on change success and benefits realization

These activities are under the direct control of the business change manager and the change management team but rely on input from other key organizational change management roles in order to effectively manage stakeholder expectations across diverse stakeholder groups. Utilizing the change agent network is especially important, and frequent communication to and receipt of feedback from change agents is critical. The business change manager and the change management team should ensure this engagement through regular meetings, formal communications, and informal feedback opportunities.

## Perform Transition

Transition is an essential part of change execution. While execution is primarily focused on doing the work, transition is primarily focused on the integration of change into business operations. The two processes are closely related and often performed together, as part of capability integration and benefits realization. From an organizational change management perspective, activities to be performed during transition include:

- Monitoring the integration of delivered capabilities into business operations with a focus on ensuring appropriate management of change, minimizing resistance, and addressing issues and risks

- Measuring business results to confirm change success and benefits realization
- Adjusting plans to address business realities through flexible approaches to transition
- Managing stakeholder expectations and responding to stakeholder concerns to ensure successful integration into business operations

The focus of the change management team's efforts in this phase is on ensuring the success of transition, so that benefits realization is achieved. This will require a certain degree of flexibility, as transition activities may not proceed exactly according to plans. This is a natural consequence of integrating program change into a dynamic business environment, and the program management team expects some adjustment during transition. Organizational change management supports this process by ensuring these adjustments proceed in an orderly way, with a focus on communication, managing resistance, and managing stakeholder expectations. In the following sections, several of the major transition activities will be discussed in further detail.

### *Monitor Integration*

Monitoring the integration of capabilities into business operations is closely aligned with the monitor results activities described in change execution. The focus here is on ensuring that as capabilities are delivered and integrated, the receiving business organization successfully receives them and integrates them in a way that achieves planned benefits. Some delivered capabilities may not meet current business needs or may be integrated in a way that reduces planned benefits realization. The organizational change management team can support the program management team in identifying such situations.

### *Measure Results*

This activity focuses on using measurements to validate the success of change in relation to business objectives. Measures of interest include measures of adoption, benefits realization, knowledge acquisition, and other indicators of the success of the change. While additional measurements will likely be undertaken by the program management team—to measure products, services, or results (e.g., conformance to specification measurement for a particular delivered product or service level agreement measurement for a delivered service)—these measurements are distinct from those that support understanding whether the relevant business outcomes have been achieved. It is entirely possible that a particular service could meet a service level agreement but fail to meet a business need, so it is critical to understand both types of measures. The latter type is typically more relevant to business stakeholders and should be the primary focus of measurement at this time.

It is not always possible to immediately validate the success of change in relation to relevant business objectives. In some cases, the delivered capabilities and corresponding integration may only achieve intermediate objectives, thus only supporting realization of intermediate benefits—as opposed to end benefits. This situation is natural, but business leaders often demand immediate data to confirm success and validate the appropriateness of their investments. Therefore, the organizational change management team must consider measures that meet the needs to deliver data supporting success within the current time frame, as well as additional measures, which may be long-term indicators. Critical factors in successful measurement of results during transition include:

- Ensuring the measures represent change to all stakeholders. Focusing only on certain critical stakeholder groups is not advisable, as change success must be viewed broadly, not narrowly.
- Ensuring the measures are appropriate for measuring business outcomes, not product or service outcomes
- Ensuring the measures can be easily and reliably supported through data gathering. During the busy transition period, there is often not time to undertake complex measurement and data analysis. Especially for organizations newly implementing organizational change management to support benefits realization management, a simple set of measures that address change success and benefits realization is most appropriate.
- Ensuring the measures have appropriate time horizons. Some medium- and long-term measures may be appropriate, but measures that provide immediate feedback on change success are necessary.

A danger in this context is defining the wrong measures for the business impact of results. For example, measuring how many people use a new process tells you about the scope of implementation but says nothing about whether the new process supports change goals. Similarly, measuring the number of people who attend training provides interesting information about the percentage of in-scope employees who met their training obligation but says little about how effectively the training supports achieving business benefits. Or, as a third example, measuring the efficiency of a new process may be nice, but process efficiency may not be strongly tied to any particular benefits objective. In all of these cases, the goal of measurement may be noble, but the practical applicability of what is being measured is limited in its ability to confirm the achievement of change objectives. An important question to ask, when confirming the set of measures to be used while monitoring integration is, "Does this measure support describing a desired benefit?" If a desired benefit is to reduce costs through automation, for example, measures that indicate whether the automation was successfully integrated into the business environment will not be nearly as valuable as measures that address whether the automation has reduced cost. Measuring the per transaction cost after implementation of the automation, against a baseline cost prior to capability integration, supports relevant reporting—measuring against the business objective, rather than against the success of capability integration.

A further danger in this context is the tendency to limit measurement to situations where clear baseline data already exists. While we prefer baseline data for measurement comparison, some measurements may not have a baseline to support ongoing validation of benefits attainment during sustainment. As such, measurement decisions must be made with an eye to the future. The measurement of change aspects that support intermediate benefits may be necessary to support validation of end benefits. The measurement requirements must be constructed in relation to both data available and reportable during transition as well as data necessary for further analysis later in sustainment.

### *Flexible Management*

This topic is worth mentioning again within the context of transition. Transition is not a one-time effort in most programs. As program work is undertaken, capabilities are delivered incrementally; often, these capabilities—individually or in combination—must be embedded into the business organization over the life of the program rather than all at once near the end of the program. This means that the organizational change management team must manage transition at multiple points in program execution. Given that programs are dynamic in nature and that some change is expected, it is reasonable to expect that during transition it may be necessary to adjust plans to respond to changing conditions within the program, the receiving business organization, or the business environment. The use of flexible management practices is important here, and the organizational change management team must be prepared to adapt plans to current conditions, ensuring communication and management of issues and resistance, as stakeholders respond to these changes.

### *Manage Stakeholder Expectations*

It is worth reiterating the importance of holistically considering stakeholders during transition. There are stakeholders who will be directly impacted by transition because of their direct roles in receiving the delivered capabilities and associated changes. Additional stakeholders may be indirectly impacted by change, but their expectations must also be managed during transition. While development of a stakeholder map and management plan identifies them, they are, occasionally, "forgotten" during transition—as the transition team focuses on the immediate needs of those most directly impacted by the change. The organizational change management team must assume responsibility for ensuring that the stakeholder community is broadly addressed during transition and that opportunities to ask questions and provide feedback are afforded to all relevant stakeholders. While the ways to address stakeholder feedback must be prioritized, the team must not ignore those stakeholders who are peripherally impacted by change. Techniques that assist with ensuring broad focus on stakeholders during transition include:

- Including them in general change communications during transition. While it is not desirable to overwhelm stakeholders with communication, including additional stakeholders in regular communications—such as e-mail project updates or newsletters—is an inexpensive way to help them feel informed
- Providing occasional communications to these stakeholder groups that are written in their frames of reference
- Leveraging change agents with end-to-end knowledge of change impacts to directly communicate with peripherally impacted stakeholders, providing them with opportunities to ask questions and offer feedback

Other techniques may be used as well, and the business change manager must assess the effort investment, balancing the interests of primary business stakeholders against those of additional stakeholders. The goals of this assessment are to maximize the effectiveness of change management activities and to minimize issues and resistance.

## Support Sustainment

Planning to support change sustainment begins early in the program life cycle. During transition, the team focuses on ensuring that stakeholder needs continue to be addressed on an ongoing basis and that realization of benefits is sustained over time. Activities required to sustain benefits are documented in the benefits realization plan, and the organizational change management team relies on this information to determine the activities required during transition to position benefits for long-term sustainment. Ensuring ongoing stakeholder engagement requires helping stakeholders understand their roles in ongoing sustainment as well as putting practices into place in the receiving business organization that support ongoing stakeholder engagement, as the organizational change management team is ultimately a temporary entity that will be disbanded during program closure. Ongoing stakeholder engagement may be facilitated through:

- Leveraging change agents in the receiving business organization to support ongoing stakeholder engagement
- Empowering a network of key users or other expert personnel

- Ensuring management's understanding of sustainment requirements and encouraging management's support of sustainment and stakeholder engagement activities
- Formalizing sustainment activities related to stakeholder engagement (e.g., production of communications or implementation of regular learning opportunities)

Other techniques may be appropriate as well. Ultimately, the senior responsible owner within the receiving business organization is accountable for ensuring sustainment activities are undertaken, stakeholders are engaged, and stakeholder concerns, issues, and risks are managed. He or she will rely on operational business functions to perform this work once the program is concluded, and the role of the organizational change management team during this phase is to position the business organization for long-term change success.

## Organizational Change Management Life Cycle Summary

The organizational change management life cycle presented here provides a practical approach to implementing business change. While presented primarily in the program management and benefits realization management contexts, the general principles and practices described are applicable in nonprogram environments as well and can be leveraged to support a variety of types of business change. An important consideration for the organization is to focus on establishing a *reusable* framework for organizational change management that can be leveraged by the organization for management of change. The investment in developing and maintaining this framework is well made if the organization focuses on developing a practical and flexible framework that is appropriately tailored for its own needs. Too often such frameworks are taken from websites, consultants, and other third parties and force fit into organizations, with little consideration of whether the practices of the framework are appropriate to the organization's culture, politics, and typical types of changes. This is a tremendous mistake. While excessive customization, attempting to address every situation that could arise is not desirable, appropriate tailoring to the organization is required. Over time this tailoring will likely be refined as the organization learns from organizational change management successes and challenges.

Ownership is important to the development, deployment, and maintenance of any organizational change management methodology. In some organizations, process ownership rests with the human resource or training and development department. In other organizations, the enterprise program management office maintains responsibility for the methodology as part of the overall project and program delivery framework. A few organizations have successfully implemented business change offices that specifically focus on change management efforts. Each organization must determine the right place for these methodologies, but having a single point of ownership within the organization—responsible for methodology development and refinement, training, communication, and other activities that ensure awareness, appropriate use, and appropriate maturity of the methodology—is a clear imperative.

## SUMMARY

This chapter presented an overview of organizational change management to aid in developing a fundamental understanding of the role of organizational change management in the program and benefits realization management domains. While not an exhaustive discussion of the many dynamics of organizational change management that are of interest for successful integration of change and benefits realization, the fundamental principles and methodology for successfully accomplishing organizational change management work presented here provide the basis for investigating the next level of detail. There is a vast array of information about organizational change management available through books, Internet resources, consultants, standards organizations, and others. While a time investment will be required, organizations seeking to develop this critical capability in the program management environment to support benefits realization should investigate several practical implementations and determine which specific methodology components, tools, and related items are most appropriate for them. As much of the guidance in this book suggests, a practical approach is: start small, learn as you go, refine as necessary, and build capability and maturity over time. In reality, implementing organizational change management techniques requires a focus on benefits realization, ensuring that the developed methodology and components are aligned with the business needs of the organization, and supporting effective use of the tools to create business value.

# 12

# BENEFITS REALIZATION MANAGEMENT IN THE PORTFOLIO MANAGEMENT CONTEXT

## INTRODUCTION

This chapter presents the role of benefits realization management in the portfolio management context. As a business function, portfolio management exists to manage portfolios of work (comprised of project, programs, sub-portfolios, and operational work) in order to achieve the organization's strategies in a cost effective way and to maximize benefits from investments in change. Often, portfolio management lies between the enterprise strategy function and the work delivery function, ensuring that the right work is accomplished in the right way to support the organization's strategy. This relationship is shown in Figure 12.1.

As depicted in Figure 12.1, the organization's strategies are key inputs to the portfolio management function. By analyzing these strategies, understanding the work required to achieve them, translating this work into constituent projects, programs, and operational improvements, and prioritizing among competing components, the portfolio management function charters, with approval from management, the projects, programs, and operational change efforts that are necessary to achieve organizational strategies. Interactions will likely exist between the project and program work and the operational work, as each influences the

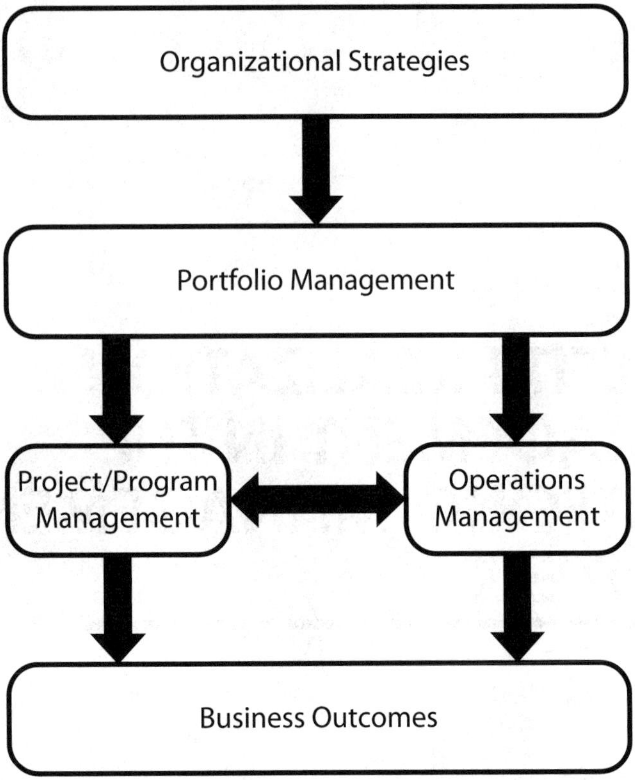


**Figure 12.1** Portfolio management context

other. The resulting output of work creates a set of desirable business outcomes which must be aligned with the strategies. The portfolio management function plays a key role in monitoring and understanding the relationship between capability creation and the resulting business outcomes with a focus on how benefits realization is supported.

The maturity of portfolio management in organizations varies widely. In some organizations, a well-defined portfolio management function is implemented through a portfolio management office that supports portfolio component selection, ensures the appropriate allocation of organizational resources to approved work, tracks and reports on portfolio components, and proactively rebalances the portfolio to respond to changing business priorities. In other organizations, portfolio management is largely nonexistent as a business function, with decisions regarding allocation of resources and chartering of projects and programs largely left to individual business units or managers. Many organizations fall somewhere in the middle, implementing components of portfolio management to assist with tracking and managing work but not performing portfolio management in an integrated way. The level of engagement from the portfolio management function in benefits realization work depends on the relative maturity of portfolio management in the organization. If the portfolio management function maintains responsibility for benefits reporting, metrics, or realization, then a partnership between the portfolio management team and the program management team will be necessary in order to ensure the needs of both parties are met. In other cases, perhaps only periodic involvement from the portfolio management function will be required. Within this chapter, the role of portfolio management in the benefits realization context is described in general terms to clarify portfolio management roles within the benefits realization management context as well as to describe opportunities to leverage portfolio management toward benefits and strategy realization.

## THE ROLE OF THE PORTFOLIO MANAGER IN BENEFITS REALIZATION MANAGEMENT

In organizations with a portfolio manager role, the portfolio manager typically engages in several key activities that are of interest from a benefits realization management perspective. Table 12.1 summarizes these key roles and their relationships to benefits realization management.

As indicated in Table 12.1, the portfolio manager supports benefits communication, issue resolution, reporting, and associated processes on the portfolio level. This interaction does not replace regular reporting to the senior responsible owner, program steering committee, and other relevant stakeholders, which are undertaken by the program management team, but rather summarizes key points from each constituent project, program, or operational initiative for

**Table 12.1** Portfolio manager activities and benefits realization management influences

| Portfolio Management Activity | Benefits Realization Management Influence |
|---|---|
| Communicates with portfolio stakeholders regarding constituent portfolio components | Benefits communication |
| Resolves portfolio issues together with relevant management | |
| Monitors portfolio and provides reporting and analysis | Benefits reporting |
| Maintains standardized portfolio processes | Influences the benefits realization plan |
| Participates in program reviews | Ensures alignment as the business changes |

portfolio stakeholders. While this may create overlap in messaging, it is important to recognize that portfolio reporting is not as detailed as that from the program management team. The key functions on the portfolio level are to identify high-level risks, issues, interdependencies, and other matters that affect overall portfolio delivery rather than to dig into the details of individual portfolio components.

## PREREQUISITES TO PORTFOLIO MANAGEMENT FOR BENEFITS REALIZATION MANAGEMENT

In order to leverage portfolio management to support benefits realization management, it is necessary to meet several prerequisites. Activities required to prepare for effective benefits realization management in a portfolio management context include:

- Ensuring the portfolio management function has visibility into the strategic management processes of the organization, including business direction and vision
- Ensuring relevant business constraints and interdependencies are understood so effective investment decisions can be made
- Ensuring relevant portfolio key performance indicators (KPIs) are established, and business case development to support portfolio selection considers these KPIs
- Ensuring the organization's appetite for risk is understood, and as appropriate, relevant risk thresholds or other indicators are defined
- Ensuring the portfolio management function implements standard processes for portfolio management, ideally aligned with recognized standards

Other prerequisites may be of interest as well. The fundamental point of interest here is that the base portfolio processes must be established and working *before* the portfolio management team attempts to integrate benefits realization management activities. For most organizations, this will be an evolutionary journey, likely starting with using portfolio management to understand the scope and resource allocation of work in progress, proceeding to establish processes related to project selection and portfolio management, then graduating to more complex analysis and reporting that includes consideration of benefits realization. The complete process of implementing portfolio management as a business function is beyond the scope of this book. The prerequisites presented here identify several key considerations that must be addressed before benefits realization management is elevated to the portfolio level.

## PORTFOLIO SELECTION IMPACTS

The portfolio management process influences benefits realization even before constituent projects and programs are chartered. A critical role of portfolio management in most organizations is selection, in which the portfolio management function facilitates relevant business stakeholders to choose among competing priorities in order to create the portfolio that best balances risks and rewards from the investment in change. Given the important role of portfolio management in achieving the organization's strategies, the portfolio manager and his or her team must be able to understand management's intent and realize it with the right mix of investments. Often, the organization has more desired investments than it has resources (financial, human, or otherwise) for the work required to capitalize on them, causing the organization to make trade-offs that best balance resource availability with business goal realization. This is an exercise in benefits realization, as return on investment is a key component of making the right investment decisions. These returns must be considered in the context of benefits realization, as the decision-making process depends upon the benefits anticipated, the alignment of these benefits with the organization's strategies, and the risks that may limit benefits attainment. The portfolio manager works with the business leadership to understand these dynamics, support data analysis and critical review to ensure a fair assessment of costs and benefits, and balance the portfolio to maximize return on investment.

These selection decisions are ongoing in many organizations. As such, some portfolio "rebalancing" may take place from time to time. This rebalancing may result in a reallocation of resources across the portfolio, potentially impacting existing projects, programs, and operational initiatives. Within the portfolio management function, reliable data on the status of existing work is required for effective decisions regarding how best to allocate resources. For this reason, a relationship between the portfolio manager and the business change manager, or the program office responsible for benefits reporting, must be established in order to ensure that reliable benefits data is available for portfolio decision making. These portfolio selection impacts may result in changes within the program, requiring the program management team to adjust benefits realization and organizational change management plans in the reallocation of work. The program management team must maintain the flexibility needed to best integrate these changes as efficiently as possible, which may involve program scope reduction or expansion, having considered the effects through the partnership between the program management team and the portfolio management team, ensuring impacts of change are considered in portfolio decisions.

In summary, portfolio selection impacts related to benefits realization management include:

- Evaluating new investments and their potential benefits to capitalize on new opportunities
- Supporting business stakeholders in making selection decisions between multiple investment options, considering anticipated benefits realization, costs, and risks
- Rebalancing the portfolio as appropriate, terminating portfolio components that no longer align with organizational strategies
- Terminating portfolio components that are not expected to realize planned benefits

Resources, such as the business change manager and benefit owners, are important for the portfolio management team as they evaluate potential investments, evaluate the performance of existing portfolio components, and consider benefits, costs, and risks associated with portfolio components to make adjustments. These resources should be engaged at the beginning of business case development to ensure appropriate focus on benefits realization management as well as to provide a critical eye in reviewing potential investments. Though perhaps not yet formally assigned to any particular investment, candidates for business change manager and benefit manager are often involved in the early development of program business cases, providing critical support to these efforts.

## PORTFOLIO REPORTING AND REVIEW IMPACTS

This section considers portfolio management reporting and review activities in the context of benefits realization management. These are two distinct activities. Portfolio reporting is an ongoing activity that consolidates data regarding the active portfolio of work, considers data for assessing and rebalancing portfolio components, and summarizes portfolio data for review. Review activities include regular portfolio review with portfolio stakeholders, review of constituent portfolio components with responsible project, program, and operations managers, and ad hoc reviews to address issues and risks that impact portfolio performance. The following sections address these two important functions separately.

### Portfolio Reporting

For many organizations implementing benefits realization management, a simple approach to reporting benefits on the portfolio level is advisable. Because benefits realization management will be a new concept, within both the program management and portfolio management domains, a learning curve will exist before the organization determines "what works" from a reporting standpoint. The temptation to capture large amounts of data and make that data available to the portfolio management function may be strong but is not advised. A simpler approach will provide significant value, while limiting the investment in reporting and allowing the organization to learn and adapt reporting over time to better meet stakeholder needs. Figure 12.2 provides a view of a basic reporting flow for benefits data in the portfolio management context.

As Figure 12.2 depicts, the portfolio management function serves as a reporting hub between portfolio stakeholders and the program. The portfolio management function defines the reporting requirements and standards to which all constituent portfolio components must adhere in reporting benefits data (and data in general) and aligns these requirements with the needs of portfolio stakeholders. Information, such as format, frequency, and other important factors, must be defined in a standard way. If possible, software tools should be employed to assist with ensuring data is provided in a common way. The portfolio management function receives benefits data as well as issue and risk data from the constituent programs. Benefits data usually includes summary data for KPIs, forecast data for benefits attainment forecasting, and key organizational change management

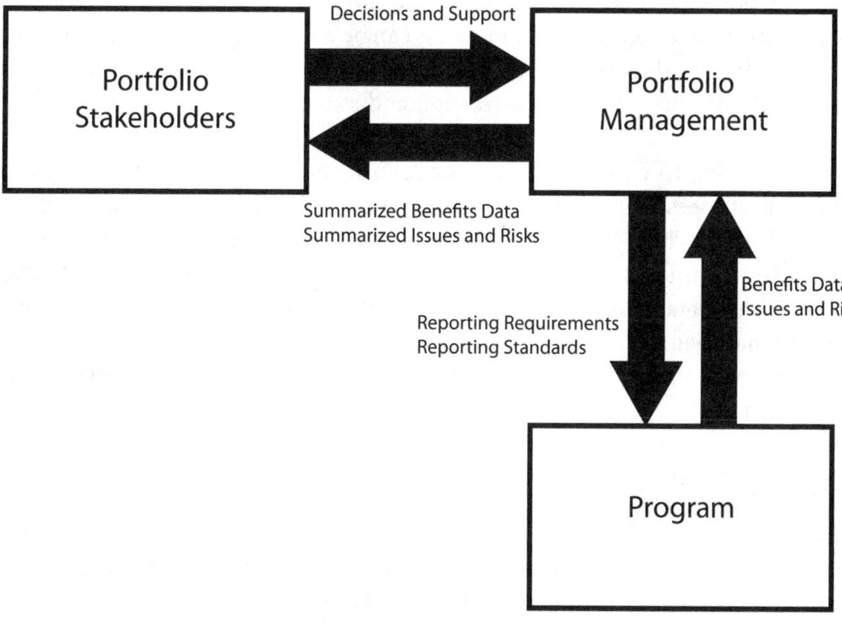


**Figure 12.2** Portfolio to program benefits reporting flow

indicators that while not directly benefits data, indicate organizational readiness for change toward benefits realization.

Data collected by the portfolio management function is analyzed, and relevant summary data is aggregated from all portfolio components for summary reporting to portfolio stakeholders. An essential component of this process is the summarization of benefits attainment and forecast data, including risks to benefits attainment. Portfolio stakeholders, who are often responsible for realizing defined organizational strategies, have a strong interest in ensuring that planned benefits are attained and that benefits forecasts support their attainment. If risks or issues limit this attainment, portfolio stakeholders may be engaged, either to directly support resolution of issues or management of risks or to make prioritization decisions that may stop work associated with portfolio components that pose risks to benefits realization. These discussions, which are facilitated by the portfolio manager but may include representatives from the program management team, require accurate and timely benefits data from the constituent portfolio components.

Portfolio stakeholders are also interested in data regarding aggregate benefits realization across the portfolio and the links between benefits realization, value creation, and strategy realization. The portfolio management team is best positioned to provide this visibility. It is possible that underachievement and overachievement of benefits may be real or forecasted, which must be considered on an overall portfolio level so appropriate decisions regarding resource allocation and prioritization of portfolio components can be made. Appropriate rebalancing activities, along with corrective actions and risk management activities required to correct issues that affect value creation and strategy realization, must be undertaken.

It is tempting to believe that the portfolio management function adds little value to this process, if the role is primarily seen as a data aggregator and reporter. This is a limited view. The portfolio management team has a strong role to play in receiving significant amounts of data from constituent portfolio components, analyzing this data, and understanding what the most critical areas of focus for portfolio management should be. The most critical issues related to performance within the portfolio should be elevated for action during portfolio review, which is discussed next.

## Portfolio Review

Regular review is an essential component of effective portfolio management. Portfolio review may include internal reviews, conducted by the portfolio management team, reviews conducted with portfolio management stakeholders, and reviews conducted with project, program or operations managers responsible for constituent portfolio components. Each of these reviews serves an important purpose and requires a review of benefits data.

### *Internal Portfolio Reviews*

Internal portfolio reviews are conducted by the portfolio management team to regularly assess portfolio performance, as well as to identify issues and risks to be either managed within the portfolio management team or escalated to portfolio stakeholders. Typically broad in nature, they review many relevant KPIs as well as the various portfolio components. Regular review and assessment of change readiness, benefits realization, and benefits forecasting should be included, with the management team focused on ensuring that the portfolio is positioned to achieve the strategic objectives elaborated by business management, including the relevant business benefits.

### *Stakeholder Portfolio Reviews*

Stakeholder portfolio reviews represent a broad category of reviews conducted with relevant portfolio stakeholders. These stakeholders may include the portfolio's governing body (e.g., a portfolio steering committee), organizational or divisional management committees, other governing bodies, and additional interested parties who have a stake in the portfolio and its constituent work. Processes for reviews with these stakeholders are part of the portfolio management plan. While many will follow a routine cadence and format, ad hoc reviews may certainly be of interest as emergent opportunities come to light, or as issues or risks present situations requiring stakeholder awareness, input, or action. A key component of these reviews will be summarized data regarding benefits attainment as well as risks and issues that impact benefits attainment. It is necessary for the portfolio management team conducting these reviews to have additional detail available to enable them to "drill down" into individual constituent portfolio components, if requested by stakeholders. For this reason, it is often necessary to collect more data regarding benefits attainment, benefits forecasting, and business change activities than will ultimately be presented as part of standard portfolio reporting. This data is used for day-to-day internal management of the portfolio as well as to support additional analysis and review, as described here.

### *Component Portfolio Reviews*

Component portfolio reviews focus on reviews conducted by the portfolio management team in concert with members of the constituent portfolio component teams. This may include reviews with program managers and members of the program management team such as the business change manager, project managers, operations managers and others with responsibility for work contained within the portfolio. The purpose of these reviews is to look deeper into component performance in order to confirm progress, identify and address issues and risks, and prepare for portfolio stakeholder reviews. Review of change management plans and benefits realization plans are important components of these reviews, allowing the portfolio management team to more deeply understand specific actions toward benefits realization. As appropriate, experts from within the portfolio management team provide advice and guidance to the program team to assist with advancing benefits realization goals.

An important component of these reviews should be discussion of, and plans to, exploit emergent benefits. The portfolio management team may need to analyze the impact of emergent benefits on overall portfolio goals in order to allocate resources to exploit emergent benefits. The program management team must ensure that the impacts of emergent benefits is quantified in order to provide defensible data to the portfolio management team to support resource prioritization decisions. As appropriate, the portfolio management team may consult with portfolio stakeholders to understand stakeholder interest in and commitment to allocating resources to support exploiting emergent benefits—if the required resources cannot be allocated within the existing program.

## BENEFITS CONSIDERATIONS IN PORTFOLIO RISK MANAGEMENT

Portfolio risk management is an essential component of overall portfolio management, and most major portfolio management standards focus significant attention on managing portfolio risk. In the portfolio management domain, the primary focuses of risk management are on understanding the sources and impacts of negative risk and considering the opportunities associated with positive risk. The concepts of risk and opportunity management are well established in portfolio management literature and are not repeated here in detail, but it is important to note that—from an overall portfolio management standpoint—the portfolio management team is interested in balancing risk across the entire portfolio, in line with the organization's appetite for risk. This often means that the portfolio will contain components with varying risk profiles, some relatively less risky and others relatively more risky. Additionally, the portfolio management team is interested in internal risks associated with poor quality data, unavailable risk data, and other risks that limit the portfolio management team's ability to provide an accurate picture to portfolio management stakeholders.

From an overall risk reporting perspective, the portfolio management team is interested in delivering risk information to portfolio stakeholders who often include members of the organization's management—including senior management. These management stakeholders are primarily interested in risks that may:

- Impact achievement of the organization's strategy and objectives
- Impact financial investments made in the portfolio
- Impact value creation and benefits realization
- Impact delivery of products and services to the marketplace
- Impact compliance with laws, regulations, and statutes

Several of these impacts are directly linked to benefits realization management activities. As such, the portfolio management team, while also focused on delivery risks—such as risks to resources and other delivery dynamics—place strong focus on risk analysis and comprehensive risk reporting related to benefits realization and organizational change activities.

From a benefits realization management perspective, the primary risk considerations are associated with failure to achieve benefits and with capitalizing on emerging benefits. From a negative risk perspective, the program management team is typically concerned with ensuring that risks that maximize benefit attainment are accepted, while also ensuring that unacceptable risks are not undertaken. The risk profile of the program may change over its lifetime, and the program management team must ensure that as the risk profile changes, the corresponding impacts on program objectives are considered. This includes their impacts on benefits realization.

From the portfolio standpoint, risk data must be included with the key data provided from portfolio components to the portfolio management team. In the benefits realization context, two types of risk data are important. The first type reports risks with the potential to affect benefits realization. These risks are likely to be reported in a standard format prescribed by the portfolio management team or via a software tool used to capture and report risks. Some portfolio managers may request a summarization of risks rather than a complete accounting of all relevant benefits-related risks, since—on the portfolio level—the risk profile of the entire portfolio is of primary interest, with summarized key risks providing an additional view into critical risks.

The second type of risk reporting escalates benefits risks to the portfolio level. Typical escalation flow for risks within the program involves first attempting to resolve the risk within the program, followed by escalating to the senior responsible owner—potentially to the program steering committee or other governance body—where resolution, based on recommendations provided by the program management team, is undertaken. Additionally, organizations with a portfolio management function may escalate to the portfolio management team or portfolio steering committee, especially for risks with mitigation actions that impact resource allocation or strategic priorities. The procedures for risk escalation are documented within the program and portfolio management plans to establish clear processes for timely escalation and management of escalated risks.

## ASSESSING THE APPLICATION OF BENEFITS REALIZATION MANAGEMENT ON THE PORTFOLIO LEVEL

The portfolio management function in benefits realization management may need to assess the effectiveness of benefits realization management within constituent portfolio components. While portfolio management is not typically seen as an assessment function, weighing the implementation of benefits realization management against the level of benefits realization management rigor required—based on the scope, complexity, risk, and other factors associated with various portfolio components—may be beneficial. This activity is only undertaken when portfolio management and benefits realization management are both successfully implemented within an organization and plays an important role in balancing resource investment against the value of benefits realization management.

Such assessment could be undertaken in the form of implementation assessment to ensure that appropriate benefits realization practices are in place within the constituent portfolio elements, or it could be undertaken in the context of rigor to ensure that the right amount of benefits realization management is implemented, according to the type of work being undertaken within the particular portfolio element. In some organizations, direct assessment work may be relegated to an enterprise program management office, or other governance function, that performs regular project and program reviews, assessments, and audits, the results of which are made available to the portfolio management team for review and action. The goal, regardless of the organization conducting the assessment, is to ensure that the benefits realization management processes to realize benefits for business strategies are implemented and effectively used. When the observed application of benefits realization management is not enough to ensure successful delivery of business change and benefits, this risk must be highlighted so that program and portfolio stakeholders can take appropriate action to correct the situation.

As a business process, assessment is never easy. Organizations implementing assessment for any process in the project, program, and portfolio management domains must ensure that: standard assessment processes are created, assessment criteria are clear and transparent to the organization, assessment measures are established and defensible, assessors are impartial and trained in assessment methodologies and the organization's standards, and assessment outcomes are presented in an appropriate, constructive way with concrete recommendations for corrective action. Additionally, the organization must institute appropriate follow-up mechanisms to ensure that identified corrective actions are implemented within agreed-upon time frames and that those actions are effective. If the organization cannot commit to managing assessment in a formal way, then assessment should not be undertaken, as research shows that informal approaches expend organizational resources with little real impact.

## PORTFOLIO MANAGEMENT CONSIDERATIONS IN BENEFITS REALIZATION MANAGEMENT IMPLEMENTATIONS

When organizations with existing portfolio management processes are implementing benefits realization management for the first time, engagement with the portfolio management team during implementation planning is important. This engagement should seek to:

- Align the goals of benefits realization management with relevant business drivers which may be shared with portfolio management business drivers
- Ensure a consistent approach to implementing benefits realization management that complements existing portfolio management processes
- Consider the impacts of benefits realization management on existing portfolio management processes and plan organizational change management activities that ensure successful process change
- Consider portfolio management data needs for reporting and review and ensure its availability
- Consider existing software and other tools and their applicability for benefits realization management use
- Assess risks to adoption of benefits realization management on the portfolio level and plan appropriate mitigations

It is advisable to begin any benefits realization management implementation initiative with a proof of concept or limited pilot first to test and validate business processes as well as benefits to the organization. This same approach applies to implementing benefits realization management into the portfolio management landscape. While some components of benefits realization management may already be in use within portfolio management, it is likely that implementation on a broader level within the program environment will lead to changes to existing portfolio management processes and the need to adopt new processes. Establishing a limited pilot of benefits realization management on the program level first, then extending this pilot to test interactions on the portfolio level before large-scale implementation is largely appropriate. In fact, successful implementation of benefits realization management on the program level may best be viewed as a prerequisite for a pilot on the portfolio level, as it helps to ensure that the appropriate foundation is laid for data reporting, risk management, review, and other activities related to benefits realization management.

## APPLYING BENEFITS REALIZATION MANAGEMENT IN PORTFOLIO MANAGEMENT IMPLEMENTATIONS

For organizations that do not currently have a portfolio management function, establishing such a function may be of interest. The application of program management principles, and especially benefits realization and organizational change management, will be extremely beneficial. Often, implementation of portfolio management is met with significant resistance, as stakeholders feel—among other concerns—that they are losing power over investment decisions, that portfolio management decreases their span of control over their projects and programs, and that portfolio management introduces unnecessary bureaucracy into the organization. Additionally, a clear business case for the value of portfolio management implementation must be elaborated in order to ensure that portfolio management efforts are done for the right reasons and with the right end goals in mind. These considerations form a strong case for managing the implementation of portfolio management as a program that has a corresponding focus on benefits realization and organizational change management.

## SUMMARY

Portfolio management and benefits realization management operate as integrated functions in organizations in which both are implemented. Establishing common ways of working between the functions, ensuring data availability and visibility to support reporting, implementing standard risk and escalation management processes, and ensuring appropriate stakeholder communication and engagement are major considerations for organizations that wish to manage strategic realization of benefits through portfolio management and to implement benefits management on the portfolio level.

13

# BENEFITS REALIZATION MANAGEMENT IN PROJECT-BASED ORGANIZATIONS

## INTRODUCTION

This chapter addresses the implementation of benefits realization management techniques in project-based organizations. A significant amount of the methodologies and literature in benefits realization management focuses on the application of benefits realization management in the context of program management. This focuses attention on the prominent role of benefits realization management as an enabler of successful business change delivery via programs. Projects typically operate with different dynamics, including a stronger focus on strict scope control, more limited capability creation versus large-scale business change, smaller spans of influence and relative initiative size, and other factors. While it is certainly possible to undertake massive projects in organizations (in fact, the scope of effort is seldom the sole distinguishing factor between project and program management methodology), it is recognized that program management is often most appropriate for implementing business change.

However, benefits realization management can play an important role, even for predominantly project-based organizations. Although program management provides the ideal methodology for blending capability creation, business change, and benefits realization, organizations that have not made significant investments in developing program management capability may still take advantage of many features of benefits realization management within project environments. Additionally, because some organizations that typically undertake projects also leverage portfolio management as a business function, it is possible for them to leverage benefits realization management on the portfolio level, with a corresponding implementation on the project level as well. As such, benefits realization management techniques may stand alone within the project management environment or coupled with portfolio management to provide project-level implementation as well as corresponding linkages to portfolio governance and reporting.

This chapter provides guidance for organizations considering the implementation of benefits realization management within project environments and assumes these organizations have chosen not to develop corresponding program management capability because of resource constraints, organizational work mix, or other factors that make program management inappropriate. Each organization must decide this for itself. There is no requirement that all businesses implement program management for work, nor is there a clear notion that benefits realization management cannot be successful in project-based businesses. Appropriate tailoring of processes to the environment may be required, but success can certainly be achieved. In addition to this chapter, general implementation advice appears in Chapter 16, which extends several topics of this chapter, together with additional guidance.

## GENERAL IMPLEMENTATION APPROACH

Implementing benefits realization management in project-based organizations requires a somewhat counterintuitive approach. In order to implement benefits realization management in a project-based environment, a program-based methodology is required. One might reasonably wonder how this manifests itself in an organization in which program management is not implemented as a business discipline. The answer is to leverage the capability you have, expanding it to meet the needs of benefits realization management.

It is likely that developing initial understanding and capability in benefits realization management will be required. Clearly, some degree of expertise within the organization is a prerequisite to implementing benefits realization management as a business function. This expertise may be obtained by hiring resources, sending existing resources for outside training to develop the necessary skills, or hiring competent consultants to provide expertise during initial implementation. Hiring resources with expertise or engaging qualified consultants are the least risky and fastest approaches to implementation; however, success is certainly achievable by training existing internal resources.

It is also likely that some capability in organizational change management will be required to effect business changes required to utilize benefits realization management in the project-based organization and engage impacted stakeholders (either directly or indirectly). This capability likely exists, though perhaps informally, within project-based organizations as project managers and project teams typically maintain implementation responsibility for some portion of their projects. Formal processes—related to stakeholder management, managing transition, turnover to steady-state organizations, and others—may exist, or, lacking formal processes, individuals within the organization may already exercise good practices that can be applied. It will be necessary to understand what capabilities exist and can be reused.

Additionally, although benefits realization management implementation may not require additional elements of program management—such as multi-tranche planning, an extensive program management plan, and other typical deliverables—the integration of management of the work, management of stakeholder expectations, management of business change to support successful implementation, and management of benefits realization will require expertise. Utilizing a senior project manager, with a track record of successfully implementing large projects within the organization or for the organization's customers, is strongly recommended. Because benefits realization management implementations typically have high visibility with senior stakeholders, the implementation leader must have organizational credibility, an ability to navigate the culture and politics of the business organization, and strong leadership qualities. Selecting an implementation leader is important, and this critical role should be viewed as an opportunity for a qualified member of the organization's project delivery staff to undertake a uniquely challenging internal project of high business importance. This individual should be appropriately empowered and supported by a team of qualified resources (to be discussed separately). While the implementation leader need not be the organization's expert in benefits realization management as a discipline, he or she should have enough fundamental understanding of benefits realization management to ensure the implementation is guided in a way that ensures successful benefits realization.

## PREREQUISITES

It is important to recognize that implementing benefits realization management as a business process is not easy. But as many organizations have learned, implementing project management as a business process is not easy either. However, the task of implementing benefits realization management in any organization—project-based, program-based, or otherwise—is made significantly harder if there is no firm foundation upon which to build the capability. The first prerequisite to implementing benefits realization management in a project-based environment is for project management to be successfully implemented as a business function in a consistent way and for projects to be consistently delivered, using the established project management processes, tools, methodologies, and associated components already defined and implemented by the organization. Some common-sense checks for this prerequisite include ensuring that:

- A defined and documented project management methodology is established in the organization, and ownership for the maintenance and enhancement of the methodology is clearly established
- The defined and documented project management methodology is implemented in the project organization
- The defined and documented project management methodology that is implemented in the project organization is regularly and consistently used in project delivery and supports effective project delivery
- Appropriate tailoring processes are established to ensure that the project management methodology can be adapted to unique project circumstances
- Project managers are provided with support when questions regarding methodologies, processes, and tools arise
- The organization plans and budgets support ongoing enhancement to the project management methodology

In many organizations, a project management office or other central body assumes responsibility for the organization's project management methodology, providing training, support, maintenance, enhancement, and other activities that ensure that it is appropriately managed and evolved as business needs change. If this organizational entity exists, its effective organization and management will help to ensure that this first prerequisite is in place.

A second and related prerequisite is organizational support for implementing benefits realization management. While program management may not be an established competency within the organization, important aspects of program management, such as business change management, will need to be leveraged for implementation to be successful. Organizational support begins with a valid and approved business case and by supporting resource allocation, sponsorship, clear objectives, and key performance indicators that will be used to monitor implementation progress and benefits realization. Organizational support should also include a defined, agreed-upon implementation scope, most likely a pilot scope, that enables the organization to test key methodological components, conduct pilot training for stakeholders, and learn lessons on a small scale before beginning a broader implementation. Initially, organizations may wish to charter a pilot scope, allocate resources to effectively support it, conduct it, and then assess results and benefits achieved, with an eye toward making appropriate adjustments prior to a broader rollout or canceling further efforts, if it becomes clear that anticipated benefits cannot be effectively obtained.

Organizational support must also specify clear ownership of the benefits realization management process. This ownership may reside with a member of the project management office, if one exists, or absent a project management office, with a designated person who will be responsible for providing methodology support, training, evolution, and other important functions to ensure that benefits realization management is sustained and that continued realization of benefits from its use occurs. Whether within the responsibility of a project management office or not, the designated owner should be reasonably conversant in benefits management methodology and ideally serves as the lead for implementing benefits realization management within the project organization, enabling him or her to establish credibility with stakeholders and actively participate in planning and implementing the capability into the business. This will provide important insights into good practices, challenges, and opportunities to enhance the benefits realization management methodology to better meet stakeholder needs.

A third prerequisite is support from ancillary business processes. Processes related to business case development, portfolio management, benefits measurement, and other components of benefits realization management may require input and support from ancillary stakeholders—beyond the immediate individual or team responsible for implementing benefits realization management. These stakeholders may include resources from finance, portfolio management, strategic planning, or other associated functions. They have a stake in the implementation of benefits realization management, either directly or indirectly, and should be engaged to support it.

## BENEFITS REALIZATION MANAGEMENT CONSIDERATIONS IN THE PROJECT CONTEXT

As a starting point for understanding the applicability of benefits realization management implementation in the project context, it is important to highlight the fundamental ways in which project-based organizations, by not implementing program management as a core discipline, differ from organizations that do use program management. First and foremost, it is likely that the project management staff has been well trained in project dynamics—on time, under budget, and to specifications. It is likely that the concepts of capability creation, business change, and benefits realization are not commonly discussed. Therefore, given the important role that project managers play in implementing benefits realization management, it is likely that education and training will be required to broaden the project manager's perspective on the role of project delivery and capability creation in the broader business context. This effort must be planned for, in order to ensure that resources understand the broader context of benefits realization management, and how their roles as project managers influence benefits realization management success.

Furthermore, it is important to consider the organizational focus on implementation of organizational change management. In some organizations that do not implement organizational change management within the program management context, business functions, such as human resources or other similar functions, provide implementation (or minimally, coaching and mentoring) of organizational change management as a business service. In these organizations, it is important to understand how their existing methodologies, tools, training, and other resources can support benefits realization management implementation. Members of the business organization responsible for business change management should be engaged in the benefits realization management implementation effort so their expertise can be leveraged to help identify opportunities to create interfaces between the functions, which ensures appropriate business change management support within the project context.

In other organizations, no formal capabilities in organizational change management exist. In these organizations, the scope of the benefits realization management implementation program needs to be expanded to create the minimal organizational change management processes and assets required to support benefits realization management. These include the processes related to stakeholder management, transition management, and others—described in Chapter 11. While this may mean extra work, it is critically important, as success in implementing benefits realization management requires a focus on organizational change management in order to ensure that the appropriate business change occurs to realize planned benefits.

A final consideration is the organization's willingness to change. This concern is not unique to this particular effort, but rather of general relevance to all change programs. It is important to ensure that the implementation of benefits realization management in the project context will be supported through implementation, transition, and sustainment. Typically, project management organizations, especially those in business environments with low change tolerance, may not be prepared to move to a benefits model of project delivery. While resistance can be overcome, it is important to consider the additional time and effort required to socialize change, communicate, conduct training, provide coaching and mentoring, and perform other activities to support successful change. Especially in these organizations, a phased or pilot approach to implementation is preferable, as such an approach supports gradual change, enables lessons learned to be effectively leveraged, and provides visible evidence of success to the organization when initial phases or pilots come to a successful conclusion.

## STRUCTURING THE TEAM

Typical program roles associated with business change implementation are slightly modified to meet the smaller scope of a pilot-based implementation of benefits realization management in a project-based organization. The organizational structure depicted in Figure 13.1 provides a basic model for structuring the implementation team.

In the team structure depicted, three primary team roles exist. These roles include the project manager, who assumes overall responsibility for the implementation effort (also called an implementation manager), a subject matter expert, who serves as the primary knowledge contact on benefits realization management, and a business or organizational change management support resource. In general, the project manager and the subject matter expert should be assigned full-time to the implementation effort. The organizational change management resource may be allocated on a part-time basis as the initial scope of organizational change in a pilot-based implementation is relatively small.

Supporting the core implementation team is an organizational program management office, if implemented, which provides support for methodology component development and is engaged in implementation and transition activities, if ultimate ownership for the benefits realization management business function

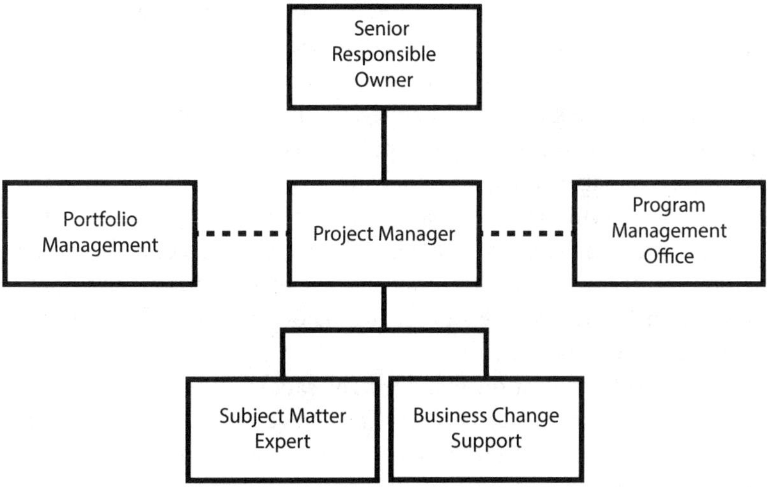


**Figure 13.1** Implementation team structure

will reside within the project management office. Additionally, support is provided by the portfolio management function, if implemented, in order to ensure that portfolio considerations are taken into account. These considerations could include data needs for portfolio reporting, and establishing interfaces between the portfolio management function and the benefits realization management business function.

Finally, implementation is supported by a sponsor (or senior responsible owner, if this terminology applies in the organization) who is responsible for providing visible leadership support to the benefits realization management implementation effort, for allocating resources to support its success, for assisting in the resolution of implementation and business change issues, and for influencing other organizational stakeholders in order to manage expectations and maintain support. The sponsor is often a key business manager who assists with developing the business case for the benefits realization management implementation and is a primary resource for validating the associated benefits to be achieved. The sponsor is also instrumental in defining the initial implementation pilot scope, ideally within his or her sphere of influence. This approach helps to overcome resistance and aids in resolving issues during implementation.

A role that may appear conspicuously missing is that of the benefit owner. In fact, while perhaps not a separate role, the benefit owner is nonetheless important. Assignment of responsibility for managing realization of benefits could rest with the project manager, the subject matter expert, or the business change resource. Assigning this responsibility to the project manager may be advisable. The logic is as follows: The business change or organizational change management resource, being assigned only part-time to the implementation effort, should focus his or her limited time on ensuring the success of the change management activities required to ensure implementation success and benefits realization. The subject matter expert should provide expert support to the organization and plays a strong role in supporting business change, but his or her time is best spent coaching and mentoring within the organization. This provides an ideal opportunity for the project manager to expand his or her knowledge of benefits realization management by serving in the capacity of a benefit owner, with support from the subject matter expert as required. In this way, the project manager gains additional knowledge and experience in benefits realization management, better enabling him or her to provide support to the organization when future implementations are undertaken.

Building benefits realization management capability is essential in the early pilot phases. As such, it may be necessary to engage additional team members on a part-time basis to support building capability toward further implementation and ongoing organizational support. Figure 13.1 has been expanded in Figure 13.2 to represent additional roles of interest within the implementation initiative.

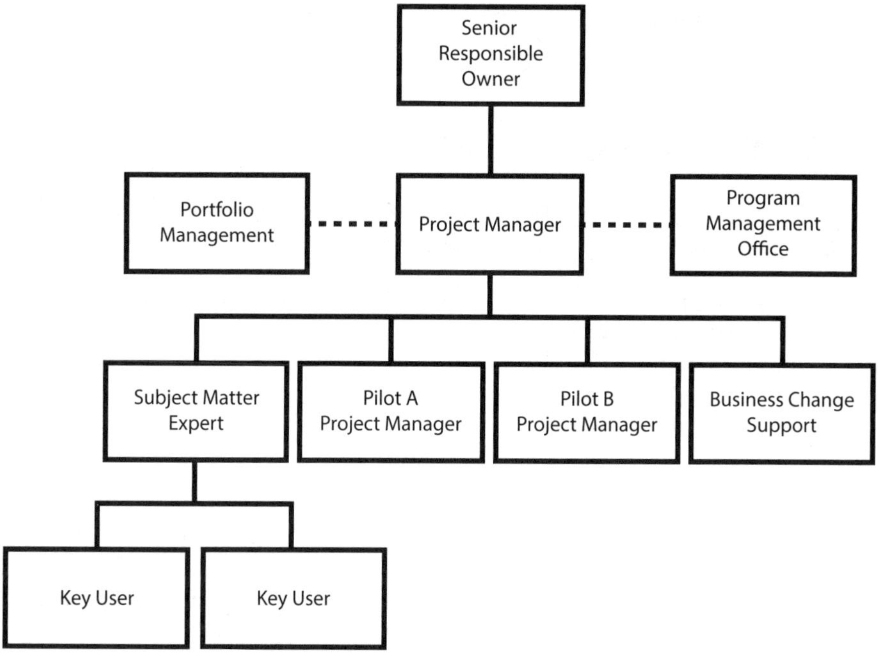


**Figure 13.2** Expanded implementation team structure

The roles added in Figure 13.2 include representatives (likely the project managers) of pilot projects in which benefits realization management is included in the pilot scope. These individuals may change over time, as the pilot(s) may involve projects with varying completion dates. While these resources are primary stakeholders more than traditional team members, including them within the implementation team is important.

The second added role is that of the "key user" who works with the subject matter expert. The purpose of this role is to build knowledge of benefits realization management principles and techniques within the organization. The subject matter expert should be relied on to mentor one or more project managers, project management office team members, or other resources who support benefits realization management as a business function, on an ongoing basis. Whether these individuals are directly involved in selected pilot projects or not, they can benefit from exposure to the pilot process and lessons learned, as well as coaching and mentoring from the subject matter expert. Over time, these key users will subsequently be able to provide training, coaching, and mentoring to the organization as knowledgeable resources. Establishing this network of key users early in the implementation process is desirable, as reliance on the subject matter expert alone will be insufficient as the implementation scope becomes larger after a few successful pilots.

## SELECTING A PILOT SCOPE

An important implementation consideration is selecting an appropriate pilot scope. Again, a pilot-based implementation is often preferred for several reasons:

- Pilots support development of capabilities incrementally, allowing new processes, tools, and methods to be tested on a small scale before broad implementation
- Pilots involve a limited number of stakeholders, simplifying communication and enabling greater collaboration between the team and pilot participants
- Pilots enable identification of issues and process gaps on a small scale, allowing lessons learned to be leveraged toward smoother implementation on a broader scale
- Pilots limit organizational investment in resources, which is attractive to leaders who are skeptical of the initiative's value
- Pilots limit resource investment risk, ensuring limited sunk costs, if benefits are not achieved as planned and the initiative is stopped
- Pilots can be localized to a single group or division, enabling sponsorship and ownership for results to be narrowly defined and easier to control

There are other advantages to a pilot-based approach as well. Conversely, there are several disadvantages of the pilot model that should be considered:

- Pilots lengthen overall implementation time
- Pilots, if not appropriately selected, may not be representative of the practices of the broader organization
- Pilots do not tend to create broad organizational impact, limiting visible benefits in the pilot stage

These and other disadvantages must be considered during implementation planning but, in general, can be managed through appropriate pilot scope selection and proactive stakeholder expectation management.

When selecting a pilot scope, consideration should be given to both the size (in number and scope) and the diversity (in range) of projects included in the pilot. Size considerations are meant to ensure that the pilot is broad enough to be representative of the "typical" size of projects in the organization—neither selecting the smallest, least complex project in the implementation scope, nor selecting the largest, most complex project in the implementation scope. Selection should also include a diversity of project types, to ensure that different potential benefits realization scenarios can be understood, that the unique dynamics of different project types are considered, and that the pilot involves reasonable stakeholder diversity. The "80/20" rule is applicable in diversity selection, representing that 80% of the representative diversity in the organization's projects could be accounted for within 20% of the projects undertaken. While these percentages may vary from organization to organization, most organizations do not undertake such a range of projects that every effort represents a completely unique type of work.

There is no "right" number of projects to include in the pilot scope. Depending upon the size and complexity of the organization, the number of pilot projects could be three, or ten, or twenty. The answer is not one, as selecting only one project limits diversity and could lead to a successful pilot but less successful implementation, and the answer is likely not 50% of the project portfolio. The key consideration is balancing risk and reward to select a small but diverse set of projects. As pilot project candidates are considered, a common-sense approach should be used to check basic appropriateness. These checks may include:

- Can benefits be identified and quantified?
- Can realization measurements be easily established?
- Is the project representative of a typical project in the organization?
- Is the project a critical project, for which including it in the pilot scope could put its success at risk?
- Are project resources available to support the required pilot work?
- Is the project manager supportive of the project being included in the pilot scope?
- Is the project sponsor supportive of the project being included in the pilot scope?

In some cases, the preferable answer may not be the actual answer (e.g., the project manager does not, but the project sponsor does support pilot participation), and these situations do not automatically disqualify a project from inclusion within the pilot scope. Understanding the relevant risks and how to mitigate them are important to determining whether impediments can be overcome.

An additional worthwhile consideration in selecting pilot projects is the selection of new, versus in-flight, projects. Ideally, the benefits realization management process is tested end-to-end in the pilot, beginning with the business case and benefits identification and concluding with transition and sustainment activities. However, depending upon how frequently the organization charters projects and how many of these projects are deemed appropriate for inclusion in a pilot, it may not be possible to limit the pilot scope to new projects because of pilot timeline considerations. In this case, it may be necessary to select projects that are already in the planning or execution phases. The benefits realization management implementation team needs to understand the impacts of this decision and determine how to proceed, either retroactively developing the benefits cases, measurements, and so forth and applying them at whatever stage the projects are already at, or deciding to pilot only the components of the benefits realization management methodology that are relevant, from the current point in the project forward.

## IMPLEMENTATION CONSIDERATIONS

This chapter does not attempt to describe a complete implementation life cycle. The implementation life cycle should follow the regular project management practices of the organization, layering in added focus on organizational change management in order to manage the business change dynamics associated with implementing benefits realization management. In this section, important considerations for implementation are described to identify a few relevant dynamics that are of interest during the planning and execution of implementation. Additional considerations are provided in Chapter 16.

### Confirming Pilot Scope

A primary consideration of interest, early in the implementation planning, has already been discussed—namely, determining an appropriate implementation approach. Assuming that the recommendations in this book have been followed, and a pilot-based approach selected, a basic inventory of candidate pilot projects should be developed early in implementation planning. While not every candidate pilot project may ultimately be selected, it is important to understand the scope of potential pilot projects. Within this scope, a high-level stakeholder analysis should be conducted for the purpose of determining project stakeholder attitudes and interests in relation to the benefits realization management pilot. Stakeholders may have valid concerns regarding inclusion of a particular project in the pilot scope, and these concerns should be understood prior to project selection. In some cases, appropriate actions may address stakeholder concerns. In other cases, significant concerns may necessitate removing certain projects from consideration. This exercise also assists in identifying the stakeholders whose expectations will need to be managed and whose support will need to be obtained for the selected projects.

The results of the stakeholder analysis, combined with size, scope, complexity, risk, and other considerations, should be used to make decisions regarding the pilot scope. Once these decisions are made, the list of pilot projects should be validated with the implementation sponsor to ensure alignment. If particular projects are outside of the sponsor's direct responsibility, alignment with the business leadership in the additional business area(s) should be obtained. The selected pilot projects should then be part of the implementation project's scope statement to formalize the pilot scope.

## Selecting Benefits Scope

An additional scope consideration, beyond the pilot scope, is the scope of benefits and measures considered for inclusion within the pilot. There is no formula for determining the appropriate number of benefits to be tracked or measures to be developed. But it is worth noting that the key reasons for conducting a pilot are to test the established benefits realization processes and to learn from issues encountered during the pilot in order to improve the processes before broader implementation.

It may be tempting to elaborate all benefits associated with each pilot project and to establish the required measurements and associated activities to track these benefits within each pilot project. However, testing the developed processes incrementally, by increasing the scope of testing over the course of the pilot, is preferable. Because not all projects will be in the same phase of the benefits realization life cycle at the same time (in other words, projects within the pilot will have varying start and end dates, and therefore will execute benefits realization management activities at different times), it is better to start with the first project entering the pilot and perform benefits identification and quantification for only one of its possible benefits. If the benefits identification and quantification process works well for one benefit, then for the next project to enter the pilot, several benefits can be identified and quantified. Then in a later project, an even larger set of benefits—perhaps encompassing the full scope of its associated benefits—can be analyzed. In this way, the initial pilot projects are not burdened with extensive work at any particular phase in the life cycle, enabling the benefits realization management implementation team to focus on potential process gaps, process improvements, training improvements, and other activities that will make it easier for later pilot projects to undertake the required benefits realization management activities on a broader scope of benefits.

The process described for benefits identification and quantification should be extended to measurement selection as well. Several measurement methods may be suited for any particular benefit. Initially, simpler measures, which support the gathering of data necessary to test reporting and analysis processes in the pilot, are preferred. Some organizations are tempted to "measure everything," and—while noble and, perhaps, applicable in some limited cases—in this case, the return on investment in developing complex benefit measurement methods early in the benefits realization management pilot is minimal. A small number of relatively easily gathered measures are sufficient for initial pilot testing. More complex measurement over a larger scope of benefits can be undertaken later in the pilot to establish additional good practices for measurement, but this should be undertaken only after the measurement, analysis, and reporting processes within the benefits realization management methodology are tested on a small scale.

## Educating People

A critical implementation consideration is educating people in benefits realization management principles, which for many may be entirely new. This education needs to be developed in a role-based way in order to align with the frames of reference of various stakeholders; but for initial awareness, a basic overview is likely to be sufficient. Subject matter experts should be engaged to lead the development of appropriate training materials for stakeholders, and if possible, the organization's training or personnel development department should be leveraged to support material development, training registration, and other functions.

Identifying training participants should be relatively straightforward if an effective job of stakeholder identification has been done. The key is to provide the right training for the right stakeholders. A standard training matrix is useful for this purpose, and it is a reusable organizational change management asset that can be leveraged for other training analysis purposes. A representative example of a training matrix can be found in Table 13.1.

The training matrix simply indicates the various training modules included within the training scope and maps those modules to the various stakeholders. It can be used as the basis for training participant lists, as well as for understanding which training offerings will require the most stakeholder groups, which aids in planning the number of offerings and associated delivery methods. It is likely that benefits realization management training will require a combination of instructor-led (either in person or virtual) and on the job training when the principles are applied in actual project situations. Involvement of subject matter experts, key users, and others will be required. Especially for key users, more in-depth training and

**Table 13.1** Training matrix

| | Training Module 1 | Training Module 2 | Training Module 3 | Training Module 4 |
|---|---|---|---|---|
| Stakeholder A | X | | X | |
| Stakeholder B | X | X | | |
| Stakeholder C | X | X | | |
| Stakeholder D | X | | | X |

practical learning is required to prepare them to effectively support the organization. Some of this learning will occur during the pilot, with help from the subject matter expert.

An additional consideration is the support tools made available to the organization. These could include making answers to frequently asked questions available; providing support via an online discussion forum where questions can be posed and responses can be provided by subject matter experts; informal "lunch and learn" opportunities to reinforce key concepts; access to recorded versions of prior training; and other mechanisms to codify information for ongoing use. If the organization maintains a project management office, any knowledge management support it has already provided to the project organization should be leveraged, and training artifacts should be provided to the project management office for its own knowledge library.

## Monitoring Progress

The mechanism, by which progress is compared to the plan, is another important component of implementation. Its focus should be on understanding, in a broad context, when the data to support understanding the effectiveness of the developed processes will be available. Because multiple projects are likely to be included in the pilot phase, and because these projects likely have varying timelines, it is necessary to have an overall view of when these projects will produce some of the key benefits realization management deliverables. A milestone format, such as the example provided in Figure 13.3, is useful for this purpose.

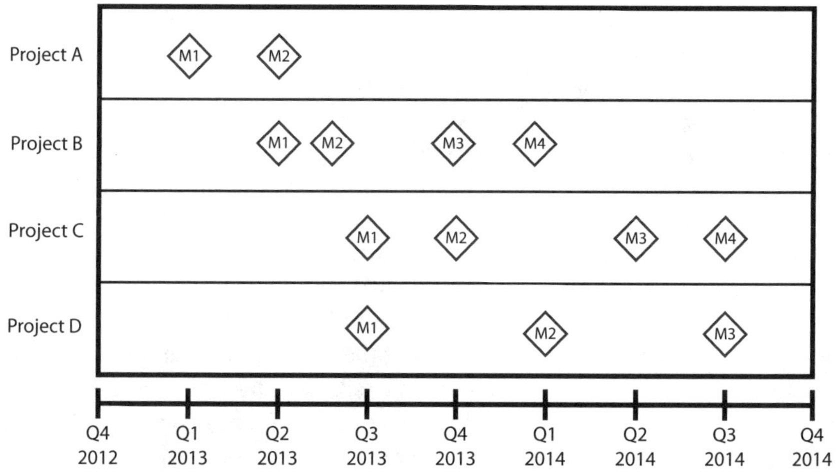


**Figure 13.3** Sample milestone chart

The format in Figure 13.3 provides an easy way for the implementation team and other stakeholders to understand when the various pilot projects will implement the benefits realization management processes that are required for the pilot. Viewing the milestones and projects in aggregate permits the implementation team and other stakeholders to easily see when critical data, such as outputs from measurement that enable first benefit reporting and forecasting, will be available. Since data from only one project will likely not be sufficient to establish the effectiveness of the process itself, the chart in Figure 13.3 can also be a useful tool for validating that appropriate pilot projects have been selected. If it is noted that the distribution of milestones across the various pilot projects will mean that an unacceptably long period of time elapses before sufficient data will be available, for example, then the implementation team may choose to select different pilot projects as in most cases, it is not appropriate to compress project schedules to accommodate a benefits realization management pilot.

Other formats that convey similar information are certainly acceptable, and if the organization implements standard project management software tools that support milestone tracking, then they may be the most appropriate tools to leverage, as they will support loading the benefits realization management implementation plan into the tool and aligning the implementation milestones with milestones within the pilot projects. Since tracking progress versus plan is a component of a project management software suite, it is also possible to capture the additional project progress data required to provide consolidated implementation status reporting by leveraging those in-place software tools.

## Establishing Reporting

An important component of any benefits realization management pilot is testing reporting. Reporting is perhaps the greatest single tangible process output of benefits realization management for stakeholders. Reports on plans, realized benefits, benefits forecasts, and other elements of benefits realization management are regularly distributed, discussed in meetings, and analyzed by business leaders to make decisions. As such, the implementation team should place a strong focus on establishing appropriate reporting processes, aligning required reports with stakeholders' data needs, and ensuring that processes are in place to validate the data's accuracy for benefits realization management reporting. This is especially critical during the pilot in order to build credibility with stakeholders. If reports are presented during the pilot that contain inaccurate information, incomplete information, or information that fails basic tests of logic, stakeholders will develop skepticism regarding the reporting and underlying data. Once this skepticism is established, it takes significant time to rebuild credibility.

In order to minimize the risk associated with skepticism, the implementation team should make every reasonable effort to closely manage the reporting process and to validate the associated data and reports prior to release to stakeholders. Some recommendations to limit risk include:

- Building reporting capability incrementally during the pilot, focusing on the few most critical reports early in the pilot and building additional capability over time
- Sharing sample reporting formats with stakeholders as soon as practicable during report development to understand stakeholder data needs and to manage expectations about the types of reports to be delivered
- Clearly marking example or draft reports as such, indicating that the data is not actual business data
- Establishing a formal reporting test plan within the pilot that establishes responsibility for checking data accuracy, validating formula and calculation accuracy, and other technical considerations that may lead to incorrect outputs
- Sharing examples of reports with project managers in the respective pilot projects to check reasonableness of data and to identify clear discrepancies

There may be additional activities required for effectively delivering reporting that is in line with stakeholder needs. Of special interest is ensuring that key stakeholders—such as project sponsors, the portfolio management office, the program management office, and other primary stakeholders who will regularly use outputs from benefits reporting—are engaged early in the reporting analysis and design process, so their data needs and inputs can be understood. Additionally, the implementation team's subject matter expert should be leveraged to provide insight into common reports, common formats, and recommended practices for effective reporting.

## Concluding and Validating Success

Appropriate pilot success measures are developed in the organization's standard project chartering approach and aligned to the specific pilot scope and anticipated outputs. A multi-project pilot that incrementally builds process capability, integrates lessons learned, and provides opportunity to build benefits realization management knowledge within the organization should be well positioned for success. The pilot phase concludes with deciding on the further course of implementation. Assuming a successful pilot, considerations for broader implementation should be made in terms of scope, business change management, and pace of implementation, balancing risk and reward to ensure that further implementation activities are undertaken in a way that considers an appropriate pace of change and the specific business needs of the organization in benefits realization management. Ideally, key members of the pilot team should be leveraged in future activities, counting on their knowledge and expertise to guide further implementation.

## SUMMARY

This chapter provided an overview of considerations in implementing benefits realization management in project-based organizations. While not an extensive overview of implementation methods in general, the information provided here can be leveraged within the context of the organization's standard project management practices and combined with other information, provided in this book on benefits realization management in general, to develop the complete benefits realization management process and associated implementation processes, relying on subject matter experts in benefits realization management, organizational change management, and project management to ensure a complete plan. While some differences between program-based implementation and implementation in project-based organizations do exist and considerations for implementation in project-based organizations are discussed, many practices from benefits realization management are directly applicable, in much the same way, to both environments, and organizations that choose not to invest in program management capability to support benefits realization management will still be able to derive value from the practice.

14

# PROGRAM MANAGEMENT OFFICE ROLE IN SUPPORTING BENEFITS REALIZATION MANAGEMENT

## INTRODUCTION

This chapter addresses program management office roles in supporting benefits realization management. Entities that provide support for the project, program, and/or portfolio management function(s) in a business are variously referred to as project management offices, program management offices, project support offices, enterprise project offices, and a host of other names. For the purposes of this chapter, the term program management office (PMO) will be used to generally describe an organization that is responsible for management of the project and program management competency within an organization, among other duties. In this context, the PMO likely maintains responsibility for establishing project and program management standards, providing training to staff, mentoring, supporting software tools, and other functions that support project delivery. In some organizations, PMOs may additionally have direct project or program delivery responsibility, support portfolio management, or perform other functions.

For the purposes of this chapter, neither the processes of establishing a PMO nor the general functional responsibilities of the PMO are discussed. Rather, this chapter provides a view of roles the PMO may play in supporting establishing and managing benefits realization management as a business function. The PMO is typically not directly responsible for the delivery of benefits, but it may provide a supporting function to the project, program, and portfolio management resources that directly support benefits management. These delivery resources may leverage the capabilities of the PMO to provide support for project and program delivery as well as for benefits reporting, process training, and other topics.

## TYPES OF PMOs AND THEIR INVOLVEMENT IN BENEFITS REALIZATION MANAGEMENT

Numerous types of PMOs, with varying names and functions, have been elaborated in literature on PMOs. And if anything from this literature is clear, there is no broad agreement on what the entity, often referred to as a PMO, should be called, nor what it specifically should do. In some organizations, PMO stands for project management office, in others, program management office. Even among entities referred to as PMOs (as opposed to any of the numerous other names used to describe similar entities), there is often broad disparity in their roles and functions. As such, a comprehensive attempt to delineate names and functions is not attempted here. Rather, several general categories of entities are described, along with several roles these entities may play.

### Enterprise Program Management Office

Enterprise program management offices (often abbreviated as ePMOs) are generally distinguished from other types of PMOs by position and focus in the organization. The enterprise PMO is typically viewed as the highest level PMO in an organization, responsible for oversight and management of activities within its scope. Enterprise PMOs often undertake strong roles in activities, such as governance, portfolio management (if an enterprise portfolio management office function does not exist), and supporting strategic planning, along with other areas of responsibility. The enterprise PMO may have subsidiary PMOs, such as divisional or group PMOs that directly or indirectly report to the enterprise PMO. The enterprise PMO is generally staffed with senior project and program management resources, who provide direct consulting and mentoring support to the project and program delivery organization, as well as with appropriate support staff to manage administrative duties, and project support staff who provide support for methodology maintenance, software tools, and other items. A common enterprise PMO structure is shown in Figure 14.1.

The structure in Figure 14.1 depicts the enterprise PMO with two subsidiary divisional PMOs reporting to it, with responsibility for project, program, and/or

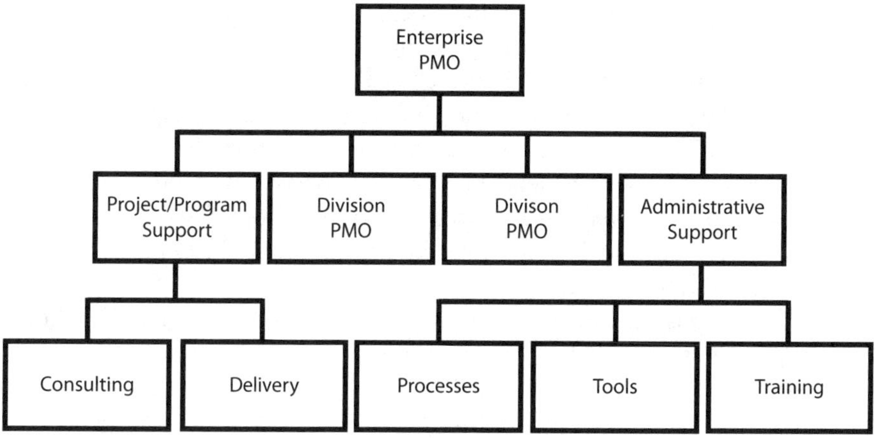


**Figure 14.1** Enterprise PMO structure

portfolio management functions within their respective divisions. Additionally, this structure depicts project and program support functions with responsibility for project and program management consulting, coaching, and mentoring, as well as an administrative support function focused on processes, software tools, and training. Some organizations add a specific portfolio management function within this structure if such a function is implemented outside of a dedicated portfolio management office.

The organizational structure depicted demonstrates a relatively large scope of responsibility for the enterprise PMO. This is often the case. With broad responsibility for functions, such as establishing process standards, managing software tools, and supporting project and program delivery on an enterprise level, the enterprise PMO staff are typically quite busy. However, in organizations that have implemented enterprise PMOs, having a single point of accountability for project, program, and/or portfolio management practice is often beneficial.

The roles of the enterprise PMO in benefits realization management can be diverse. Its most common role is methodology governance. The enterprise PMO maintains responsibility for managing the benefits realization management methodology—including its associated processes, tools, templates, and associated artifacts—ensuring that consistent ways of working are defined across the organization and that support, training and mentoring is provided to meet the needs of benefits realization management stakeholders. While this role for the enterprise PMO may appear to be more tactical than strategic, it is important to note that process consistency is tremendously valuable, especially in larger organizations. Ensuring that benefits realization management practices are defined and consistently implemented supports consistent reporting and process governance, which enables greater confidence in the process. Important considerations for the enterprise PMO in this context are the required staffing to support process definition, maintenance, and maturity, as well as the required organizational capability within the enterprise PMO to provide consulting, mentoring, and process guidance. While the enterprise PMO does not need to provide staff to support subject matter expertise in benefits realization management, if a network of key users or subject matter experts has been established within the organization, it is important that appropriate personnel within the enterprise PMO understand the benefits realization management framework, as well as how the framework is used within the business organization, so they can intelligently engage stakeholders to support building process capability and maturity over time.

In enterprise PMOs in which the PMO is responsible for portfolio management, the role of the enterprise PMO in benefits realization management is significantly more involved. These enterprise PMOs often support a strategic planning function, engaging with business stakeholders to provide support for organizational direction setting, portfolio planning, business case managing, and benefits planning. While the PMO does not directly set the strategy of the organization, its critical role in supporting decision analysis and managing the portfolio of approved work makes benefits realization management a logical competency to retain within the enterprise PMO. In some sense, the implementation of benefits realization management within organizations with an enterprise PMO that is responsible for both portfolio management and benefits realization management is ideal. With business function accountability for both portfolio management and benefits realization management resting with the enterprise PMO, process integration between the two processes is significantly easier. Additionally, because the same resources are likely engaged in both functions, process maturity tends to occur faster because the process limitations and gaps are more easily identified. It is not necessary to implement an enterprise PMO, or to ensure the integration of portfolio management and benefits realization management via an enterprise PMO, to successfully implement benefits realization as a business function. But where this integration does exist, the benefits tend to be clear.

## Portfolio Management Office

In some organizations, portfolio management is implemented with a variation on the program management office that is called a portfolio management office. The portfolio management office serves as the process ownership and governance body for portfolio management within its scope of responsibility and performs functions, including, but not limited to:

- Engaging with stakeholders to ensure strategic alignment between business strategies and the organization's portfolio

- Prioritizing activities and engaging stakeholders in determining investments that balance risks and rewards
- Allocating resources to support the organization's approved portfolio, resolving issues as appropriate by balancing risks and rewards
- Managing risks to identify, understand, and mitigate them across the portfolio
- Supporting portfolio reporting to meet the expectations of portfolio stakeholders
- Managing benefits realization activities to ensure that appropriate benefits are planned across the portfolio and that the portfolio is positioned to deliver planned benefits

Many of these activities involve processes that are relevant to the benefits realization context. These include but are not limited to:

- Understanding of organizational strategies and benefits required to meet planned objectives
- Business case development to support portfolio prioritization, which requires a strong focus on benefits identification and associated quantification
- Portfolio reporting, which includes a benefits component in reporting realized benefits as well as forecasts for future benefits attainment
- Risk management activities, which include identifying risks to benefits realization and determining appropriate responses

The portfolio management office typically interacts with projects and programs that use benefits realization management either by direct contact with the project and portfolio management teams or by interaction with the PMO structure that supports them. Regardless of the specific interaction, regular interaction between the project and program delivery functions and the portfolio management function is required to ensure that benefits realization management data is available to the portfolio management team and that outputs of the portfolio management function—relevant to the project and program management organization—are appropriately considered and managed.

Portfolio management office leaders should be keenly aware of the importance of a strong working relationship between the portfolio management office and the project and program delivery function. This relationship must include coordination of benefits realization management processes—as they influence, or are impacted by, the portfolio management function—coordination of data to support reporting, and ensuring that as processes change the corresponding impacts on associated processes are considered. If the portfolio management office exists outside the context of an enterprise PMO or similar entity, the appropriate working relationships must be established. If the portfolio management office is part of an enterprise PMO, another PMO entity, or is organizationally aligned with the enterprise PMO, then some coordination may be assured by that relationship. Even then, however, the portfolio management office does not have direct responsibility for the benefits realization function but rather serves as a data provider and consumer.

In some organizations, however, the responsibility for the benefits realization management function rests within the portfolio management office. This approach clearly has its advantages. In this case, the end-to-end process—from business case development through benefits realization—is overseen by a single organization. Reporting tends to be significantly simpler since the same organization considers the relevant stakeholder needs and defines the benefits reporting requirements, both for portfolio management and for the project and program delivery functions, and resources may be optimized by leveraging a single organization that manages these two tightly connected processes. For organizations performing a new benefits realization management implementation and already have an existing portfolio management office, strong consideration should be given to including benefits realization management within the scope of the portfolio management office. While this does not mean that the portfolio management office directly manages benefits realization on the project or program level, the portfolio management office serves the important role of providing governance to the overall process, in line with stakeholder expectations. As many outputs of benefits realization management are of interest to the portfolio management function, this approach may seem perfectly natural.

## Project Office

Unlike the enterprise program and portfolio management offices, the project office most often exists as a temporary entity as opposed to a permanent function within the organization. The most common implementation of a project office is to provide operational support to a particular project or program. Especially in large programs, it may be difficult for the program management team to directly address the myriad operational and administrative functions required to effectively manage the program. Even relatively basic business functions, such as proper time or cost accounting, can be daunting for the program management team on larger programs. As such, the project office is most often positioned to support such activities as:

- Management of data and associated software tools that collect, analyze, and report data
- Coordination of required governance activities, such as phase gate reviews
- Activities to support project or program reporting requirements

- Methodology implementation and support to ensure consistent application of the organization's project or program management methodology
- Administrative support to the project or program management team

In the benefits realization management context, the project office, if staffed with personnel who have a basic understanding of benefits realization management processes, reporting requirements, and related functions, can be leveraged to provide support to the program manager and the business change manager in accomplishing benefits realization. A primary support area often lies in benefits realization management process administration. The project office may support data management for measurement and benefits tracking purposes, support such activities as benefits reviews, ensuring timely reporting of benefits data to stakeholders (such as the portfolio management function), and perform other activities to reduce the administrative overhead associated with benefits realization management within the direct project or program management team. This support does not absolve the project or program team of accountability for management of the benefits realization management process, fidelity of data, and reasonable assurance that the benefits being tracked and managed are appropriately accounted for, achieved, and reported.

The project office may also be positioned to provide support for organizational change management activities. The large number of stakeholders, stakeholder interests, and communications, training, and other change management activities that must be tracked and managed provide an opportunity for the program office to play a critical role, enabling members of the organizational change management team to focus on the highest priority change management activities while being assured that other important, yet less critical activities are being effectively managed. Because of the importance of effective organizational change management in benefits realization management, the program office should be leveraged to provide this and other necessary support.

## Center of Excellence

A center of excellence is an entity on the organizational level, or within divisions or departments, created to build project or program management capability. The center of excellence is often responsible for the development, deployment, and maintenance of standards, methodologies, and processes, as well as for topics, such as training and mentoring, that enable project and program managers to be more effective. Often more tactical than the strategic enterprise program management office, the center of excellence is a support organization for project and program managers, providing a point of contact as well as representative good practices. The center of excellence does not typically maintain a direct staff of project managers (who typically reside within the business organization) but rather relies on formally appointed center of excellence team members who provide support to project and program managers. In some organizations, the center of excellence is staffed with full-time employees. In other organizations, the center of excellence may be staffed with resources who have other job responsibilities as well or with interested project and program managers who primarily focus on project or program delivery but "donate" time to center of excellence activities.

The center of excellence may also provide strong support for talent management, supporting training, career development, mentoring, informal peer learning activities, maintenance and reuse of lessons learned, and other activities for growing personnel capability. While formal career management functions and associated processes likely rest with human resources, the center of excellence is well positioned to be a conduit to the project and program management community.

In the benefits realization management context, support through the center of excellence is occasionally challenging. If the center of excellence is formally established, with a dedicated staff and a clear charter, then support for benefits realization management is easier to ensure than when the roles are less clear, the staff is not dedicated, or the center of excellence relies on "volunteer" resources from the existing project and program management community. In these cases, several problems may emerge:

- Prioritization of benefits realization management may be difficult as the center of excellence faces resource constraints or focuses on more fundamental methodology or process challenges
- Knowledge and experience in benefits realization management may be limited, depending upon its resources' origins
- Training budgets and associated resource commitments may be difficult to allocate to benefits realization management
- Ability to influence the organization to comply with processes and standards may be limited, hindering the center of excellence's ability to enforce benefits realization management standards and compel project and program managers to provide reporting or other deliverables

None of these challenges are insurmountable. However, an awareness of such challenges is important as these improve the odds of making informed decisions about how to most effectively leverage the center of excellence.

Assuming that any relevant challenges are viewed as addressable, the scope of the center's participation in benefits realization management must be considered. Often, because centers of excellence are more tactical, it makes sense to limit the scope of their involvement to more tactical matters. If the center of excellence represents the single center of project and program management competency within the organization, then its primary focus may be on supporting development, implementation, and maintenance of standards and processes related to benefits realization management. The center of excellence can assure that these processes, once validated by the benefits realization management implementation team through pilots and implementations, are appropriately integrated into the organization's overall methodology and that the benefits realization management methodology components are regularly reviewed and updated, consistent with the center's methodology management processes.

Additionally, because centers of excellence support peer learning, training, mentoring, and similar functions, the center can be a valuable resource for supporting ongoing education, training, and mentoring in benefits realization management techniques. Assuming the benefits realization management implementation team provides initial training to the center or engages its members in the key user community during implementation, the center of excellence will be well equipped to support the organization when questions and additional training needs arise. This approach supports the center's broader role in project and program knowledge management, enabling it to better serve the project and program managers who rely on it.

Finally, because centers of excellence do not typically play a strong role in portfolio management, they often have a limited role in supporting the portfolio aspects of benefits realization management. Topics, such as data management to support reporting, are not generally included within its scope as these activities are not the types of activities the center undertakes in the broader project management context. Unless there is a compelling case to include such activities, they are often best left to coordination between the organization's portfolio management team and the responsible project and program managers.

## Organizational Unit Program Management Office

The concept of an organizational unit PMO generally refers to a broad category of PMOs that are aligned with particular divisions, groups, geographies, or other logical segments of the organization. The organizational unit PMO has responsibility for the project, program, and/or portfolio work within its domain, operating on a similar model to an enterprise PMO but on a smaller scale. It is not unusual for organization unit PMOs to take on responsibility for portfolio management within their domains, be responsible for methodology and process, engage in education and training activities, and so forth. The level of direct involvement in these efforts may primarily be driven by whether the organizational unit PMO represents the highest level PMO within the organization, or whether the organizational unit PMO reports to an enterprise PMO that provides governance on the overall enterprise level. When an organizational unit PMO represents the highest-level entity, there may be several organizational unit PMOs, each with its own processes and methodologies to support the needs of its individual units. In organizations with an enterprise PMO, coordination across organizational unit PMOs is often managed through the enterprise PMO, which standardizes the ways of working, with each organizational unit PMO tailoring processes, methodologies, tools, and other items to its own unique needs—within the guidelines set forth by the enterprise PMO.

Organizational unit PMOs without an overarching governance structure (such as an enterprise PMO) can pose special challenges for integrating benefits realization management and more generally, can create special challenges for organizations. If not self-coordinating, there is significant risk that each organizational unit PMO will develop its own discrete processes and methodologies to meet its own "unique" needs, with little standardization across the various organizational unit PMOs. This may make it difficult, if not nearly impossible, to effectively implement benefits realization management, and integrating a standardized benefits realization management process into disparate organizational project, program, and/or portfolio management methodologies is a significant challenge—both technically and from an organizational change management perspective. In many cases, these "unique" needs are preferences rather than needs, a form of convenience to allow each organizational unit to work in its own way, often considering its own group's interests without regard for the organization's broader interest in standardized ways of working. This is unfortunate, as establishing standardized project, program, and portfolio management processes, with appropriate tailoring for truly unique challenges, provides better value to organizations than managing disparate methodologies.

When there are disparate project and program management methodologies, as well as diverse portfolio management methodologies, it may be possible to integrate benefits realization management processes into the organizational unit PMO's processes by a gap fit exercise in which individual organizational unit PMOs assess the best integration points according to their unique methodological components. If portfolio management is centralized in the organization, the processes by which the individual organizational unit PMOs provide data to it can be leveraged to ensure consistent delivery of required benefits realization management data, still allowing the individual organizational unit PMOs to determine the best methods for integrating benefits realization management into their operations.

Building benefits realization management capability within organizational unit PMOs may also pose a challenge. The benefits realization management implementation team will need to assess the best approach to equipping members of the various organizational unit PMOs with the training necessary to enable them to support benefits realization management processes. Ideally, the implementation of benefits realization management is timed to ensure delivery to organizational units in a phased way, which enables the benefits realization management implementation team to integrate appropriate organizational change management activities into its plans to engage the organizational unit PMO during implementation.

When the organizational unit PMO reports to a centralized enterprise PMO, the implementation is much simpler, as processes and standards can be driven by the enterprise PMO. As noted, some process tailoring may be required during implementation of benefits realization management into a particular organizational unit, but this tailoring should be relatively minor and limited to addressing mandatory deviations, such as those required to comply with laws or regulations and to meet valid process deviations that have significant business impacts. While it is seldom desirable to force processes onto an organization, a certain amount of inflexibility is necessary for organizations to standardize its ways of working. Benefits realization management lends itself to standard ways of working, and many organizations have implemented benefits realization management in a relatively standard way, with perfectly acceptable results in varying business units and geographies. A preference should be given to standardization in most cases.

## Other PMO Types

There are certainly other types of PMOs beyond those described here. Some have a much stronger direct project and program delivery role and are staffed with many qualified project and program mangers that directly deliver project work. In these PMOs, benefits realization management is embedded to some extent, by default, by virtue of the fact that the project and program management resources are themselves key users of the benefits realization management methodology. In these cases, the PMO already provides centralized management of the projects and programs within its direct control, and thus, the additional data management to support benefits realization management simply extends processes that are already in place.

Other PMOs function like business change offices, responsible for implementing business change programs within the general focus on organizational change management. In these PMOs, a strong focus on organizational change management already exists, and the benefits realization management implementation team needs to consider how the existing practices should be integrated into the benefits realization management methodology. These PMOs may be tightly integrated into benefits realization management, from an organizational change management perspective, but have insignificant roles in providing training and support for the benefits realization management process or in performing data management and other types of functions.

Other types of PMOs exist as well. The benefits realization management implementation team needs to consider how, if at all, these PMOs can be leveraged to support benefits realization management.

## DETERMINING AN APPROACH

The benefits realization management implementation team must consider the PMO, regardless of type, as a stakeholder in benefits realization management implementation. The interests and influence of a particular PMO vary from organization to organization and even within different PMOs in a single organization. Therefore, the benefits realization management implementation team must consider PMO entities in their plans and determine the appropriate steps to manage the expectations of these stakeholders. They must also be strongly considered during implementation planning, so appropriate processes can be built to support the ways of working between the constituent projects and/or programs and the PMO. Additionally, appropriate business change management activities must be planned, so these PMO entities are regularly engaged during implementation. Finally, as these entities will often become the support organization for benefits realization management after the formal implementation program concludes, effective planning for transition and sustainment of support for benefits realization management must be planned, with clear alignment and agreement among business stakeholders regarding the support model, how ongoing support costs will be managed, and so forth.

## KEYS TO SUCCESS

When considering the roles of various PMO entities in the benefits realization management process and how to leverage them to support benefits realization management, a few points are important:

- Focus on developing a single point of ownership for benefits realization management and a single way of working. Multiple variants of benefits realization management are not desirable. A single organizational entity should own the benefits realization management business function within the organization and be responsible for its ongoing implementation, support, and maturity after initial implementation is complete. An enterprise PMO or other high-level PMO is well suited to perform this function.
- Clearly understand how PMOs function in the business organization. It is critical to understand the roles, responsibilities, resource capacities, spheres of influence, and authorities of any PMO that will play a role in benefits realization management, so realistic assumptions can be made regarding the support a particular PMO can provide. It is unlikely that the implementation of benefits realization management will dramatically change the roles of PMOs within the benefits realization management scope.

- Focus on standardized processes. While some degree of tailoring may be required, a strong focus should be placed on ensuring that most processes are standardized across the organization.
- Focus on building people capabilities. Engaging a PMO to support benefits realization management must include engaging the appropriate people within the PMO and providing them with training and support to become knowledgeable in both benefits realization management principles as well as the specific processes being deployed in the organization.
- Clearly articulate the value. It is critical to articulate the benefits to be obtained from PMO engagement in benefits realization management. This value will vary from organization to organization, but it must be understood and articulated.

## CASE STUDY EXAMPLE

A case study, describing a role for the PMO in supporting benefits realization management, is provided in Appendix A. It includes a general model for PMO roles in supporting benefits realization management and describes a small-scale scenario that can be easily amplified to accommodate implementation in many organizations.

## SUMMARY

This chapter provided an overview of several types of PMOs that are common in organizations as well as guidance on roles that these PMOs may play in benefits realization management. Because of the diversity of the PMO landscape, providing definitive roles and responsibilities is not easily accomplished. As such, this chapter provided a starting point for understanding potential roles, enabling productive discussions with stakeholders to determine how best to leverage the organization's investment in PMOs to support benefits realization management goals. It is easy to ignore the fact that benefits realization management must be supported in the ongoing operations of the organization until late in the implementation program. This is a tremendous mistake. Planning for ongoing support must begin early in implementation planning, and engagement of PMOs to be involved in this support should be started as early as possible in order to avoid unnecessary organizational change management challenges during benefits realization management implementation.

# 15

# BUSINESS CASE CONSIDERATIONS

## INTRODUCTION

This chapter examines benefits realization management in business case development. The business case is a fundamental deliverable of business planning processes as well as a key input to program and portfolio management processes. Through the business case, issues, problems, and opportunities are articulated in a way that enables organizational stakeholders to make choices between potential investments, and effective business case development is important for making these decisions. A brief overview of business case development will be provided in this chapter; however, the intent is not to extensively address the finer points of developing effective business cases. Rather, the use of business cases to support benefits realization management activities will be discussed.

Additionally, this chapter addresses business case review and ongoing stewardship during project or program execution. From a benefits realization management perspective, these ongoing activities seek to ensure continued alignment between benefits realization management activities and the business case, ensuring that changes to planned benefits, the business case, or other factors are appropriately analyzed and understood, so stakeholders can be engaged to provide input or make decisions to ensure the work meets organizational objectives.

## BUSINESS CASE OVERVIEW

In organizations with formal business case development practices, the business case is one of the first documents that project and program managers encounter when assigned to new projects or programs of significant size and scope. The development of the business case typically begins well before project or program management work begins, as it is a key tool for business stakeholders in deciding how to allocate limited resources among all viable business initiatives. The business case provides a basis for informed comparisons and decisions, presenting various investment opportunities in a common way, which helps business stakeholders understand business challenges, solution alternatives, required investment, anticipated benefits, relevant risks, and other important information.

Business cases are reviewed, and decisions are made in planning processes. In organizations implementing portfolio management as a business function, the portfolio management team plays a strong role in supporting business case development, validating the appropriateness of information contained in the business cases, and assisting stakeholders with understanding their resource allocation options based on business priorities and proposed business cases. In organizations not implementing portfolio management as a business function in the organizational project management context, a strategic planning or general management function typically operates as a portfolio management organization, assisting stakeholders with the necessary analysis to support effective decision making.

Business case development is not easy. Defining the anticipated benefits in uncertain investments creates challenges. It may be tempting to address the uncertainty through extensive investment analysis and detailed project planning, but the investment in initial business case development must be tempered by the understanding that not all business cases will be approved. As such, while business cases should be underpinned by thoughtful analysis, detailed scope decomposition, estimates, risk analysis, and related processes, full development at the initial business case stage could result in significant work devoted to investments that are ultimately not selected. While business case development cannot be a "back of the napkin" analysis, organizations must balance investment in business case development with other organizational priorities, gathering enough information to make informed decisions while not overburdening business case developers and analysts with undue detail. It is important to recognize that project and program managers undertake detailed planning and that the same detailed analysis at the business case development stage is inappropriate, as the business case may be refined as more information becomes available during project or program initiation and planning. At the conclusion of planning, the business case will be more detailed than at its initial stage; this additional detail may drive further investment decisions—if, for example, further elaboration of project scope, costs, and risks during project initiation and planning reveal that the business case has changed in a significant way. As appropriate, projects or programs may be expedited or terminated, based on the additional information obtained during this refinement process.

## RELATIONSHIP BETWEEN THE BUSINESS CASE AND BENEFITS REALIZATION MANAGEMENT

Business case development and benefits realization management are tightly aligned. Benefits-related activities start at business case inception when stakeholders begin to define required business changes and their associated impacts. These business changes are defined in the context of planned benefits, which are meant to support the organization's strategy. As such, in some sense, the business case development process is a benefits realization management process from the start. As business case development continues and is refined, the corresponding benefits are similarly refined, producing a set of benefits at its conclusion, that represent stakeholder desires and organizational intent and align with the organization's strategy.

During project or program delivery, benefits are monitored to ensure that realization is in line with plans. As business needs change or challenges limit benefits realization, their impacts on the approved business case are analyzed, with the appropriate business stakeholders to review impacts and choose appropriate courses of action. Project and program management teams, with an eye toward capitalizing on opportunities, similarly scan the environment to identify emergent benefits and consider these emergent benefits in relation to the business case in order to present proposals to stakeholders for capitalizing on some of them. Stakeholders evaluate these proposals in the context of enhancing the business case, considering their risks and rewards. These activities, in addition to regular benefits reviews that are part of normal project or program governance activities, support ongoing validation of the business case in the benefits context.

## BUSINESS CASE STRUCTURE

Specific formats for business cases vary from organization to organization, and the literature in management and related disciplines suggests that many formats may be used. Given the lack of agreement on a common business case format, it is easier to describe its general content. The specific presentation and level of detail attributed to any portion of a business case may vary. In this section, common components of a business case are briefly described, along with further information and supporting data for benefits realization management that may be contained in each section.

## Executive Summary

Like many formal business documents, the business case begins with an executive summary that provides an overview of the document's substance. For a business case, this executive summary typically contains a brief overview of the business challenge or opportunity being addressed, the proposed solution to address it, anticipated financial investment and corresponding returns, discussion of critical risks or issues, and a recommendation on how to proceed. The executive summary is typically brief and designed to permit stakeholders to understand the substance of the business case quickly and enable them to focus their attention, within the more detailed business case document, upon their particular interests.

The business case should provide a high-level overview of the benefits anticipated from the work articulated in the business case. The executive summary should focus on the critical few benefits of interest to business stakeholders and their corresponding quantification. A comparison of benefits to costs is often included within the executive summary to provide stakeholders with a view of potential returns. These comparisons are presented financially and underpinned by detail within the business case. While some discussion of intangible benefits is often appropriate in business cases, the executive summary, to the extent possible, should focus on articulating key tangible benefits.

## Business Challenge or Opportunity

This section provides an overview of the current business challenge or opportunity that the business case addresses. Relevant business background, competitive analysis, stakeholder analysis, SWOT techniques, and related analyses should be detailed here to enable stakeholders to understand the current situation as well as the compelling business need to undertake the work outlined in the business case. Challenges and opportunities should be provided, along with a discussion of the corresponding priority, urgency, or risk of inaction associated with the business case. General statements of planned benefits may be made in this section, but it is usually not appropriate to detail specific benefits here.

## Alternatives

This section of the business case provides an overview of ways to address the business challenge or opportunity from the previous section. In some cases, there may be only one viable alternative to address the articulated business need. In many cases, however, there are multiple alternatives, each representing varying levels of risk, investment, and return. Business stakeholders often wish to review these alternatives in order to balance investment and return, understanding that limited organizational resources must be allocated across potentially many investment alternatives.

Alternatives must be presented in a way that enables comparison of the alternatives in terms of their differences in investment, benefits, risks, and other important factors. As such, these alternatives are often presented with their corresponding costs and benefits, as well as appropriate financial analysis and metrics (NPV, IRR, etc.). Considering the many factors that may be of interest in this comparison, scoring grids or similar techniques are often used. An example of a scoring grid is shown in Table 15.1.

The scoring grid in Table 15.1 is a weighted criteria model, which places the various solution alternatives at the top and agreed-upon evaluation criteria in the columns at the left. The evaluation criteria are given a weight (in this case, from one to five) based on the relative importance of each criterion, with the highest value representing the greatest relative weight. Each alternative is rated according to an agreed-upon scale (in this case, a scale from one to five) based on how well the alternative meets the criteria. Multiplying the score by the weight, and summing the results for each alternative yields a corresponding score, which can then be compared against the scores of other alternatives to provide an initial prioritization. In this case, alternative "C," with an overall score of 55, represents the best alternative based upon the assumed model.

Evaluating solution alternatives must consider the benefits associated with each alternative and the degree of confidence in benefits attainment associated with each. While it is always tempting to "shoot for the stars," it is important to balance this desire with an understanding of the relative risk to benefits attainment that each option presents. For this reason, if scoring grids or similar techniques are used to evaluate alternatives, it is appropriate that benefits-related criteria consider both the relative anticipated benefits as well as their likelihood of being attained. An alternative with high benefits potential but high risk to benefits attainment must be differentiated from an alternative with lower benefits

**Table 15.1** Sample alternatives scoring grid

| Criteria | Weight | Alternative A | Alternative B | Alternative C |
|---|---|---|---|---|
| C1 | 3 | 3 | 5 | 3 |
| C2 | 2 | 3 | 4 | 3 |
| C3 | 4 | 3 | 4 | 3 |
| C4 | 1 | 4 | 2 | 3 |
| C5 | 5 | 3 | 2 | 5 |
| Score | | 46 | 51 | 55 |

potential but low attainment risk. While benefits are not the only concern, they are often weighted heavily in the models and, as such, can impact overall rating outcomes.

## Financial Analysis

While financial considerations are usually discussed in the context of solution alternatives, they are underpinned by more detailed financial analysis. The substance of this analysis appears in this section. As appropriate, the relevant financial models and calculations should be described along with their corresponding assumptions and other factors. It is likely that business cases will be reviewed by business stakeholders who hold direct financial management responsibility within the organization, so it is important that this section clearly articulate the financial case(s) being presented within the business case. As appropriate, the organization's accounting or finance departments may be engaged to support the financial analysis section.

Financial analysis related to benefits is included here. This analysis may include the basis of quantification information for benefits that are expressed in financial terms, cost assumptions that could impact benefits estimates, dependencies between benefits and their potential impacts on financial aspects, and other topics. Resources familiar with the financial modeling and forecasting practices of the organization should be engaged, together with resources familiar with benefits quantification techniques, to ensure an alignment between these practices. Additionally, the financial context of benefits should be reviewed and validated as part of business case review, which will be discussed in the business case review section of this chapter.

## Risk Analysis

Risks associated with the business case are articulated in this section. Ideally, risk identification and quantification techniques from the project and program management domains are leveraged here to create a high-level risk summary that considers overall business case risk as well as the specific risks of particular alternatives. This may be presented graphically, in a risk grid format, as in Figure 15.1 or in other appropriate formats. A simple picture is often most appropriate for providing a high-level view of relevant risks, with corresponding detail provided as text within this section of the business case. High-level mitigation actions are included to show plans for mitigating these risks.

As part of risk analysis, risks to benefits attainment are identified, and if possible, inputs from potential benefit owners should be sought for their perspectives on risks to benefits attainment. Potential mitigation actions should be specifically articulated for identified risks. It is important to keep in mind that more detailed

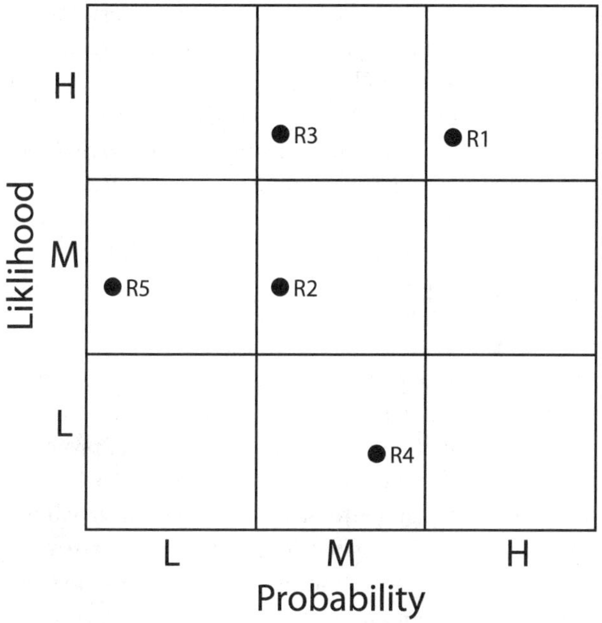


**Figure 15.1** Business case risk grid

risk analysis will be undertaken during project or program initiation and planning. Undertaking this work will likely result in identification of new risks, as well as reprioritization of others. The business case stage should focus on the critical few risks to benefits realization that are relevant to business stakeholders for the business case review and approval process. More risk analysis at later stages will be used by the project or program management team as the basis for developing a detailed risk management plan. Such rigor is usually unnecessary at the business case stage.

## Recommendation

This section provides a definitive recommendation on how to proceed. If multiple solution alternatives exist, a recommended alternative should be provided along with any relevant justification for the selected solution. Alternatively, if only one option is proposed, then its justification is provided. Additional reasons for the recommendation are detailed, and the business case identifies its required funding, human resource allocation, approximate timelines, and other relevant information that provides context for the recommendation.

A restatement of anticipated benefits should be made in the recommendation so that the benefits associated with the recommendation are clear to those reviewing the business case. These benefits were already articulated, but it is not uncommon for some stakeholders to focus solely on the executive summary and recommendations sections of the business case. As such, this section supports selling the business case to stakeholders, as does the executive summary. Proposals to mitigate benefits realization risks are included here as well, in order to assure stakeholders that the relevant risks have been considered and that high level plans are already being devised.

## Future State Blueprint

A business blueprint is a common artifact in several popular program management methodologies. The blueprint describes the future operating state or model to be achieved through change. As business cases often involve one or more dimensions of change, articulating a future state blueprint provides a view of the business after the changes from the business case are realized. The blueprint provides a view of the specific changes to be undertaken (via capability integration), as well as the related impacts on business processes and the corresponding transition path which moves the organization from the current state to the future state. The blueprint is further elaborated in program planning, providing significant detail on changes to people, the organization, technology and information, and other aspects of the business that will be affected by the change program.

Typically, a blueprint is a visual representation of a plan, such as a construction blueprint that provides dimensions and other information about a building. The business blueprint may contain drawings and other visual artifacts, but it will primarily contain a significant amount of supporting documentation. A typical business blueprint includes details, such as:

- Process or other models that describe changes in ways of working
- Organizational structures depicting future business relationships, lines of reporting, responsibilities, and other details
- Technology impacts and descriptions of changes to technology, information systems, and other aspects
- Data, information, and knowledge impacts, including changes in data capture, information flow, reporting mechanisms, and other facets
- Documentation of benefits from change, including relevant metrics and realization considerations
- Elaboration of other relevant program management artifacts, including program vision statements, charters, and related documents

This detail will be elaborated in further planning if the business case is approved. For the purposes of the business case itself, an overview of future ways of working and changes needed to achieve the future state are sufficient and provide a solid basis for further elaboration of the blueprint during planning. As noted in the list of business blueprint components, elaboration of benefits is an important aspect of the blueprint. Since benefits have already been identified within the business case, repetition is not necessary here. The business change articulated in the business blueprint *should* consider and describe corresponding impacts on benefits however. These descriptions aid in understanding how the changes described in the blueprint support achieving benefits.

An example of an outline for a business blueprint is shown in Table 15.2.

Table 15.2 provides an example of typical business blueprint contents. Organizations may wish to adapt the example here to meet their unique needs, but in general, this example outline contains the critical sections that enable effective elaboration of the current and future state business organization, as well as the associated changes needed to realize the future state. A focus on benefits is included in the business blueprint to ensure that benefits from change are appropriately highlighted.

## Project or Program Overview

The project or program overview describes the implementation plan associated with the work articulated in the business case. At this stage, milestone charts or

**Table 15.2** Business blueprint outline example

| Section | Contents |
|---|---|
| Purpose | • Describes the current organization and need for change<br>• Elaborates the vision statement |
| Benefits | • Describes high-level benefits<br>• Describes associated measures and timelines |
| Business Model | • Describes the future state business model<br>• Compares future state to the current state |
| Organizational Structure | • Describes the future state organizational structure<br>• Includes organizational charts, roles, and required staffing levels as appropriate |
| Technology | • Describes the implementation of technology to support change<br>• Includes infrastructure, equipment, facilities, software, and other technology |
| Information | • Describes information requirements in the future state business model<br>• Elaborates the future mode of operation to support information requirements |
| Risks | • Describes high-level risks<br>• Describes mitigation plans to address identified risks |

other graphical depictions of plans are perfectly acceptable. Detailed planning will only be undertaken after the business case is approved, so it is not necessary to attempt it at the business case development stage. The relevant timeline, key capabilities delivered, key business change implemented, and key benefits realization milestones are articulated here to provide context and to help manage expectations concerning when the elements of the business case will be realized. A focus on when intermediate and end benefits will materialize is important, as it ensures that stakeholders understand when to expect these benefits, which avoids unrealistic expectations that arise from not presenting realistic achievement timelines in the business case.

## WHO DEVELOPS AND VALIDATES THE BUSINESS CASE?

Business stakeholders with a vested interest in the business case typically initiate business case development. They may not have prior business case development experience and as such, may rely on an organizational strategic management or portfolio management function to provide training and/or mentoring in business case development. Ideally, a standard template exists for business cases, which provides not only required inputs but also guidance on how to use the template, proposals for formatting critical business case information—such as financial models—and so forth. Effective business case review requires that business cases are similar in format, content, and level of detail, so meaningful comparisons can be made.

Business case development input should be obtained from relevant subject matter experts as part of the process. This input could include financial models from the organization's accounting or finance function, required business change from relevant stakeholders, potential risks from project or program managers who are experienced in risk management, and information from other sources. Business case development is collaborative, involving a number of parties. This ensures that the business case is developed in a way that includes the requirements, inputs, and opinions from a number of representative stakeholders.

Input regarding potential benefits and benefits attainment is of critical importance for business case development. If possible, an initial list of potential benefits owners should be identified, and they should be engaged in the benefits identification and quantification components of business case development. Additionally, engaging a resource familiar with organizational change management principles and methodologies may be beneficial—not only for input into change aspects of the business case but also for support and review of the relevant benefits.

It is not uncommon, when organizations are newly implementing benefits realization management, to find that business case development processes do not support effective benefits articulation. Often, such business cases contain only broad statements of potential benefits, are primarily underpinned by intangible benefits, or have benefits attainment targets with no basis in sound analysis. While it may be tempting to say that some benefits articulation is better than no benefits articulation at all, the reality is that insufficient or inappropriate articulation of benefits contributes greatly to projects and programs not achieving business objectives. Understanding how benefits are defined and quantified, determining the gaps between current practice and recommended practice, and adjusting business case development practices to align with good practices in benefits identification and quantification are critical activities for the benefits realization management implementation team. The implementation process should place a strong focus on elaboration of benefits in the business case, as the business case serves as a critical input to further benefits realization management work in the delivery project or program itself. While minor adjustments to the business case are anticipated during further project or program initiation and planning after the business case is accepted, significant revisions are not appropriate. Significant revisions can represent challenges for organizations as choices may have been made to pursue a particular business case at the expense of others. If an approved business case is significantly revised, the impact could be that the organization would have been better served by selecting an alternative investment. While changing the investment mix is possible later, opportunity costs and sunk costs may be created by radical revisions now. These situations are not ideal and can be minimized by sound initial business case development with a correspondingly clear focus on benefits.

## BUSINESS CASE REVIEW AND EVOLUTION

Many organizations undertake multiple business case reviews within their overall management processes. This approach reflects the fact that at initial business case development, the level of available detail to support accurately reflecting costs, schedules, risks, benefits, and other important considerations is less than that following project or program initiation and planning approaches. As a result, analysis that might otherwise support better cost and schedule estimating, for example, may not be available. We understand this situation and expect that during initial business case review and approval, the level of estimating accuracy will be better than rough but not nearly as precise as after detailed project or program planning. As subsequent planning occurs, additional detail will drive the clarity required to revise plans and estimates. A representative view of this relationship is shown in Figure 15.2.

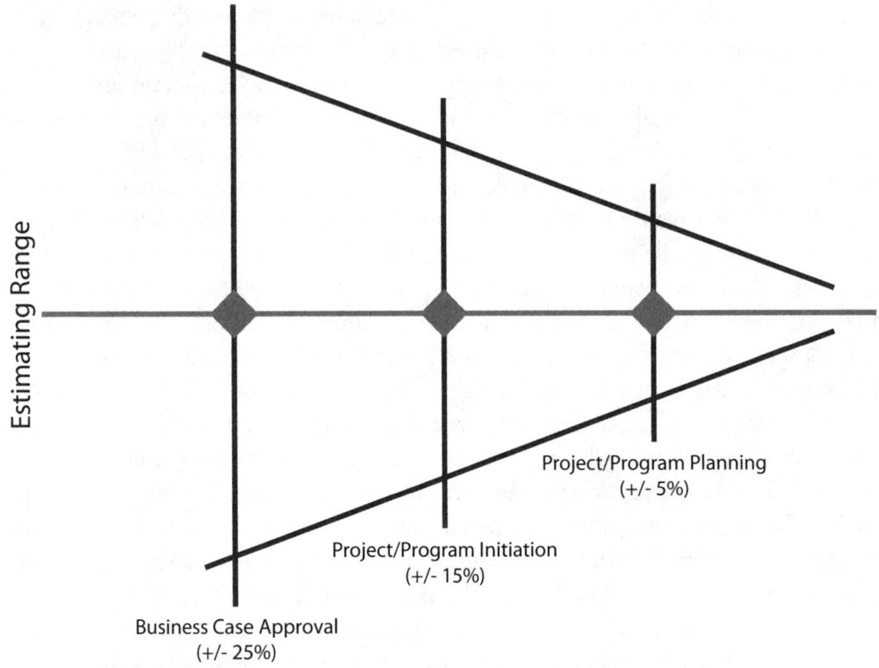


**Figure 15.2** Business case revision and review

As Figure 15.2 illustrates, the estimating range associated with the various phases of business case development and revision narrows as time goes on. At initial business case development and approval, one might expect a margin of estimating accuracy as large as +/–25%—although in many cases, this range is narrower. Through work done after business case approval (during project or program initiation), it is likely that details will become available that permit revisions to estimates presented at initial business case review and approval, narrowing the estimating range to roughly +/–15% (some organizations aim for +/–10%). Further work, leading up to review and approval plans at the conclusion of the project or program planning phase, should narrow this gap significantly due to the significant amount of detailed planning undertaken during this phase. These efforts should narrow the estimating range +/–5%, which is an acceptable range if appropriate risk allocations are made in scheduling and budgeting for remaining unknowns. These final estimates are carried forward into project or program execution, with appropriate monitoring and controlling, to assess performance versus plans, and appropriate responses to deviations.

Figure 15.2 depicts three key milestones (indicated by diamonds). An initial business case review and approval must be undertaken as the basis for establishing organizational intent to proceed with the work proposed in the business case. This first review may be part of a broader prioritization effort that seeks to establish the organization's portfolio of work and charters the initiatives to support portfolio goals, or it may be part of an ongoing organizational process of regularly reviewing new business cases for potential integration into existing portfolios of work. Regardless of process, a decision-making body—comprised of appropriate business stakeholders—must authorize appropriate business cases. This authorization assigns initial resources to support project or program initiation and establishes governance and oversight for the approved business case. This governance and oversight may name a specific project or program steering committee or more often, formally appoint a senior responsible owner (or sponsor) who will be accountable for the continued evolution of the approved business case for the organization.

A second business case review is conducted at the conclusion of project initiation activities. At this stage, the initial project or program management team will have conducted due diligence activities, elaborated additional deliverables to clarify scope, risks, and other important items, and will have made updates to the business case that reflect the added understanding gained during initiation. At this stage, the business case is reviewed to ensure that it remains aligned with organizational strategies and that the revised business case continues to offer value to the organization.

An additional business case review occurs during a broader review conducted at the conclusion of project or program planning. This review is established as a key phase gate in the project or program delivery life cycle, allowing stakeholders to review detailed project or program delivery plans, timelines, budgets, and other factors prior to commencing project or program execution. Review of the revised business case at this stage permits a final validation that the business case remains acceptable to the organization and that appropriate resources are committed to ensuring delivery of the planned capabilities, changes, and benefits associated with it. Given the significant increase in resource investment that occurs when projects or programs enter execution, this critical review serves to ensure that if the business case is no longer appropriate, action is taken prior to additional investment. Action could include revision to the project or program scope, allocation of additional resources to facilitate additional benefits realization, or termination of the project or program.

Benefits need to be considered during each review. Though well thought through plans, schedules, budgets, and other items may be created in initiation and planning, a well-executed project or program that does not deliver the benefits articulated in the approved business case is not likely to be viewed as successful. Additionally, revisions to the business case may cause revisions to the planned benefits, which could lead to a reduction in value from the work. The project or program sponsor, together with the steering committee or other governance body, must address such situations, to ensure that business stakeholders understand potential impacts on benefits realization in the context of the organizational investment required to complete the project or program. In some cases, changing business priorities, reductions in benefits potential uncovered through due diligence and planning activities, and other factors lead stakeholders to conclude that the anticipated returns do not justify the required investment. Making these decisions requires clear, timely, and accurate data to support options analysis, and a strong component of business case review is the review of supporting data and analysis created during initial business case creation and subsequent refinement. Benefits data should be internally reviewed by the project or program management team, together with relevant stakeholders and subject matter experts, prior to formal business case reviews to validate whether it is reliable and should be presented in the formal review.

## BUSINESS CASE DURING PROJECT OR PROGRAM EXECUTION

At the conclusion of project or program planning, the business case should be "final," with respect to the work planned and approved in the project or program planning phase review. This does not mean the business case will not change. There may be opportunities during execution to take advantage of emergent benefits and there may be a need to modify the business case because of changes in scope if business conditions, or project or program conditions, change the benefits outlook. There may also be a need to periodically revalidate the complete business case for subsequent project or program reviews (especially in larger programs). The processes for business case review and modification should be documented within the organization's methodology framework, with a focus on ensuring there are clear rules to govern who may authorize changes to the business case, how business case reviews and updates are made, and the roles of the project and program management team in ongoing business case monitoring.

From a benefits realization management perspective, the benefits components of the business case are built into key deliverables of the benefits realization management life cycle—such as benefits profiles and the benefits realization plan, among others. These benefits-relevant deliverables should remain aligned with the business case, and impacts to one should be understood in relation to impacts on the others. Ensuring this alignment is an important component of benefits realization management governance. Additionally, it may become clear that certain benefits will not be achieved or will be achieved at a lower level than predicted in the benefits realization plan. These situations must also be assessed in the context of the business case to understand potential impacts on achievement of the overall business case. Such situations must be brought to the attention of the senior responsible owner so decisions can be made regarding how best to proceed. Early warning is critical, and thorough analysis of potential mitigations and impacts must be undertaken in order to ensure that the senior responsible owner and other relevant stakeholders are informed of the precise nature of potential challenges to benefits realization and their impacts on the approved business case.

## SUMMARY

This chapter provided an overview of key business case elements and their relationship to benefits realization management. Additionally, the chapter provided an overview of benefits realization management considerations in business case review and in ongoing business case monitoring. Participants in benefits realization management activities—such as benefit owners, business change managers, program managers, and others—must understand the business case and its constituent components, in detail, in order to ensure that planned benefits realization management activities align with the articulated business case and remain aligned throughout the life of the work undertaken to achieve it.

16

# PRACTICAL GUIDANCE FOR IMPLEMENTING BENEFITS REALIZATION MANAGEMENT

## INTRODUCTION

This chapter provides practical guidance for implementing benefits realization management in an organization. Rather than provide a complete implementation methodology, the chapter addresses important areas of emphasis to be taken into account when introducing benefits realization management into an organization. The specific implementation methodology should follow the general methodologies of the organization, which typically results in the implementation being run as a project or program, following the project or program management methodology of the organization. Benefits realization may be implemented in different organizations in diverse ways: in some organizations, it may be part of the implementation of program management methodology; in others, it may be embedded into existing program management methodologies; in still others, it may be part of a project-based methodology; and in still other organizations, benefits realization management may be implemented only on the portfolio level or as a discrete business function, completely separate from project, program, and portfolio management. Because of the diversity of implementation processes and methodologies, proposing a single implementation methodology is not possible.

This chapter proposes ten key recommendations for successful implementation in a business organization. These recommendations include guidance for practically realizing the recommendation during implementation planning and execution. Additionally, it provides perspective on common roadblocks to success and how to manage them.

It may seem strange that implementation guidance is provided at the end of the book rather than at the front. The implementation aspects are best appreciated once the context of benefits realization management is understood, potential roles and interfaces with other business functions are considered, and key considerations in benefits realization management in the context of other processes—such as program management, portfolio management, business case development, and others—are understood. With this background, one can apply the principles offered here, with one's own knowledge of project, program, and portfolio management, to working together with others in the organization and detailing an achievable benefits realization management implementation plan. For additional context regarding implementation approaches, Chapter 13, on implementation of benefits realization management in project-based organizations, provides guidance that can be leveraged in a general way for program-based or portfolio-based benefits realization management implementations.

## PRACTICE #1: BEGIN WITH THE END IN MIND

The decision to focus on benefits realization management does not typically appear out of nowhere. Some relevant organizational driver has caused the organization to consider benefits realization management either as a solution to an existing problem or as an opportunity to contribute to something the organization values, possibly both. As discussions regarding benefits realization management are undertaken, it is important to focus these discussions on how benefits realization management contributes to an end state goal the business values. This focus helps to ensure that early discussions focus on *why* benefits realization management is being considered, rather than on *what* benefits realization will accomplish or on *how* benefits realization management will be used. Beginning with the end in mind places the focus on the value to be created through its implementation or, minimally, on the end state of the organization (as opposed to the current state) and the enhancements that are achieved through implementation of benefits realization management. Of course, these are logically viewed as the benefits of benefits realization management, but—given that little may be known about benefits realization management methodology within the organization—discussions with stakeholders, which are focused on benefits *before* training in benefits realization management is conducted, risks causing confusion. Most people can readily understand the simple "begin with the end in mind" mantra, as it drives their thinking toward the desirable goal they wish to achieve.

Additionally, beginning with the end in mind relates to considering the overall scope of the benefits realization management implementation effort. Creating a high-level vision statement for benefits realization management may assist with this effort and be a useful tool for early discussions with stakeholders. It is recognized that this vision represents an end point that lies well into the future. It may include a broad organizational scope (e.g., multiple geographies or business units), inclusion of multiple business functions (e.g., program management or portfolio management offices, strategic planning functions, etc.), and a significant process scope—including the full benefits realization management life cycle, from benefits identification through benefits sustainment. Starting with a broad scope is a potentially challenging approach. In most cases, a more reasonable scope is established early, capitalizing on approaches like the pilot implementation approach. However, although it is nearly certain that some portions of the elaborated vision will not be realized for some time, an understanding of the complete end state can help with building stakeholder support for benefits realization management. Showing a complete vision instills confidence that the full impact of benefits realization management has been considered. It also helps to engage stakeholders in discussions about the "ideal" end state, recognizing that the initial vision may be subject to refinement. This refinement is best performed early, as opposed to after significant investments in building capability have been made. A clear vision statement, articulated succinctly and refined with feedback from organizational stakeholders, provides a firm foundation for success and utilizes the notion of beginning with the end in mind quite well.

Finally, organizations implementing benefits realization management should consider the end state within their overall efforts to mature project, program, and portfolio management in their organizations. The concept of "organizational project management," as the holistic and integrated management of the scope of project, program, and portfolio management to create value, is relevant here. Benefits realization management is one component of an overall view of project management within the business context. As such, organizations that focus on maturing their processes and managing holistically—in the broader context of organizational project management—should understand how benefits realization management contributes to these efforts, the relevant activities and timelines that drive organizational project management efforts, and how benefits realization management is best aligned with these broader plans and timelines. An extensive discussion of organizational project management cannot be provided here. For more details, refer to the Project Management Institute's organizational project management literature.

## PRACTICE #2: ESTABLISH ORGANIZATIONAL COMMITMENT

Establishing organizational commitment for implementing benefits realization management requires three primary activities:

1. Socializing benefits realization management with stakeholders
2. Understanding and addressing stakeholder concerns
3. Formalizing organizational commitment

The process may seem simple. In some sense, it is not particularly different from the initiations of most projects and programs. Socializing benefits realization management requires understanding who the stakeholders are and producing materials that explain key benefits realization management concepts and benefits to them. Stakeholder identification processes and tools should focus on the primary stakeholders to be involved in the decision to proceed with implementation, as well as on stakeholders who, though perhaps not direct decision makers, will provide critical input to the early scoping and planning needed to secure approval.

In addition to stakeholder identification, relevant collateral needs to be developed for presentations, discussions, and other opportunities to build support. The vision statement is a key document for this. Additional documents—such as case studies from other organizations that have successfully implemented benefits realization management, white papers describing common benefits realization management methodologies, and examples of opportunities to leverage benefits realization management in the organization—are also helpful. While a formal communications plan may not be necessary at this stage, it is minimally necessary to ensure that identified stakeholders receive information that helps them to understand the implementation vision and how they will be impacted.

It is possible that some stakeholder resistance will remain, even after general discussion of the organizational vision for benefits realization management and specific discussions with stakeholders. At this stage, common causes of resistance are discomfort with change, not understanding how benefits realization management benefits individual stakeholders (it is often initially viewed as an "organizational" benefit), concern regarding how rigorous tracking of benefits will impact stakeholders (especially those who are used to presenting a list of intangible benefits, which are then approved), as well as concerns about how greater visibility to benefits attainment and sustainment will impact stakeholders. These sources of resistance may all be valid and they may be prevalent in organizations that currently offer limited visibility into project and program success in terms of quantified returns on investments.

To be sure, benefits realization management supports stronger, more data-based initiative selection on the portfolio level, as well as stronger, more data-based reporting and management of benefits attainment and achievement. Thus, stakeholders may view the process as providing visibility they do not desire. Fewer "pet projects" with questionable benefits may be approved, and managers may be held more accountable for ensuring that projects, which are approved, return the value elaborated in their business cases. This can cause significant concern for stakeholders, and addressing all stakeholder concerns is not easy, as benefits realization management is more about "what's in it for us" than "what's in it for me." At the organizational level, better initiative selection and better returns on investments through effective management of benefits realization presents a significant improvement to the overall utilization of resources and investments in supporting the organization's strategies. But, for individual managers who will be held accountable for the processes and results within a division, group, or other lower level, this improvement may be great for someone else but means additional work for them. In fact, this may be true. There may be disbenefits at the individual work group level—as measurement, reporting, and associated activities, both within the initiatives themselves and as part of benefits sustainment—rests on these divisions or groups.

Addressing such concerns as these is not easy. At this stage, establishing organizational commitment requires addressing some of these concerns by specifying actions that will be taken to minimize disbenefits. A few general suggestions for allaying these worries include:

- Discuss the balance between the organizational good and the individual good. Implementing benefits realization management should result in better benefits realization, which leads to more consistent deliveries of business goals. While this impacts the organization overall, it also impacts stakeholders individually, as better business results can lead to more job opportunities, bonuses, more stable working environments, and so forth.
- Note that change is an evolutionary process. Benefits realization management will not be implemented overnight; as such, there will be a gradual transition during which stakeholders will have significant opportunities to contribute to the process, which provides for balancing their needs with implementation objectives.
- Describe the implementation approach if possible. Stakeholders may be more comfortable if they know that the proposed implementation will be tested, piloted, and reviewed prior to a broad rollout. Sometimes, organizational stress from past failures of other programs leads to general resistance to change. Focusing on how this implementation will be positioned

for success from the start and managed in a reasonable way may alleviate this resistance.

- Be clear about what will change and what will not. In some organizations, modifications to existing processes may be necessary for implementation; in other organizations, building and deploying completely new processes may be required. Where possible, focus on what will stay the same or be reasonably enhanced.

Realistically, some basic organizational change management must begin at the business case and vision development stage. It will not be possible to address all stakeholder concerns, but understanding them early makes the subsequent processes run more smoothly, especially as further work is done toward more detailed planning.

Formalizing organizational commitment should follow the processes the organization already has in place for approving investments. These processes likely involve approving a charter as well as assigning initial resources. Ideally, the implementation program has a specific initial scope, which includes one or more pilot efforts, as well as an approval—in principle—of the full implementation vision. It is important to ensure that organizational commitment includes not only the approval to proceed but also the commitment to provide ongoing, visible senior leadership support for implementation. This support may be in the form of a steering committee, or other body, representing organizational stakeholders who are able to provide support to the implementation team and who socialize the implementation and associated benefits within their spheres of influence. This body, together with a senior responsible owner, is often better for implementations, as the steering committee may have a broader range of stakeholder representatives, enabling the implementation team to receive a broader scope of feedback and to leverage the broader group for support of communication, management of resistance, and other important activities.

## PRACTICE #3: START SMALL AND GROW

This suggestion is broadly applicable to all benefits realization management implementations. While it may be tempting to undertake a broad implementation scope in order to return value from the implementation investment to the organization quickly, I recommend a pilot approach. Pilots provide significant insight into what works, and what doesn't, from a process, tools, and management perspective. This feedback is extremely valuable, as no two benefits realization management implementations are the same. Differences in organizational processes, culture, politics, and other factors often mean that relatively "basic" benefits realization management processes may require tailoring and testing to ensure their effectiveness. It is unreasonable to believe that an organization will be able to take a prepackaged benefits realization management methodology and implement it with no tailoring. For organizations who prefer to build their methodology themselves or significantly tailor processes, tools, templates, and other items in existing methodologies, the process will be even more of a challenge, requiring testing the developed processes, adjusting them as appropriate, and seeking stakeholder feedback. Pilots permit this testing and adjustment without impacting a large number of stakeholders.

When determining an appropriate scope and process for the pilot, the following considerations are important:

- Selecting the pilot scope
- Creating the pilot timeline
- Determining the pilot success criteria
- Establishing organizational commitment to the pilot

## Selecting the Pilot Scope

An appropriate pilot scope is critical and considers two dimensions—the scope of process and the scope of implementation. From a process perspective, the implementation team will need to determine whether to deploy the entire scope or to focus on specific elements in the initial pilots. This is worth repeating. It may be appropriate to focus on piloting one process, for example benefits identification, in several projects or programs, and once validated, additional processes can be piloted and validated. Or, it may be appropriate to test the entire end-to-end process on a small number of projects or programs at once. This decision is not easily made and must consider:

- The time commitment required; testing end-to-end processes can be time consuming, depending upon project or program duration, and these timelines are often longer than is appropriate for a pilot.
- The need to return value to the organization; even if end-to-end processes are not tested, implementing some processes can provide beneficial returns. For example, better benefits identification through deployment of a benefits identification process, training, and so forth may be beneficial, even if benefits sustainment processes are not yet implemented.
- The nature of the projects or programs; a six-month project may be a candidate for end-to-end process testing, while a five-year program may be a candidate for testing specific processes. There is no right or wrong answer, and organizations must understand that some testing of "in flight" projects or programs may need to occur.

I recommend an incremental pilot approach, in which specific developed processes are piloted and implemented, leading to end-to-end capability over time for the organization. The selection of these processes must be aligned with organizational priorities, ensuring that the processes likely to yield significant return are developed and deployed as early as possible. For example, if the organization has difficulty articulating benefits in business cases, it may make sense to begin by focusing on benefits identification and revision to business case processes. Of course, some precedence relationships will drive these choices as well. For example, organizations having trouble measuring the returns on investment in change may benefit from the measurement and reporting aspects of benefits realization management, but these processes rely on effective benefits identification and quantification, thus necessitating that benefits identification activities are implemented prior to addressing measurement and reporting challenges.

An additional consideration is the number of projects or programs to be included in the pilot. It is not possible to propose a specific number of projects or programs that are appropriate for a pilot scope, as considerations of project or program size, duration, complexity, and other factors are important. For most organizations, a number greater than one but less than ten is usually appropriate. Selecting one or two projects or programs may not create a representative sample of the types of work undertaken by the organization. Selecting twenty or thirty projects or programs for a pilot can be overwhelming and will feel more like a full implementation.

Candidates for inclusion in the pilot should represent the fundamental types of work the organization typically undertakes, should be of a reasonable size and complexity, and should be efforts the organization typically undertakes successfully. Selecting pilot projects that are very complex, risky, or of a challenging nature will not make life easy on the benefits realization management implementation team and will not likely lead to success and appropriate capture of process improvements and lessons learned, since inherent complexity or risk may divert the core project or program management team to focus too much attention on these items rather than on the activities required to successfully pilot benefits realization management.

## Selecting the Pilot Timeline

Another important consideration is the pilot timeline. When chartering the benefits realization management implementation, stakeholders will have expectations about when results—especially for initial success—will be available for review. As such, the pilot timeline must balance stakeholder interests in results with the need to effectively develop, implement, test, revise, and prepare processes for broader deployment. As all implementations will be different, it is not possible to provide a single timeline that is applicable for all situations. However, a general process view is provided in Figure 16.1.

Figure 16.1 depicts the key work phases of implementation planning; process development; pilot execution, review, and validation; and preparation for implementation. These phases are common to many project and program management efforts. The end-to-end timeline from implementation planning to preparation for implementation of any particular iteration—recognizing that a number of iterations may be made for incremental deployment of processes—averages three to six months. This permits sufficient time for planning and conducting the pilot, while allowing the organization to see value from the efforts in a timely manner. In a sense, this approach supports an incremental benefits delivery model, for which intermediate benefits from implementation can be seen and put into practice by the organization while end-to-end processes are built and eventually, fully implemented to achieve the desired end benefits.

## Determining Pilot Success Criteria

A third important component will be the selection of appropriate success criteria. These criteria should be developed in the context of stakeholder expectations and benefits described in the business case and vision, and should be developed in a way that validates incremental success as well as contribution to end goals. As such, it is important to establish the implementation scope, pilot scope and timeline, implementation approach (iterative or end-to-end), and other elements before finalizing success criteria.

## Establishing Organizational Commitment to the Pilot

Establishing organizational commitment to the pilot requires obtaining approval from the stakeholders who will be impacted by pilot activities. This primarily involves ensuring that sponsors of projects or programs, which are within the pilot scope, are in agreement with the selection of their projects and ensuring that they understand the specific expectations of themselves and the project or program teams. This requires discussions of activities to be undertaken by the

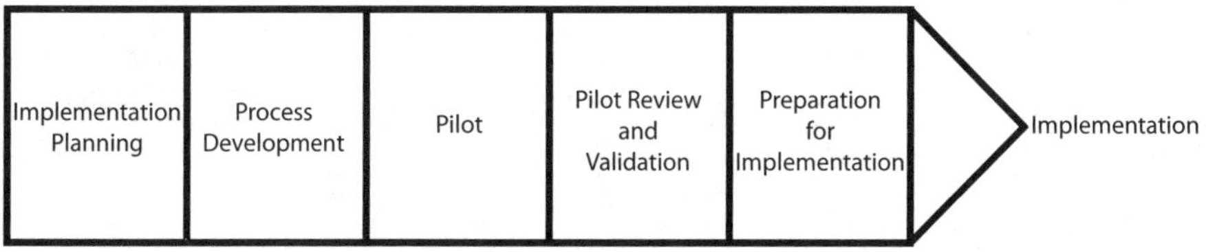


**Figure 16.1** General implementation process

project or program teams, activities to be undertaken by the implementation team, and interactions between these teams during the pilot. A RACI chart—distinguishing between responsible, accountable, consulted, and informed stakeholders—or responsibilities assignment matrix format may be used to establish clear expectations for the roles to participate in the pilot and their responsibilities, which will assist in establishing clear expectations. An example format can be found in Table 16.1.

Managing expectations is critical as the project and program management teams are primarily focused on delivery of the projects or programs, thus creating the danger that focus on benefits realization management is not primary. Being clear about the work to be done, its timeline, and the specific roles of the project and program management teams in that work assists in planning the appropriate resource commitment. Commitment from the project or program sponsor will go a long way toward ensuring proper focus.

In some cases, pilots may not focus directly on projects or programs. For example, initial process pilots may focus on processes at the portfolio management level that have little direct impact on projects or programs. In these cases, establishing organizational commitment requires obtaining the commitment of the stakeholders concerned with these processes. Regardless of the specific areas of the organization that are in scope, obtained commitments should be documented and formally approved so that the implementation team has clear authorization to proceed.

## Growing over Time

Given that the elaborated vision for benefits realization management likely includes a broad implementation scope, it is necessary to plan pilot activities with an eye toward the future. While initial pilot activities may be elaborated in great detail, further implementation activities may be less well elaborated. The use of milestone charts or similar tools is often appropriate for this purpose, enabling the implementation team to show near-term milestones associated with the pilot activities (coupled with underlying detail regarding the work encompassed in

**Table 16.1** Sample RACI chart format

| | Implementation Team | Project Manager | Project Sponsor | PMO | Portfolio Manager |
|---|---|---|---|---|---|
| Activity A | R, A | C | I | | |
| Activity B | A | R | I | I | C |
| Activity C | A | R | C | I | I |
| R = Responsible A = Accountable C = Consulted I = Informed | | | | | |

these pilots) alongside longer-term plans for implementation. While these timelines may be adjusted as pilots progress, it is important to ensure that sufficient advanced planning is included in overall implementation planning and that longer-term timelines are aligned with overall implementation goals and are socialized with stakeholders early, so that commitment to these timelines can be established and maintained during regular implementation review activities.

## PRACTICE #4: BUILD A COMPETENCY NETWORK

Establishing and building benefits realization management competency in the organization is a critical success factor for benefits realization management implementation. While competency most likely initially resides in the implementation team, that team will eventually be disbanded. Competency must be developed in the business organization so that as implementation proceeds and ultimately concludes, the business organization is left with qualified personnel to continue to support and evolve benefits realization management practices over time.

Initial benefits realization management expertise likely resides with one or more subject matter experts that the organization either externally engages or builds from within its population. While engaging internal resources and sending them to training or other learning opportunities to develop them to be able to support benefits realization management may appear desirable, a challenge does exist with this approach. Qualified consultants or externally hired resources bring perspectives from other implementation efforts that enable them to understand an organization and determine what practices are likely to be effective and how to tailor those practices to the unique case. Unfortunately, this experiential learning cannot be easily obtained in a training class. Retaining the services of a qualified consultant or external subcontractor to provide initial support, training, and mentoring to benefits realization management implementation efforts may be beneficial. While they may not be needed to lead the implementation as such (existing project or program management resources are often most appropriate for this role), their support in a consulting capacity can save significant time, reduce implementation risks, and support internal competency with training, coaching, and mentoring.

As part of implementation planning, a competency development plan should be established to ensure appropriate support for benefits realization management as well as to define the key roles, responsibilities, training needs, mentoring needs, and other factors that are important for implementation progress. This plan may be developed together with organizational change management resources, training resources, human resource professionals, or others who are skilled in processes associated with training, competency development, and related disciplines.

Competency development should be focused around a broad competency model that defines the specific roles to support the organization and to maintain and build competency over time. A general model is shown in Figure 16.2.

As the model in Figure 16.2 illustrates, four levels of resources are defined. At the base of the pyramid, business users form the broadest segment of individuals in the model. These are the "day-to-day" users of benefits realization management who require training in relevant components of benefits realization management that are related to their specific job functions. These business users may include benefit owners, project and program managers, portfolio managers, members of project and program steering committees, and others who either directly participate in the benefits realization management process or provide inputs or receive outputs from the process. While these users do not need to be process experts, they do need to understand benefits realization management in the context of their roles and the impacts of their roles on the overall process. They usually require training and support and, due to potential turnover, may

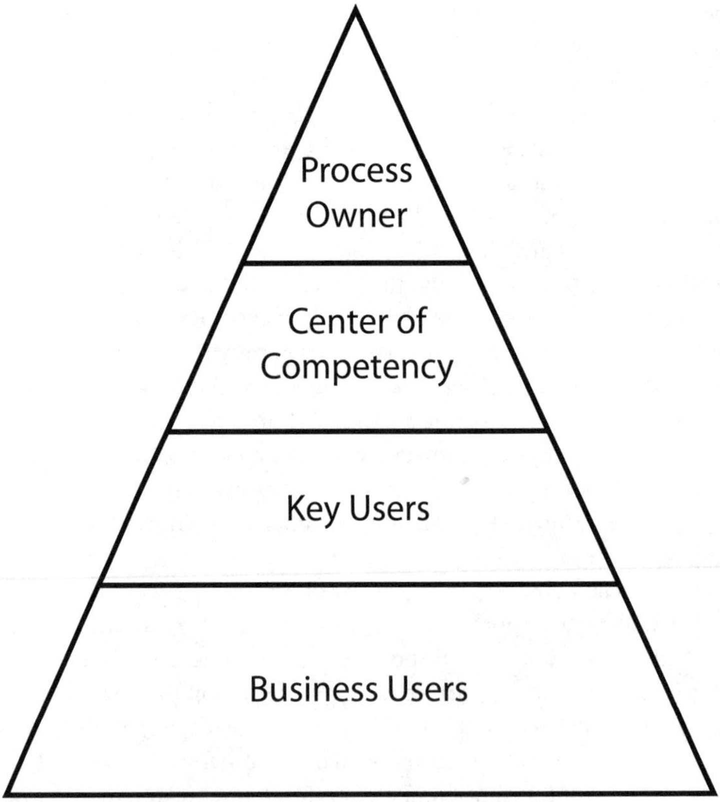


**Figure 16.2** Basic competency model

require ongoing support from others within the competency model, as employees leave, and new employees—potentially with less knowledge of benefits realization management—assume new roles.

Above the business users in the pyramid sit key users. These are typically a subset of the business users who are directly involved in benefits realization management activities and support building competence within the business organization. They are typically experienced users of the process who have gained significant experience in benefits realization management through regular participation in benefits realization management activities, and who have received specific, advanced training that enables them to support the business users for many common questions and issues that may arise on a day-to-day basis. Early pilot participants, who are trained by the implementation team and actively participate in pilot activities, are strong candidates for key users, as they have both knowledge from training and experience from pilot participation that enables them to actively support further implementation activities and the ongoing business processes once the implementation is complete. Building an effective network of key users should be part of any benefits realization management implementation plan, and leveraging them for training, mentoring, and support during further rollout activities is an effective way to reduce reliance on the core implementation team and subject matter experts for initial training and business user support activities. Of course, resource allocations need to be made with this approach, as key users are typically not allocated on a full-time basis in that role and thus must often perform key user activities in addition to their day-to-day job functions.

Above the key users sits a center of competency. This is the "home" for benefits realization management within the organization, where process and methodology are maintained, where responsibility for ongoing process maturity rests, where training and associated activities are coordinated, and where other activities in support of benefits realization management as an overall business function resides. Often, this center of competency is part of an existing organizational structure, such as an enterprise PMO, as opposed to a separate entity. Placing the center of competency within the same organizational unit of project, program, and/or portfolio management competence creates the opportunity for significant collaboration and development of relevant synergies to ensure that as the related project, program, and portfolio management processes evolve, the corresponding evolution of benefits realization management is also considered. The center of competency may consist of one person, a small team of people, or merely a portion of one person's time, depending upon the scope of benefits realization management implementation and of responsibilities assigned to the center. Some typical responsibilities include:

- Maintaining and evolving the benefits realization management methodology

- Providing training in processes and tools to the business organization
- Supporting key users with ongoing training and mentoring, as well as helping them to resolve questions or issues from business users
- Maintaining alignment of benefits realization management practices with organizational project, program, portfolio, and associated management practices
- Supporting action on business user concerns, lessons learned, and other information that supports effective ongoing processes within the business organization
- Acting as evangelists for benefits realization management within the business community and supporting communication and stakeholder engagement to ensure ongoing organizational support
- Providing regular communication to benefits realization management business users regarding process changes, tips for success, recommended practices, and other aids to competency development
- Providing regular communication to benefits realization management stakeholders regarding process effectiveness, improvement opportunities, and other factors affecting the process and its effectiveness in the organization that are of interest to key stakeholders

Centers of competency may not be involved in managing the benefits realization management process within the organization directly, but they may have additional responsibilities for data management, reporting, and other activities on a business unit or organizational level that do directly support benefits realization management.

Finally, at the top of the pyramid sits the process owner. The process owner is a single, named individual who provides overall leadership to the benefits realization management process and business function within the organization. The process owner should be a recognized benefits realization management expert in the organization and ideally leads the benefits realization management center of competency. In smaller implementations, the business process owner and the center of competency may be the same person. In other cases, multiple resources comprise the center of competency, and the business process owner is responsible for ensuring appropriate focus by the center of competency. The business process owner serves several important roles, including, but not limited to:

- Liaising with senior stakeholders to understand their expectations and to ensure continued alignment of benefits realization management with their needs
- Providing leadership to the center of competency through direction setting, issue resolution, and proactive management

- Overseeing required process monitoring activities to ensure the effectiveness of the benefits realization management process
- Providing visible management support for benefits realization management and encouraging key stakeholders to provide similar support
- Ensuring appropriate organizational change management activities to mature practices within the organization
- Remaining abreast of industry practices, attending conferences and training as needed, and determining how best to leverage emerging practices toward continued benefits realization

The process owner, if also acting as the center of competency, is generally assigned on a full-time basis. If such an assignment is being considered on anything less than a full-time basis, thought should be given to the variety of functions filled by the center of competency and the process owner. If the process owner role is a distinct role to be supported by a center of competency, full-time basis allocation should be evaluated. It is not uncommon for organizations to empower one person with process ownership for multiple processes. This situation is perfectly acceptable as long as the constituent workload is appropriate for one resource. Regardless of the work mix, it is critical to ensure that the responsibilities associated with the process owner and center of competency are formally assigned, that sufficient resource capacity is allocated to perform the work, and that the appropriate reporting and related organizational structures are established to ensure proper support.

The competency pyramid requires a strong focus on communication and collaboration. Figure 16.2 has been redrawn in Figure 16.3 to show the common communication and collaboration channels within the competency model.

As Figure 16.3 illustrates, communication channels must be established between the various levels within the pyramid, ensuring that business users have support from the key user network, that the key user network is supported by the center of competency, and that regular interaction occurs between the center of competency and the business process owner. It is certainly possible that "skip level" communication will occur. As an example, the business process owner might also engage with key users and the business user community to gather feedback, address challenges, or for other reasons.

Figure 16.3 depicts communication between the center of competency and relevant benefits realization management (BRM) stakeholders, as well as communication between the business process owner and relevant senior benefits realization management stakeholders. The specific stakeholders vary from organization to organization, but may include such groups as PMOs, portfolio managers, participants in strategic planning, business unit leaders, and others impacted by benefits realization management activities.

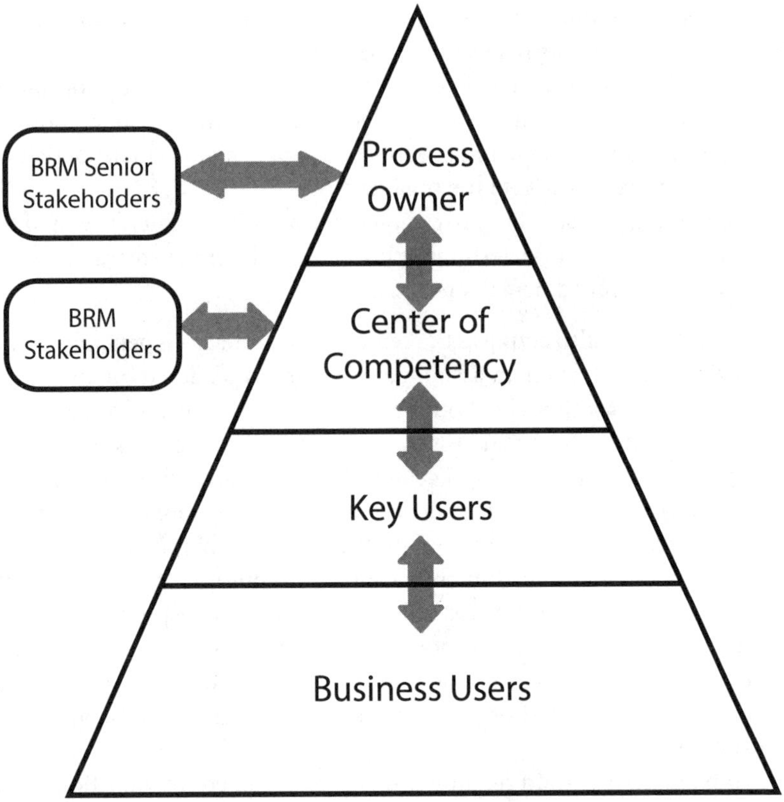


**Figure 16.3** Basic competency model with communication channels

Establishing a network of competency (as in this model) provides opportunities for training, peer learning, and associated activities at all levels. The center of competency, in consultation with the business process owner and relevant stakeholders, should ensure that a competency development plan is established, describing how business users, key users, and other stakeholders will be regularly engaged and how appropriate training and mentoring activities will be implemented to enhance competency over time. Especially in the business user community, peer learning and mentoring activities are often highly successful and should be leveraged to enable members to share knowledge, grow skills, and provide peer support.

## PRACTICE #5: FOCUS ON THE PROCESS

Having spent some time in consulting, I appreciate a good consulting aphorism, and one of my favorites is "a fool with a tool is still a fool." It is certainly possible to purchase or build fancy software packages to solve many problems, and in many arenas, there are plenty of vendors who are more than happy to visit your company to show off their capabilities. And in many cases, these vendors have prepackaged methodologies or other enablers that are designed to integrate their software tools into an organization. These solutions potentially have a time and a place in benefits realization management implementation efforts, but to be sure, the time and place is not at the beginning of the process. While some people may disagree, I firmly believe that starting with tools and using them to drive processes is a mistake. Even when the organization has limited processes, initial focus should be on the design of appropriate processes to support a common way of working within benefits realization management and on the integration of these processes with other organizational processes as appropriate. Certainly, understanding the use of tools in process development is acceptable, but efforts should not be exclusively focused on tools.

Some tools may already exist in the organization's landscape. Common examples include project management tools such as scheduling and resource management tools, portfolio management tools that support the organization's portfolio management processes, and other tools that support such processes as risk management or budgeting. These may range from customized spreadsheets and databases to multimillion dollar integrated software packages with functionality spanning the entire project, program, and portfolio management landscape. Understanding how these tools can support benefits realization management efforts is important, and if tools that can be leveraged to support benefits realization management exist already, then their capabilities and current uses should be understood in order to determine possible integration points, or points where the tools can support benefits realization management processes. However, it is strongly advised to avoid the urge to leverage tools before the processes and ways of working are established and tested in the organization, unless there is a strong organizational mandate to integrate them immediately. Proceeding in this way may risk effort duplication, in terms of manually performing some processes for data integration and so forth, but these effects are temporary and well worth the effort. It is too easy for tools to "muddy the waters" in an implementation, causing unnecessary resistance, complexity, issues, or other negative impacts on early implementation efforts, which is a time when building confidence in the success of benefits realization management is critical.

If the organization does not already have a significant investment in software tools, tools should not be implemented until a later implementation phase and should be managed with a separate business case after implementation demonstrates a clear need for them. Because the tools landscape is large, and tool prices can vary significantly, a vendor evaluation and selection process is necessary in order to properly evaluate them according to business needs. Critical work to determine the specific business problems or opportunities that may profit from tools prior to their evaluation is necessary. This analysis may go beyond the scope of benefits realization management as there are few tools in the marketplace that focus exclusively on benefits realization management. Consequently, organizations may need to focus on more comprehensive tools—suited for the project, program, and portfolio management market—that integrate benefits realization management in their functionalities. These tools might focus primarily on execution such as common project and program management toolsets. They might focus primarily on portfolio management. Or, they might be comprehensive tools that integrate project, program, and portfolio management with other functions. Many tools are quite impressive with interesting features and prices to match their extensive capabilities. The organization must evaluate which specific business processes are best suited for integration with tools and the specific benefits expected from tools implementation. This is not something to be left to the vendor. It is something the organization must derive for itself, based upon a critical analysis of its own processes. Proceeding in this way helps the organization to frame the specific functionalities it desires before engaging extensively with vendors, and it may help the organization narrow its tools search to the few vendors whose products most closely align with their needs.

As a matter of general guidance, it may be appropriate to start considering the role of tools in benefits realization management once the core benefits realization management processes required by the business to support its expected benefits have been designed, tested, and initially implemented. By this time, some level of benefits realization should already be achieved, demonstrating the success of benefits realization management implementation. The success of the implementation and corresponding realized benefits are strong selling points for investing in tools, when it can be shown that benefits realization will be enhanced by the further work to implement tools. A compelling business case for this added work is the cornerstone for success, and it is more easily made when process success has already been established.

A common objection to the recommendations here is that by implementing processes and then returning later to implement tools, inherent inefficiencies are built in from the start, requiring rework to correct these inefficiencies when tools implementation is undertaken. The logic seems to go that the tools somehow reduce these inefficiencies and minimize rework by "getting everything right the first time." In practice, I have rarely seen this work out. In reality, one set of inefficiencies is traded for a greater set of problems when process and tool change occur at the same time in an area with little preexisting capability and experience. Implementing benefits realization management processes and tools is different from, for example, changing processes and tools for existing practices in the accounting department. In the accounting department, processes exist. Standards govern how accounting is done. Accountants are well versed in their profession. Change is not necessarily easy in an accounting department, but it occurs in a relatively stable, existing context.

For many organizations, benefits realization management is completely new. There are no—or few—existing processes. If processes do exist, they are typically informal, ad hoc, or inefficient. It is unlikely that many people are already familiar with benefits realization management. Capability must be built from the ground up. This is a much different environment and requires a different way of working. Driving process consistency *first* ensures appropriate focus on building the right processes to meet stakeholder needs. If these processes exist for some period of time without corresponding software tools, it is not the end of the world. Driving tools implementation later avoids the tendency to split focus between the process and the tools, which can occur when tools are introduced too early. In most cases, software tools support a well-developed process that is aligned with recognized standards with minimal rework. While training, data conversion, and other activities are required, later implementation of a software tool to support the organization does not typically turn the benefits realization management process upside down, requiring significant changes to processes. If it does, the root causes are commonly either inherent inflexibility in the tool or a cumbersome process that introduces complexity the tools cannot easily overcome. The former problem is addressed with a gap analysis, before purchasing the tool, which seeks to understand whether the selected tool can support the in-place process. The latter problem is addressed by reducing complexity and understanding how to leverage the software tool to simplify processes in a beneficial way.

## PRACTICE #6: PRACTICE WHAT YOU PREACH

This simple advice is a cornerstone of organizational change management. If you want to build support for change, you need to visibly support the change yourself. If you want to successfully implement benefits realization management, you must execute the benefits realization management implementation using benefits realization management principles. This includes the entire landscape of benefits realization management—from vision, to business case development, to benefits identification, to managing benefits realization, to organizational change management, to appropriate transition and sustainment activities. These plans must be built at the start and managed throughout the implementation. Additionally, utilizing sound practices during implementation provides an opportunity to demonstrate benefits realization management to stakeholders prior to its introduction in pilot projects. While the practices at the time of implementation planning and initial execution may differ from the final practices that are built and deployed during pilot work and subsequent roll-out, the fundamental principles do not differ and provide an opportunity to demonstrate how the implementation team applies the principles of benefits realization management, on a day-to-day basis, to support the critical implementation work.

Of special importance during implementation is a focus on organizational change management. While some may view organizational change management as a supporting process for benefits realization management, it is—in its own right—critical. Building a solid organizational change management plan to support the implementation is work that must be undertaken by the implementation team, with support from resources with experience in managing organizational change. Ideally, a business change manager supports the benefits realization management implementation and assumes responsibility for the required organizational change management efforts. If the organization possesses this capability, those resources should be engaged. If the organization does not have capability in organizational change management, building it to support benefits realization management implementation, is desirable. Even if developing the capability does not result in a full organizational change management methodology, key elements of stakeholder expectation management, communication, training, and other topics will be developed, which may be generally applied to other work and serve as a starting point for more comprehensive development of an organizational change management methodology.

## PRACTICE #7: MANAGE AND MEASURE

A second common consulting aphorism is, "you can't manage what you can't measure." While not entirely true, it is true enough to work as a general guideline. Organizations frequently do not place sufficient focus on understanding what can and cannot be measured in a way that creates more value than cost. Have you ever encountered an organization that captures significant amounts of data but only uses a portion of it for making business decisions? Or, an organization with little management based in real data that rather makes decisions using intangibles or questionable data? These situations rarely inspire confidence. In fact, observant outsiders almost always see the inherent limitations in such approaches immediately—wasted organizational effort, poorly made or poorly executed decisions, indecision, or other inefficient ways of working.

Because of benefits realization management's focus on measurement, an emphasis on measurement carries over into implementation. Management and measurement during implementation must focus on the activities required to proactively manage both the implementation itself (process metrics, training metrics, and so forth) as well as the measures to support benefits realization reporting. This is a common approach in many programs, requiring the team to understand which measures are relevant for ensuring capability creation, as well as which measures best support gauging integration into the business environment and benefits realization. In some cases, there may be overlap. In other cases, the measures will be distinct. In total however, they need to address these key questions:

- Is the implementation proceeding according to plan (e.g., on budget, on time)?
- Are the developed processes appropriate and effective?
- Is business change occurring according to plan?
- Will the planned benefits be achieved?

These questions apply across the project management domain (basic delivery metrics, such as cost and schedule), the program management domain (benefits realization), and the organizational change management domain (business change metrics). Establishing key performance indicators (KPIs) in these areas is an important part of implementation planning, as is ensuring that provisions for data gathering, analysis, and reporting are built into the overall implementation plan.

The developed metrics set need not be extensive or complex. A set of basic metrics, which address key stakeholder expectations and permit effective management of the implementation work, is sufficient. In fact, complexity can be problematic and should be avoided. A direct link should exist between each developed KPI and an output that is valued by a stakeholder with a strong focus on the critical few KPIs that are the most relevant to the greatest number of stakeholders. Of course, KPIs should also support effective monitoring and controlling of the implementation, with a focus on the few metrics that assist the implementation team in managing performance according to the targets or objectives set forth in the business case, charter, and other key documents that govern the implementation work.

In this context, management refers to utilizing the developed measures to assess progress and report it to stakeholders. Again, a direct link must exist between the developed measures and something that is valued by stakeholders. Thus, as reports are developed to assist with management, these reports should be clearly linked to the measures in use. Some measures will be largely internal, supporting the implementation team in managing day-to-day work. These measures could be simple, such as number of open issues, relevant schedule position on the work package level, and the like. They are not typically reported in detail to stakeholders outside the implementation team, but they are effective for managing work. Of greater importance are measures that support progress reporting to stakeholders outside the implementation team. These stakeholders commonly include the senior responsible owner, implementation steering committee, portfolio management or PMO functions, and others. Regular status reporting is part of the overall implementation plan, so the relevant reports, reviews, and related items should be concretely established. Ensuring timely availability of data, sufficiency of data analysis, and appropriate "early warning" systems to correct for variance from plans are important management components in this context. Regular, consistent use of data to support guiding the implementation, reporting to stakeholders, and responding to emergent issues is of primary importance.

## PRACTICE #8: DEMONSTRATE SUCCESS EARLY

The world is waiting. Well, not literally. However, the business organization is keenly interested in the progress of the benefits realization management implementation and expects results. Clearly, results do not occur overnight, and some time is required to build processes, train people, and produce initial data and results of relevance to stakeholders. But, in the interests of good organizational change management practices, the implementation team should not wait—potentially months—before sharing indicators of success with the organization. Success does not have to mean "ultimate success," nor does it have to come only at the end of implementation. Incremental "wins" along the way should be shared with stakeholders, as well as the boarder business organization, to demonstrate tangible results from the implementation team's hard work. To support this idea, refer to Figure 16.4, which is an enhanced version of Figure 16.1.

Figure 16.4 depicts incremental outputs at each phase of the initial implementation work that are integrated into the overall organizational change management framework to form the basis for incremental reports for stakeholders. Consider an example. At the conclusion of implementation planning, certain deliverables—such as high-level milestone schedules, confirmation of initial pilot scope, and others—will be available. Portions of these deliverables may be packaged together into a newsletter, blog, website post, or some other distribution mechanism and shared with stakeholders to demonstrate the tangible outputs of implementation planning work as well as to preview some of the key next steps in implementation. While these initial outputs may not indicate success, they do demonstrate appropriate planning which should inspire confidence within the stakeholder community that the implementation is being managed properly. Similarly, at later stages, additional incremental deliverables, or other relevant outputs, may be leveraged through organizational change management to demonstrate progress toward implementation goals.

In reality, it may be several months before data is available that demonstrates the direct value of benefits realization management in the organization. Waiting

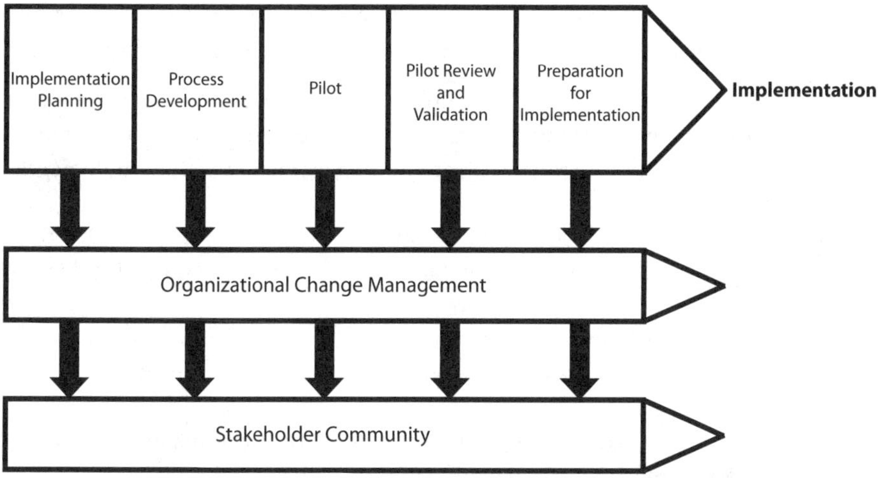


**Figure 16.4** Implementation process with incremental outputs

this long to demonstrate progress with the implementation is not advisable. Previewing the work ahead and predicting the first direct tangible outputs from the implementation is important for managing stakeholder expectations. It is especially important to be transparent when issues or risks put key deliverables at risk. Early success inspires confidence. Early challenges, if not managed well, erode confidence or cause confidence not to be built at all. Neither situation is desirable. But, sometimes, unavoidably the implementation does not proceed according to plans. If so, the implementation team must ensure appropriate communication with a focus on maintaining confidence and momentum through appropriate organizational change management activities. There is no single formula for success. Different circumstances require different approaches, and the implementation team should be prepared to address challenges as they arise. Relevant challenges should be put into context, referring to successes already achieved, and noting that it is not uncommon for occasional issues to arise in change programs. The team should keep an eye to the future, focusing the organization on successes already achieved and the end goals that are desired, and remembering that appropriate management of issues ultimately leads to successful outcomes.

## PRACTICE #9: PUBLICIZE SUCCESS

This practice is closely related to demonstrating success early (Practice #8). It is critical to publicize success. This is not only important for team morale, but it also gives a visible indication to the organization that benefits realization management is real and working. While extensive efforts to publicize success could be undertaken, simple steps are often sufficient. Some ways to publicize success include:

- An e-mail or letter from the implementation sponsor acknowledging a key milestone, thanking the team, and encouraging the organization to learn more about benefits realization management and the implementation efforts
- An implementation newsletter or article highlighting a successful pilot and the teams (both implementation and business) responsible for the success
- Informal "lunch and learn" or similar sessions with pilot participants to share successes and respond to questions asked by members of the business organization
- A celebratory gathering in which members of the implementation and business teams are recognized in front of their peers
- Success mentions in broader organizational publications, such as employee newsletters or company-wide conference calls
- "Team member of the month" or similar designations that enable the implementation team to recognize members of the business team who make important contributions to implementation success

Recognizing members of the business teams that participate in the implementation—especially those who are active pilot participants—is important. Not only does such recognition build morale, it demonstrates to the organization that the implementation is not simply being performed by a small group of people. Rather, the implementation is being shaped by a diverse group of organizational stakeholders with clear input from members of the business organization. As the implementation progresses, more stakeholders from more areas of the business are likely to be engaged, building the implementation community to include representatives of a broad cross section of the organization. Demonstrating that these diverse stakeholders are engaged and that their engagement is leading to success goes a long way toward building confidence within the business organization that the implementation will succeed in general and that benefits realization management will make significant contributions to organizational results. Publicizing success to support these goals should not be overlooked.

## PRACTICE #10: PICK YOUR BATTLES

This practice is already known to most people. Practical business experience teaches us that not every battle can be won and that some battles are not worth waging. While true battles in a benefits realization management implementation are uncommon, there are likely to be situations in which the implementation teams need to make choices about how best to handle stakeholders who are difficult to manage, or how best to respond when implementation aspects are questioned in unproductive ways. Other situations may require balancing risk and reward when engaging stakeholders who are overly resistant, hostile, or questioning the implementation with facts or circumstances that are slanted in their favor or outright untrue. These situations are never easy, and managing them requires business acumen. The key point is to keep your eye on the goal and to choose responses that balance the need to deal with the situation at hand with the need to align the implementation progress with the business case, charter, and expectations of the senior responsible owner. Creating significant deviations to appease stakeholders is not desirable, and the implementation team must remain focused on the approved plans, relying on the senior responsible owner, steering committee, and other relevant stakeholders to assist in managing any situations that may have negative impacts on perceptions of the implementation work or of benefits realization management in general.

## SUMMARY

This chapter offered practical guidance to support a successful implementation of benefits realization management in the business organization. This guidance is general in nature and is applicable regardless of whether benefits realization management implementation is undertaken on the project, program, or portfolio level. This chapter did not address detailed planning activities, which should follow the organization's normal project or program planning processes, and which should rely on qualified project or program management personnel to expertly support detailed implementation planning and execution. Their expertise, combined with subject matter experts from benefits realization management resources and appropriate engagement of organizational change management resources, positions the implementation for success and for long-term value in the organization.

# Appendix A

# CASE STUDY—A PMO ROLE IN BENEFITS REALIZATION MANAGEMENT

**Contributed by Hayley Douglas**

## INTRODUCTION

This chapter presents a case study describing a PMO role in benefits realization management. The purpose of this case study is to introduce a representative example of how principles of benefits realization management can be leveraged together with support from a PMO to advance a business goal. The case study focuses on a nonprofit organization, but the principles are applicable and scalable in a variety of organizations. While the roles and responsibilities of PMOs vary widely, it is clear that for many organizations, a PMO can provide critical support for organizational project management as well as more directly managing the organization's projects.

## BRIEF HISTORY OF PMOs

In 2013, many organizations have a PMO in their corporate structure. The difficulty is: Are these organizations using the PMO in a way that enhances their positions in the business world? For example, the practices of managing projects, people, and methodologies are well established. But the text, *An Inside Look at High-Performing PMOs*, by Crawford and Cabanis-Brewin, explains the struggle of a newly implemented PMO, "Linking strategy to projects . . . remains revolutionary thinking in some organizations."[1] This succinctly describes the struggle companies continue to face when it comes to managing their project portfolios in a way that supports benefits realization management and strategy realization.

Data suggests that PMOs do, in fact, effectively contribute to benefits realization. The caveat to this data is that, the longer the PMO is established in the business structure, the more successfully the company's benefits are realized. According to *The PMOSIG Program Management Office Handbook: Strategic and Tactical Insights for Improving Results*, by Craig Letavec and Dennis Bolles: ". . . PMOs that had been in place for four years or longer seemed to be making a definite difference in organizational performance. [. . . They] showed a 16 percent budget or schedule performance improvement compared to those organizations without."[2] This performance increase could translate into benefits for the company. For example, if a company delivers a product under budget and ahead of schedule, it may enhance its reputation and generate added goodwill with clientele, as other potential benefits, such as increased revenue, arise.

Even mature, top performing PMOs, often do not have a system that allows them to track their baseline results, according to a study presented in *An Inside Look at High-Performing PMOs* by Crawford and Cabanis-Brewin.[3] This study suggests that fewer than one-third of top performing PMOs have systems that track these results, which would show whether the use of a PMO does, in fact, link directly to meeting the end benefit. Projects can be completed successfully, but, in most cases, there is no system to measure the success of the capability linkage to the end benefits and corresponding strategies. As PMOs become increasingly mature, this value measurement tool will provide insight into the benefits of a PMO. For now, many believe that it is a vital instrument for success.

How can we elevate PMOs to improve the benefits realization of any given company? We need to implement a model that is practical for companies across industries. The model must be targeted to improve the processes by which delivered capabilities are applied, integrated into a business, and help a company attain the end benefit.

# CASE STUDY

## Program Description

A ten-year-old, not-for-profit professional etiquette forum for young business people, called "Hire Me" is located in Nebraska at a private institution. The forum's management made a target to increase attendance for the year from out-of-state schools, aiming at attendees from all 50 states. One program management thought that would lead to the end benefit of increased attendance across the nation was implementing an early registration, cold calling project directed to prospective out-of-state universities.

The private institution had one leader spearheading the cold calling project, Bruce. He was in charge of other duties in addition to the cold calling project. And in addition to managing the cold calling project, he was responsible for contributing to the cold calling program itself. For example, Bruce had to participate in the cold calling effort as well as oversee it; he had to book speakers for the forum, and was in control of organizing the logistics of hosting events in a small college town. To support his efforts, he had forty volunteers at his disposal to use as cold calling agents. These agents were sourced from the forum's network and instructed on how to execute the cold calling process.

To support the cold calling effort, each agent was provided a list of roughly fifty universities with numerous contacts. The contacts were administrators, professors, department chairs, club heads, and so on. Since the universities spanned the nation, agents had to take time differences into account when making calls. Agents were given a six-week deadline to contact one person from each university on their list, evaluate whether they were interested in having students attend the forum, and register the school. E-mailing in advance of a call or leaving a voicemail to schedule an appointment for a phone call was strictly prohibited, as it was important to the executives of Hire Me that prospective attendees talk to an agent over the phone directly, so the agent could record the conversation to collect feedback. Management wanted information about why universities did not want to attend the program, as well as what it would take to interest them in attending (e.g., decreased costs, a more impressive speaker line-up, an increased social aspect to the forum, etc.).

In order to incentivize volunteers to complete the calls and register participants, the management created a monetary reward system to motivate them for making reservations with universities. These incentives included bonuses for registering schools that had never attended the forum ($25 per university), those that had not attended in the preceding year ($15 per university), and those that attended the last forum ($5 per university). Both the conversations and registered universities were documented through a shared electronic file that stored information, so all users with access could view and update the file to record status.

## Results

By the deadline, the program was fairly successful. The number of schools that Hire Me booked in advance exceeded the amount for any previous year, but it did not succeed at registering a school from each state. The program secured schools from thirty-three states across the country—only 66% of the target. Looking back on the cold calling process and the incentive program, there were a variety of complications that could have been improved with the use of a PMO:

- Work priorities: The agents had obligations outside the Hire Me cold calling program.
    - These agents did not fully dedicate their time to the goal for the Hire Me program.
    - Feedback indicated that members struggled with scheduling calls to schools across time zones.
- Work redistribution: Some agents became overwhelmed and forfeited their lists of universities to other agents as competing priorities created constraints on their limited volunteer hours.
    - Head executives questioned whether the work that was turned in was adequate since the agents completing multiple lists had so many universities.
- Coordination and leadership: Bruce, in his capacity as manager for the effort, was overextended, as both a manager and participant in the work.
    - It was unrealistic to expect him to complete the work, organize the agents, and oversee all the projects.
- Data format ease of use: Feedback suggested that the process of recording and entering the information from the calls, registered schools, and the incentive program into the electronic tracking document was too intensive and confusing.
    - The data collected from the conversations lacked useful information about why schools did not want to attend the forum because agents did not completely fill in the complicated forms.

These obstacles hindered the organization's ability to realize the planned benefits. These unanticipated complications demonstrate that the project was not executed to the standards by which it was to be completed. Perhaps if the structure of the cold calling program had been more tailored to each cold calling agent, the agents would have had more time to dedicate to actual calling and would have spent less time figuring out when to call. Further, if the project leader, Bruce, had been able to focus his time on organizing the work and tracking the results to understand benefits realization potential instead of making calls, the process might have been improved. This would have enabled him to better monitor the results and see that the agents were struggling with their roles and recording registrants and conversation details. Benefits realization depends heavily upon the successful execution of the planned work. Since the cold calling project was not carried out as well as executives had hoped, the benefit was not fulfilled to the extent it could have been.

### Benefits Realized and Lessons Learned

The result of the cold calling project was that only thirty-three schools from out-of-state registered for the Hire Me forum—66% of the target of fifty states. The number of universities registering early exceeded previous years, but it did not meet the goal advertised by the host college. It is reasonable to say the cold calling program made a significant contribution to the 66% success and was directly linked to the end benefit of increasing attendance. Also, agents made connections with all of the universities on their lists. These connections meant that the cold calling capability was leveraged for an indirect benefit—new contacts for the Hire Me forum. Even though not all contacted universities attended the forum, those connections led to an intermediate benefit of increased awareness of the program among identified schools of interest across the nation. The connections with universities that had attended in the past, but not in the previous year, additionally provided the forum with extremely useful and relevant feedback on how the program had evolved and what those schools would like to see in the future. This feedback could be used to support better future quality for the Hire Me forum.

The unforeseen challenges and realized benefits opened the door for improvement; the utilization of a PMO would be beneficial for the forum as a PMO implementation would support work management, reporting, and benefits realization management that could lead to greater realized benefits associated with such work as that of the Hire Me forum. In the future, if the Hire Me forum followed a structured PMO approach, complications would decrease and benefits would increase. The following section presents a general model that may be applied to a variety of organizations to demonstrate the potential power of a PMO model to support benefits realization management.

## PMO MODEL

A basic model for a PMO role in managing benefits realization can be described in the context of this case study. The volunteers, management, and customers of the Hire Me etiquette forum all had a role in directly supporting or providing input (directly or indirectly) to the realization of the benefit of increasing attendance. For the purpose of describing a general model, volunteers from the case study will be called employees here. Management will mean the management who desires benefits from work and provides resources to support the work. Customers will mean the end customers of the organization.

One of the key lessons learned from the case study is that lack of efficient coordination of work and data management led to decreased focus on achieving the goal, which led to diminished realized benefits versus the benefits plan. This is clear from the fact that only 66% of the planned benefit was achieved. A revision to the ways of working in the Hire Me case study could include establishing a small, focused PMO role to provide coordination, work allocation, benefits tracking, and benefits reporting to support ensuring the achievement of stated business goals. Figure A.1 simplifies this relationship and illustrates the PMO as the central "hub" for coordination between interested parties.

Figure A.1 depicts the PMO and points of interaction between the PMO, the customer, the employee, and management in a general way that supports the case study provided. More details of the interactions between these parties appears in the following section, but in general, the PMO plays several key roles to support benefits realization, including serving as an information broker between interested parties, as a work manager to ensure that project efforts support planned benefits, and as a benefits manager to support tracking attained benefits and reporting to interested parties. Information sharing between parties is important

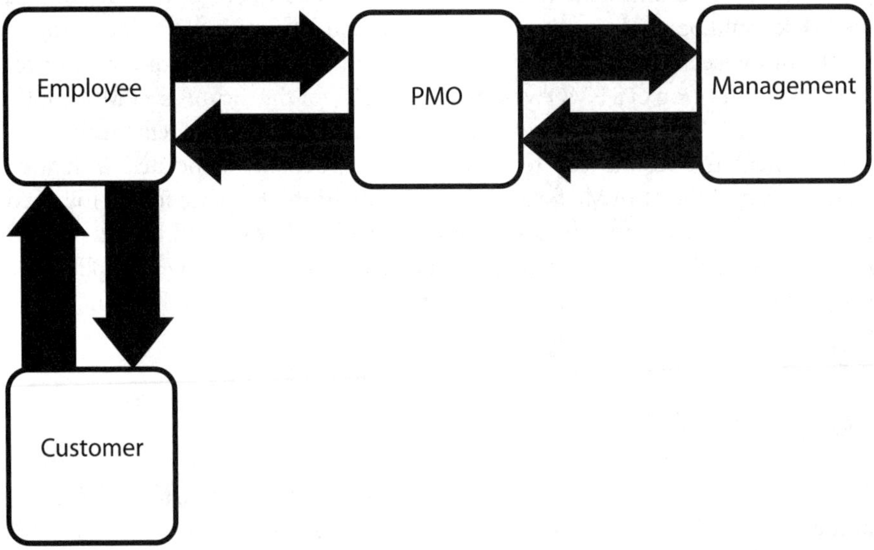


**Figure A.1** General PMO relationship overview

for success, and the PMO plays a central role in that function and in additional coordination work.

## Role 1: Information Broker

In the information broker role, the PMO works as a mediator of information between parties, ensuring consistent communication. The PMO's information broker role facilitates required communication, as shown in Figure A.2.

It is important to note that Figure A.2 represents a limited subset of all potentially necessary communications, and for simplicity, feedback is not shown. However, even with the representative example of communication in one direction, the information broker role can be easily understood. For example, the PMO will be directed by management to accomplish a goal and provide a corresponding set of planned benefits. The PMO will initially respond with feedback on how the projects to achieve those benefits would be accomplished. And then, when the two parties agree, the individuals within the PMO will break down the work required into constituent work packages for employees, essentially undertaking the project coordination via project or program management principles. The employees will provide information regarding work accomplished and feedback from customer interactions—before, during, and after project completion. The PMO will collect this feedback from the employees and translate it back to management in the form of reporting and other communication. With many potential goals to

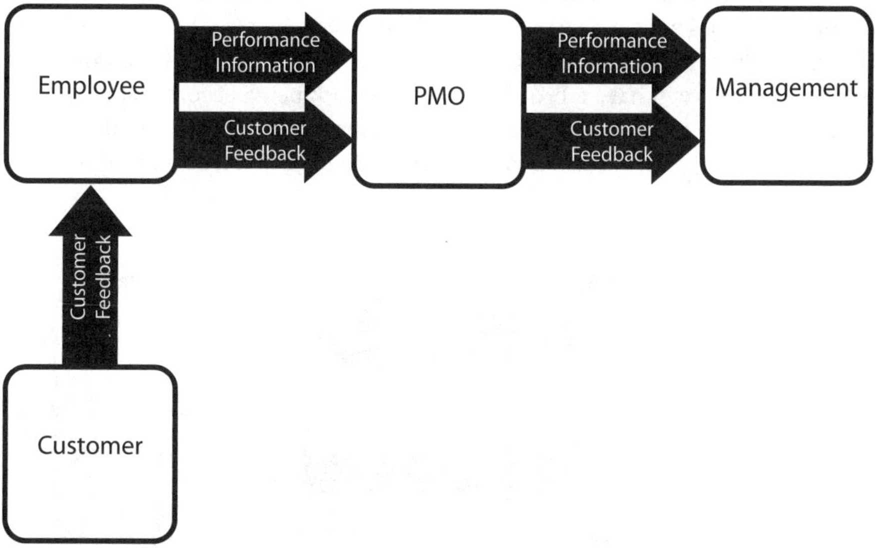


**Figure A.2** PMO information broker role

be met (and thus many potential benefits to be achieved), the PMO would play a central role as a reporting manager, ensuring appropriate communication to management, as well as providing internal planning and execution support, as in the work manager role described next.

## Role 2: Work Manager

In the work manager role, the PMO will act in a directing capacity, meaning it will allocate and reallocate work between parties as necessary, in order to ensure that work is allocated in the way that best supports desired benefits. This may entail direct management via project and program management practices or, for smaller efforts, more informal management. In either case, the role of managing work supports benefits realization by ensuring the appropriate allocation of resources. Figure A.3 illustrates the work manager role relationship.

When the PMO translates the benefit goals of management into the project work required to achieve those goals, decisions are made regarding which projects the PMO believes will accomplish the goal—which results in allocating the work to employees to support these goals. If the employees are struggling with a project or see that one project is not accomplishing the goal, the PMO can alter the project's focus or scope according to this performance information—which entails the reallocation of work. Information obtained in the information broker role supports this analysis and assists the PMO in making appropriate reallocation decisions to support benefits realization.

Understanding the performance of the work and how that work performance supports (or does not support) achieving the desired benefits is an important role the PMO plays, but it requires performance information from those doing the work. The PMO will have a broad view of the work being accomplished, which enables it to take received work performance information and use it to determine whether the work is progressing toward achieving the desired benefits. If it is not,

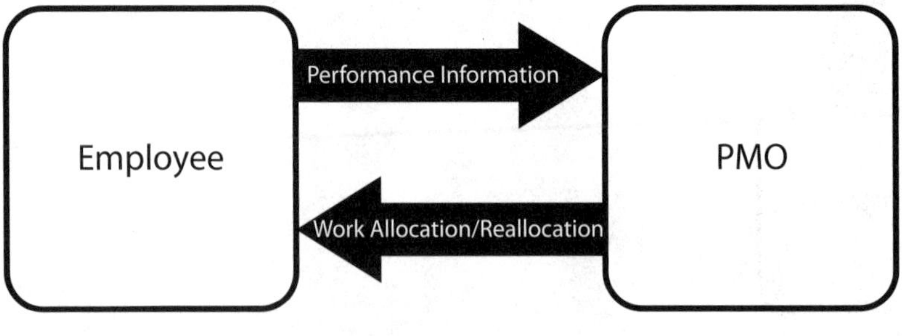


**Figure A.3** PMO work manager role

the PMO's information broker role may provide feedback to management, which allows management to assess how to proceed.

## Role 3: Benefits Manager

Lastly, the PMO functions as a benefits manager. As such, the PMO determines the project's success in terms of management's final goal by tracking the benefits created and reporting to management on how benefits have been achieved. Figure A.4 illustrates this relationship.

This role of the PMO aligns closely with the work manager role. The PMO receives its understanding of planned benefits from the organization's management and determines how the corresponding work supports those benefits, allocating and reallocating work as needed. Using work performance information, the PMO determines whether the outputs created support the desired benefits. If the PMO determines a project's success is unattainable or may not result in achieving the planned benefits, it organizes steps to improve the situation. They could increase training for a project, take customer feedback and apply it, or stop the project altogether.

The PMO will provide regular work performance information and benefits realization information to management with reports. These reports will include actual work performance data as well as information to help management understand whether their benefits goals are likely to be met. If a project is successfully completed, the PMO will summarize data from the project and inform management on the benefit realization status. If a project is experiencing challenges, these challenges are reported to management, so management can understand the situation and take action.

## Model Application in General

The roles described here present a mix of responsibilities, generally spanning project or program management, as well as elements of portfolio management. Essentially, the PMO role in this model is to blend elements of execution management—traditionally within the scope of project and program management—with

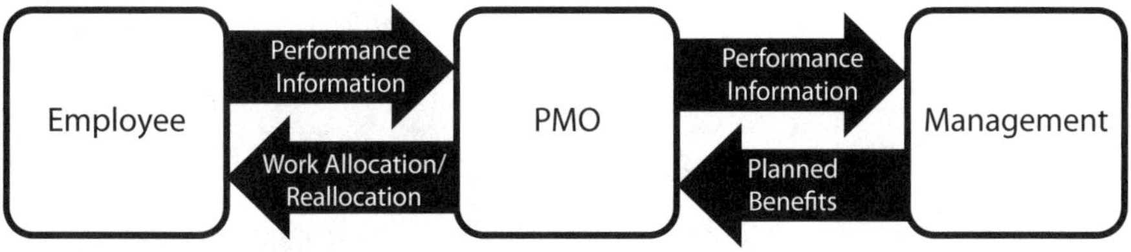


**Figure A.4** PMO benefits manager role

reporting and tracking elements of portfolio management to support ensuring that work is aligned with desired benefits goals as well as to provide transparency to stakeholders regarding the status of efforts within the PMO's scope that support desired benefits. In large organizations, these roles are typically segregated into distinct execution management roles undertaken by project and program managers (often not under the PMO's direct control), the PMO as a standards and process manager, and a distinct portfolio management function responsible for project and program prioritization, tracking, and reporting—traditional portfolio management business functions.

However, for smaller organizations without such distinct roles, this model provides a simple view of how the PMO can effectively support benefits realization management, providing coordination, direction, and reporting that may be absent—especially in less mature project organizations. Even if only one or two of the three described roles are implemented, benefits are possible. For example, the PMO may be the information broker and benefits manager without directly supporting work management, which may be relegated to business units with assigned project and program managers. While the PMO may not directly manage the work in this scenario, providing visibility to management about the work and its contribution to benefits realization, as well as supporting appropriate allocation of work, can still be beneficial.

There is no necessity that all three roles be implemented; however, it is important to recognize the value of including one or more of these roles within the scope of the PMO, especially in organizations for which distinct program management and portfolio management competencies are not yet implemented. Essentially, these roles, especially in smaller organizations, can be the first steps toward formalizing work to support benefits realization management. A smaller PMO wanting to expand its core focus could begin to align one or more of the described roles, which may already be implemented to some extent, with benefits realization management in order to provide some degree of formality. Even if not perfectly implemented initially, the foundation for tracking and managing benefits in a more formal way can be built, simply by leveraging the PMO as the central broker for coordinating this work. Over time, as focus expands, development of more formal competency in benefits realization, portfolio, and program management could be achieved, but this could be a long term goal, rather than an immediate need. Simple application of one or more roles is a starting point that may be appropriate in some organizations.

## Model Application in Case Study

If the model had been applied to the case study, many struggles of the cold calling project could have been avoided. If the project had been executed with a

PMO, the goal of management (registering a school from each state) might have been reevaluated and reworked into something more realistic, based on the PMO's understanding of available resources and the required work allocations. Or, if the PMO found the goal attainable, it would break the work down into projects to reach the goal and manage it in a more formal way. One of the project's goals that was broken down in the case study without a PMO was the cold calling project. The cold calling project was seemingly effective, but—with the use of a project manager role from the PMO—it could have been more successful with better tracking and understanding of how the work supported realizing the desired benefit.

When all of the issues with work prioritization arose in the case study, the PMO could have reallocated the work, in conversation between the employees, the PMO, and as appropriate, the management. The work could have been reallocated to agents with the time and resources to complete the calling, or it could have been distributed to projects—other than the cold calling project—which may also have supported the desired benefit.

Finally, if the PMO had been used during the Hire Me program, the cold calling's success would have been evaluated as the project was being completed, and reporting would have been provided to help management understand whether cold calling was on track to deliver the desired benefit of gaining participation from all fifty states. This is the benefits manager role of the PMO. The PMO would have informed management that cold calling alone was not accomplishing the goal, and it may have reevaluated the benefits plan, potentially allocating more agents to the task or discontinuing cold calling altogether if it determined that cold calling could not meet the desired goal.

## SUMMARY

The history of a PMO shows that the longer it is implemented within a company, the more successful the company is at delivering projects and programs. This case study demonstrates the challenges a company without a PMO may face, including lack of clear work priorities and work coordination, lack of management awareness of progress toward goals, and lack of constant project evaluation to ensure alignment with strategies and benefits realization. With the implementation of a PMO, these challenges can be foreseen and potentially avoided. The benefits plan is more likely to be realized, organizational resources are more likely to be appropriately allocated, and overall success is more likely to be achieved. PMOs can ensure benefits are realized by managing work, providing data to managers, and performing benefits management functions. The basic model presented here builds a strong foundation for any organization, and especially for smaller organizations that are not able to commit time and resources to the full development of PMO, program management, portfolio management, and benefits realization management competencies.

## REFERENCES

1. Crawford, J. Kent, with Cabanis-Brewin, J., *An Inside Look at High Performing PMOs*, PM Solutions Research, 2011, 37.
2. Letavec, C. and Bolles, D., *The PMOSIG Program Management Office Handbook*, J. Ross Publishing, 2010, 83-85.
3. Crawford, with Cabanis-Brewin, *An Inside Look at High Performing PMOs*, 53.

# Appendix B

# SAMPLE PgMP®
# EXAMINATION QUESTIONS

## INTRODUCTION

This chapter provides sample examination questions related to benefits realization management to assist candidates preparing for the Program Management Professional (PgMP®) examination. The questions are designed to test the reader's understanding of core benefits realization management concepts in the context of the Project Management Institute's standards and relevant literature. The PgMP credential requires a significant amount of knowledge across a broad range of topics, and the PgMP examination, though only one component of the overall certification, is challenging. Readers are advised to consult a range of resources, including this book, to prepare for the examination.

## SAMPLE QUESTIONS

1. Programs or projects deliver benefits primarily through:
   a. enhancing existing organizational capabilities or creating new capabilities through project or program work.
   b. creating outcomes that are deemed beneficial by stakeholders.
   c. enhancing existing capabilities or creating new capabilities that support the organization's strategies and objectives.
   d. creating benefits that stakeholders deem beneficial.

2. Devising the benefits metrics for reporting on benefits attainment occurs during:
   a. benefits identification.
   b. benefits analysis and planning.
   c. benefits delivery.
   d. benefits transition.
3. Ensuring continued realization of benefits occurs during:
   a. benefits transition.
   b. benefits delivery.
   c. benefits sustainment.
   d. benefits analysis and planning.
4. Which of the following is not typically an input to initial development of the benefits register?
   a. Business case
   b. Strategic plan
   c. Benefits realization plan
   d. Program objectives
5. Key performance indicators are:
   a. identified together with quantitative measures during benefits identification.
   b. identified during benefits identification.
   c. identified together with quantitative measures during benefits analysis and planning.
   d. identified during benefits analysis and planning.
6. Which of the following is not a primary activity of benefits analysis and planning?
   a. Developing the benefits realization plan
   b. Establishing benefits metrics
   c. Establishing the benefits monitoring and controlling framework
   d. Establishing key performance indicators
7. A program mandate:
   a. includes statements from a governance board, or other decision-making body, indicating the expected benefits to be realized.
   b. is a component of the program business case.
   c. includes quantified metrics used to assess benefits realization.
   d. is created to assess the sufficiency of the program business case's planned benefits.
8. Which of the following is not true about the benefits realization plan?
   a. Is a component of the overall program management plan
   b. Describes roles and responsibilities required to manage benefits

c. Describes activities required to transition capabilities from the program to the receiving business organization
d. Describes the intended benefits defined by the program's sponsoring organization

9. A representation of a program that includes the relevant dependencies between program work and its associated timelines is known as a:
   a. program schedule.
   b. program architecture.
   c. program roadmap.
   d. program plan.
10. Benefits analysis typically occurs:
   a. once, during benefits planning.
   b. iteratively, throughout benefits delivery.
   c. during benefits planning and benefits transition.
   d. as part of benefits sustainment activities.
11. Validating the program value proposition is part of:
   a. strategic alignment.
   b. value delivery.
   c. business case management.
   d. organizational change management.
12. A focus on value delivery is a key consideration in:
   a. benefits identification.
   b. benefits analysis and planning.
   c. benefits delivery.
   d. benefits transition.
13. Value has been delivered when:
   a. capabilities are created.
   b. capabilities are delivered to the receiving business organization.
   c. delivered capabilities are able to be used in a beneficial way.
   d. program transition is complete.
14. Benefits transition:
   a. is the responsibility of the program management team.
   b. occurs at the completion of the program.
   c. requires the receiving business organization to execute preparation activities for successful transition.
   d. is not planned until during benefits delivery.
15. Benefits are typically sustained through:
   a. the ongoing operations functions of the organization.
   b. the program management team responsible for transition.
   c. the ongoing operations functions of the organization or new projects or programs.
   d. the product support group responsible for the delivered capabilities.

16. During benefits identification, several business stakeholders identify potential benefits that the program management team believes will be difficult to quantify. The program management team should:
    a. disregard these benefits because intangible benefits do not support the development of the program business case.
    b. capture these benefits in the program benefits register.
    c. develop a measurement system for quantifying their attainment.
    d. group these benefits together with tangible benefits and determine the aggregate impacts.
17. During transition activities, the program management team discovers that a planned capability cannot be integrated into the receiving business organization without a previously undocumented impact on ongoing business operations. The program management team should:
    a. proceed with the transition but defer the capability transition for the impacted business operations until a later transition.
    b. assess the impact to ongoing business operations and proceed in the way that creates the least disruption to ongoing business operations.
    c. assess the impact to ongoing business operations and make a recommendation to the senior responsible owner on how to proceed.
    d. proceed with the transition but minimize the associated disbenefits as much as possible.
18. During transition activities, a benefit owner identifies an improvement opportunity that could lead to further benefits realization. This emergent benefit is best handled by:
    a. apprising the receiving business organization of the emergent benefit and including it in the transition documentation, so the receiving business organization can determine how to exploit the emergent benefit in its operations.
    b. documenting the emergent benefit in the program's benefits register.
    c. assigning the task of analyzing and determining the benefits opportunity to the benefits owner who identified the emergent benefit.
    d. including the emergent benefit in the sustainment activities planned for the receiving business organization.
19. The primary responsibility of the program management team during benefits identification is to:
    a. ensure that all benefits are captured in the benefits register.
    b. identify all appropriate benefits and document them in the benefits register.
    c. ensure that all appropriate stakeholders are involved in the benefits identification process.
    d. ensure that all identified benefits are appropriately quantified.

20. A stakeholder has been identified by the organizational change management team as a strong supporter of several key program benefits. The program management team should:
    a. engage this stakeholder to maintain his or her support.
    b. recruit this stakeholder into the organizational change management team.
    c. assess the stakeholder's influence to determine whether he or she should be a benefit owner.
    d. assess the stakeholder's influence to determine how best to engage this stakeholder to support the program.

## ANSWERS TO SAMPLE QUESTIONS

1. The correct answer is **C**. Benefits are delivered through enhancing capabilities or creating new capabilities to support the organization's strategies and objectives.
2. The correct answer is **B**. Benefits planning includes: planning metrics and measurement systems to track benefits attainment.
3. The correct answer is **C**. This activity, which may be the responsibility of the receiving business organization in the long run, occurs during benefits sustainment.
4. The correct answer is **C**. The benefits realization plan is established during benefits analysis and planning and is not available or an appropriate input to developing the benefits register.
5. The correct answer is **B**. Key performance indicators are identified during benefits identification, and their quantified measures are identified during benefits analysis and planning.
6. The correct answer is **D**. Key performance indicators are established during benefits identification.
7. The correct answer is **A**. The program mandate states the organization's intent regarding benefits to be realized and is an important input to development of a program business case and benefits realization plan.
8. The correct answer is **D**. The program mandate describes management's intent regarding benefits.
9. The correct answer is **C**. The program roadmap depicts the program work, dependencies between the work, and corresponding timelines, so the program management team and stakeholders can understand the overall program architecture.
10. The correct answer is **B**. Benefits analysis typically occurs iteratively, in conjunction with benefits delivery, as emergent benefits are identified and as the program responds to the changing business environment.

11. The correct answer is **A**. Strategic alignment includes the processes that ensure the program value proposition remains viable and aligned with the organization's strategy.
12. The correct answer is **C**. While understanding value is important at all phases in the benefits realization management life cycle, a primary focus on value delivery is important during benefits delivery to ensure that the program delivers planned benefits.
13. The correct answer is **C**. Value has been delivered when delivered capabilities are transitioned and in use in the receiving business organization in a beneficial way.
14. The correct answer is **C**. Benefits transition is a partnership between the program management team and the receiving business organization and requires significant preparation by the receiving business organization to ensure that it is prepared for transition.
15. The correct answer is **C**. While A and D may also be true, C best captures the fact that sustainment may be accomplished through operations as well as through new project or program work.
16. The correct answer is **B**. Although initial analysis may show that the benefits cannot be easily quantified, such benefits should not be ignored. Developing a measurement system is not appropriate during the benefits identification phase, and grouping these benefits together with other benefits does not provide appreciable value. Documenting these benefits in the benefits register for later evaluation and consideration is the most appropriate approach.
17. The correct answer is **B**. The program management team should assess the impacts and then proceed in the way that creates the least disruption to ongoing business operations. Performing only a partial transition is less desirable. Involving the senior responsible owner may be necessary, if the proposed transition approach is not acceptable to the receiving business organization. Minimizing disbenefits is a general benefits realization management activity.
18. The correct answer is **B**. The program should not immediately transfer this emergent benefit to the receiving business organization through transition or sustainment. Performing analysis on the benefit is premature. The best course of action is to document the emergent benefit in the program's benefits register and ensure that discussion of it occurs during regular benefits register reviews.
19. The correct answer is **C**. The program management team should ensure the involvement of all appropriate stakeholders in the benefits identification process. The program management team is not able to identify all potential business benefits (a task primarily involving stakeholders,

rather than the program management team), and it is likely not possible during benefits identification to quantify every identified benefit.

20. The correct answer is **D**. The stakeholder's influence must be understood in order to determine the best strategy for engagement. The stakeholder may be a candidate for the role of champion or change agent, but the way that he or she can best support the program must be understood in the context of both his and her interest and influence.

# INDEX